PENGUIN COOKERY LIBRARY
EASY TO ENTERTAIN

Patricia Lousada was born in New York City. Her Italian
mother was a singer and an inspired cook. She danced with
the New York City Ballet before leaving to live in Paris for
two years, where she attended lectures at the Cordon Bleu
School. This deepened her interest in cooking and she now
gives lectures and demonstrations on various kinds of cooking. She has written three cookery books for Sainsbury's:
Pasta Italian Style, *American Sampler* and *Food for Presents*.
She is also the author of *The Book of Chocolate* and *The Book
of Sweets* and was one of the eight cooks featured in Arabella
Boxer's *Sunday Times Cook Book*. Patricia Lousada is
married and lives in London.

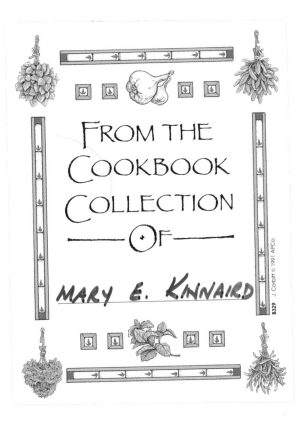

FROM THE
COOKBOOK
COLLECTION
—·OF—

MARY E. KINNAIRD

Patricia Lousada

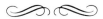

Easy to Entertain

ILLUSTRATED BY PHILLIDA GILI

PENGUIN BOOKS

FOR
THE TWO CARLAS

Penguin Books Ltd, Harmondsworth, Middlesex, England
Viking Penguin Inc., 40 West 23rd Street, New York, New York 10010, U.S.A.
Penguin Books Australia Ltd, Ringwood, Victoria, Australia
Penguin Books Canada Limited, 2801 John Street, Markham, Ontario, Canada L3R 1B4
Penguin Books (N.Z.) Ltd, 182–190 Wairau Road, Auckland 10, New Zealand

First published 1986

Filmset in Linotron Bembo by
Rowland Phototypesetting Ltd
Bury St Edmunds, Suffolk
Made and printed in Great Britain by
Richard Clay (The Chaucer Press) Ltd
Bungay, Suffolk

Designed by Judith Gordon

CONTENTS

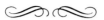

INTRODUCTION

Entertaining should be a pleasure. It should give you the chance to see friends, talk and relax over a good meal. But often your enjoyment is marred by having to spend too much time in the kitchen away from your guests. You can't even stir the pots in peace because your mind is in the other room. You can hear people laughing and talking, and you naturally wish you were with them; or, if it is quiet, you feel anxious and know you should be in there helping to liven things along. Entertaining can be a dilemma when you want to treat your guests to delicious food and also enjoy their company.

The answer seems obvious. Do your cooking before your guests walk through the front door and plan your meal like a military battle. Then you can spend time with your friends with an easy mind, knowing everything is under control and the work done.

This is the point of this book. It contains a wide range of dishes, and the recipes have been worked out so they can be prepared ahead of time with a minimum of last-minute work; some can be prepared quickly and others will take a little longer, but in all cases you can do the work in advance, even several days before your party. The recipes cover hors-d'œuvre, first courses, main courses, vegetables and salads, desserts, basics, sauces and extras.

There are lots of options for trouble-free first courses. You can start with a *salade composée* such as a salad of mixed smoked fish or a duck-breast salad. There is a light terrine of skate with vegetables or a heavenly dish of seafood with ginger if you want to start with something fishy. These are visually exciting ideas inspired by *nouvelle cuisine* and are particularly well suited to home entertaining. As you will no doubt take time over the table decorations and the flowers, it makes good sense to spend a few moments making the food look nice too, especially when the place settings can be arranged in advance. If you don't feel like a salad or fish, try a new soup – either hot or cold. The Coriander Soup and the Asparagus and Courgette Soup are both delicious and different. Here, too, a few minutes spent toasting almonds or chopping fresh herbs can stimulate the eye and appetite. If you are feeling more adventurous, serve a soufflé. The mixture can be made a day ahead and the egg whites folded in just before the guests arrive. Try using individual dishes, which make serving that much easier: the soufflés will cook in under ten minutes and look terrific. All you have to think about is seating your guests in time.

The main course is the most important choice and where you are most likely to run into problems. Casseroles are always a good solution. They take kindly to reheating and neatly combine a vegetable or two. They can be lightened for today's tastes by using less flour and cream and adding bright crisp vegetables. Venison, farmed rabbit and game are now available in supermarkets and make more unusual braises and stews. Tender cuts of meat such as fillets of pork and beef, duck and chicken breasts, can also be prepared ahead. They need more careful cooking initially and equally careful timing when you reheat them before serving. But they can be excellent if they are not overcooked and will look elegant on the plate. Fish makes a wonderful main course, particularly today as we think more about our health. It must be bought as fresh as possible and is best cooked at the last minute. Luckily, the cooking is just a matter of minutes and so not too daunting. There are lots of simple but excellent ways that fish can be baked. These dishes involve almost no preparation and no last-minute worries, and are ideal if you work and don't have much time to devote to cooking.

Sweets are usually cold, so that is easy. But what will you have? Should you tempt your guests with a fabulous chocolate marquise that they will happily scoff up, or balance the meal with fruit? The decision is up to you, but let the rest of the meal help you decide. Many desserts can be arranged ahead on individual plates and kept cool in a larder or refrigerator, leaving one less thing to worry about.

To help you decide what to have, check best buys weekly in newspapers and learn what's in season. Balance the menu – not only easy dishes with more complicated ones, but, more important, the ingredients. No one really wants to be loaded down with rich food. Confine the butter and cream to one course. Many people have been brought up to eat everything on their plate, so it is up to you to give small portions and well-balanced food. If you have special cheeses you are planning to serve, why not do away with a first course altogether? This is a new trend in France and a sensible one. Texture is also important. After a mousse you want something with more substance. After crunching your way through a salad, a fish dish is more appreciated. Don't be afraid to keep it simple. Fresh ingredients cooked simply so they taste of what they are cannot be bettered. Visualize how the menu will look and what contrasts of colour would look good. Buy vegetables, fruit or garnishes with that in mind, as well of course as the taste combinations. This may be the moment to splash our on the edible flowers that even supermarkets now sell. Think what little extras will give the meal more zip: spiced kumquats for the ham, a home-made loaf of bread, a brandy-snap *tuile* to contain the fruit salad, or chocolate truffles to serve with coffee. Recipes are in the 'Extras' section and are not time-consuming.

Another useful idea I have found is to keep a notebook with a guest list and menu, and comments on how the food tasted and any snags. It is invaluable as a reference. It is surprisingly easy to forget who you invited with whom and what you served. The other bit of advice is to entertain regularly. It becomes easier and easier the more often you do. You get better and better at it and there's a lot of enjoyment all round.

ACKNOWLEDGEMENTS

I would particularly like to thank Sue Oury for her invaluable help and recipes, which include Chicken Breasts Stuffed with Crab; Duck Breasts with Ginger; Roast Pork with Lemon and Coriander; and Sue's Ossi Buchi. Friends and neighbours have shared their recipes and I am very grateful to Jo Pattrick, Mary Trevelyan, Barbara Newman, Heather Platt, Patricia Trumper, José Manser, Jane Nissen, Marguerite McBey and Henrietta Green. My thanks to Jane Grigson, Bobby Fizdale and Arthur Gold for the use of their recipes. And special thanks to my family for all their encouragement and interest.

NOTE ON QUANTITIES

All recipes in the book give ingredients in both Imperial (oz, pts, etc.) and Metric (g, ml, etc.) measures. Use either set of quantities but not a mixture of both in any one recipe. 1 tsp = 5 ml and 1 tbls = 15 ml.

The Recipes

All the recipes are set out so you can see at a glance how much freedom you have to cook in advance. The instructions entitled 'Before serving' tell you how much time is needed for final cooking or reheating. This varies considerably: Cooking a roast may take 1½ hours and heating a casserole only 15 minutes, but *no more work is involved with the longer cooking times*. In most cases the sauce or stuffing is made well ahead and it is simply a question of calculating when to pop the roast or dish into the oven. In many instances this can be timed to coincide with starting the first course but the longer cooking times may have to be started before your guests arrive. Make a timetable of the time it takes your oven to reach different temperatures. This is a convenient bit of information to have pinned up nearby. You will then be able to calculate exactly when to turn the oven on for the different recipes. Make a countdown for each dish as a reminder of what you have to do and when. This is really essential for success and it will make you more relaxed and less likely to forget the nice biscuits you have so carefully baked or the garnish so finely chopped. A kitchen timer can also be helpful.

General Information

Casseroles: For tender, succulent meat never allow the meat to boil but keep it at the lowest simmer possible. The surface should just tremble. Adjust the heat accordingly, lowering the oven temperature when necessary. Place a piece of greaseproof paper on top of the meat and tuck it around the edges so it touches the liquid in the casserole. It will baste the meat as it cooks. Use a lid as well.

Stocks: The ingredients for making chicken and fish stocks are inexpensive and easily available. A stock used in a sauce makes all the difference and can upgrade your meal in a spectacular way. Simmer stocks for the recommended times; if they are simmered longer the bones can impart a bitter taste. If you need a more concentrated stock for a sauce, reduce by boiling rapidly after the stock has been strained. Add the salt after this reduction. If a stock is simmered gently enough initially, it will be quite clear and can be used for consommé without clarifying. Strain without pressing on the bones and vegetables. Avoid cubes – the monosodium glutamate is instantly recognizable and unsubtle, to say the least.

Roasts and meat portions: It is the thickness of the meat that determines the length of cooking time. The weight provides a general guide but obviously a thin piece of meat needs less time than a thicker piece even if they have the same weight. A meat thermometer is a great help for large roasts. For smaller cuts use your finger to determine if it is cooked enough. Meat should still be springy to the touch if you want it pink and tender.

Dariole and soufflé moulds: Individual moulds can be used to great advantage for entertaining. Buy good-quality moulds with a rim around the edge to facilitate covering. Soufflé moulds should be made from fine porcelain and have a good ½-pt (300-ml) capacity. They are expensive but will last forever with care. Always place them on a tray before putting them in a hot oven.

Cling-film: Darioles, terrines and other dishes baked in a *bain-marie* can be lined with cling-film. It eliminates the need to grease the dish and peels off easily after turning out. Chopped herbs or blanched vegetables prepared in advance will stay fresh if sealed with cling-film. Cold mousses or charlottes can be lined with cling-film. Don't worry about any creases; they will not be noticed when the pudding is turned out. Cling-film can also be used to cover meat or vegetables when you are keeping them warm in a low oven – about 170°C/325°F/Gas Mark 3 maximum.

Salads: Lettuce can be washed, dried and stored in a clean pillowcase overnight in the refrigerator, where it will keep beautifully crisp.

Shortcrust and puff pastry: When the recipe lists 6 oz (175 g) of pastry in the ingredients, this refers to the amount of flour, and not to the total weight of the pastry; it is a guide for the amount of pastry to make up.

Sauces: The strength of stocks, vinegars, wines and other flavourings can vary considerably, so this is an area where you must taste and adjust the quantities. English vinegars in particular are stronger than those of other countries, so go cautiously. Use only half the amount stated, then simmer to combine the flavours and taste before adding the rest.

Extras: Special oils, vinegars and mustards can enhance many salads and other dishes. A few suggestions to try are: Balsamic vinegar, sherry vinegar, raspberry vinegar, walnut oil, hazelnut oil, sesame seed oil and *mostarda di Cremona*. Store the oils in the refrigerator once they are opened and use within a month or two.

HORS-D'ŒUVRE

The fillings for these hors-d'œuvre can be made one day in advance. They can be assembled several hours before serving.

QUAILS' EGGS

Boil gently for 5–6 minutes for hard, 1½ minutes for soft eggs. Place in ice water, but peel while still warm. Cut in half, slice a tiny piece off top and bottom to make egg stand. Sieve the yolks with butter or mayonnaise, season, then spoon or pipe back into whites.

ROQUEFORT GRAPES

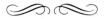

8 oz (225 g) cream cheese
2 oz (50 g) Roquefort cheese
3 tbls cream

toasted chopped nuts
1 lb (450 g) Italia or other
grapes

Mix cream cheese, Roquefort and cream together. Dip grapes in mixture, then roll in nuts. Refrigerate until set.

SESAME CHICKEN BITES

Bite-sized pieces of chicken covered in sesame seeds are tempting with drinks.

4 chicken breasts
2 oz (50 g) sesame seeds
4 tbls brown sugar

For the marinade
4 tbls tahini paste

2 cloves garlic
juice of 3 lemons
2 tbls soya sauce
4 tbls sesame oil
4 tbls sunflower oil

1. Cut the chicken into 1-in (2.5-cm) cubes.
2. Mix marinade ingredients with chicken and refrigerate overnight.
3. Toast the sesame seeds lightly in a moderate oven for 10 minutes.

——————— BEFORE SERVING ———————

Drain the marinade into a frying-pan, add the sugar and simmer for a few minutes. Add the chicken and sauté until tender. Roll in the sesame seeds, skewer with toothpicks and serve hot or cold.

STUFFED CHERRY TOMATOES

Sieve cottage cheese with a bit of cream. Add finely chopped fresh herbs. Cut tomatoes in half, scoop out some of the insides with a melon baller and fill with the cheese.

Alternatively, make a taramasalata and use as a filling.

STUFFED MANGE-TOUT

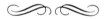

8 oz (225 g) crab meat	squeeze of lemon juice
4 tbls cream	salt and pepper
1 tbls mayonnaise	12 oz (350 g) mange-tout

Blend the crab meat, cream and mayonnaise together. Season with lemon juice, salt and pepper. Blanch the mange-tout in boiling salted water for 30 seconds, refresh under cold water and drain. Split open and spoon or pipe a thin layer of the cream in the pea.

1 lb (450 g) prawns in their shells	2 tbls walnut oil
	pepper
juice of 2 oranges	12 oz (350 g) mange-tout
3–4 tbls fresh mint, chopped	

Peel the prawns and save the shells for stock. Marinate the prawns in the orange juice, mint, oil and some pepper for at least 2 hours. Wrap a blanched mange-tout around a prawn and secure with a toothpick.

OTHER IDEAS

Carpaccio or gravad-lax on buttered bread.
Chevrons of smoked trout served with a horseradish sauce (whipped cream with horseradish added).
Melon or pear slices with Parma ham.
Tiny boiled new potatoes scooped out and stuffed with soured cream and lumpfish caviar
Celeriac rémoulade (see p. 51) served in small chicory leaves.
Cold fish mousseline baked in a terrine (set in a *bain-marie*) and served in small cubes (see p. 36).
Filo is the answer for delicious, hot hors-d'œuvre that can be made well in advance and frozen. Wrap it up with all sorts of good fillings, freeze it and bake it at a moment's notice. See the following recipes.

FILO SAUSAGE ROLL

1 onion, very finely chopped	10 oz (275 g) frozen spinach, thawed
1 tbls oil	2 small eggs
1 lb (450 g) good sausage meat (use good sausages and remove casing)	1 tsp fennel seeds
	salt and pepper
	1 pkg of filo pastry
	melted butter

1. Sauté the onion in the oil until soft. Add the sausage meat, breaking it up with a fork until browned. Remove any fat and turn into a bowl.
2. Place spinach in a sieve and press it to get rid of the moisture. Add to the meat. Add the eggs and fennel, and season if it needs it.

3. Unroll the filo sheets and keep covered with plastic. Use 8 sheets; brush them in turn with melted butter and lay them on top of each other. Spoon or pipe a 1-in (2.5-cm) wide row of the sausage mixture along the near edge. Roll it up like a Swiss roll and place seam-side down on a baking sheet. Repeat with remaining filling.
4. Brush the top with melted butter and freeze on a tray overnight. Wrap in cling-film and continue to freeze until needed.

BEFORE SERVING

1. Preheat the oven to 200°C/400°F/Gas Mark 6.
2. Cut frozen roll into ½-in (1.3-cm) rounds. Place on a greased baking sheet and bake about 12 minutes. Serve hot.

FILO CHICKEN ROLL

6 oz (175 g) chicken breast, boned and skinned	2 egg yolks
1 tbls oil	4 oz (100 g) freshly grated Parmesan cheese
1 oz (25 g) butter	1 tsp grated nutmeg
4 oz (100 g) lean pork loin	salt and pepper
12 oz (350 g) ricotta cheese	1 pkg of filo pastry
2 oz (50 g) mortadella sausage, very finely chopped	melted butter

1. Sauté the chicken in the oil and butter until lightly browned. Remove the chicken and brown the pork. When cool, chop as finely as possible by hand. Mix with all the other ingredients and season.
2. Follow the instructions for Filo Sausage Roll (see above) from No. 3 onwards, substituting the chicken filling for the sausage mixture.

FILO SPINACH ROLL

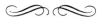

2 lb fresh spinach
salt and freshly ground
  black pepper
2 onions, very finely
  chopped
2 tbls olive oil
8 oz (225 g) ricotta cheese

3 small eggs
3 oz (75 g) freshly grated
  Parmesan cheese
grated nutmeg
1 pkg of filo pastry
melted butter

1. Wash the spinach in several changes of water, then drain. Cook with a pinch of salt and any water left clinging to the leaves, about 8 minutes. Drain in a sieve, pressing to get rid of extra moisture. Chop the spinach finely.

2. Sauté the onion in the oil, stirring, until soft. Stir in the spinach and cook together for a minute or two. Scrape into a bowl. Mix with the ricotta and then the eggs. Fold in the Parmesan and season well with nutmeg, salt and pepper.

3. Follow the instructions for Filo Sausage Roll (see p. 18) from No. 3 onwards, substituting the spinach filling for the sausage mixture.

FILO TRIANGLES

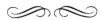

Bite-size filo packages are easy to make. Folded in the traditional triangular shape, they can contain any number of good things. You will need 8–10 sheets of filo pastry for each recipe.

For the smoked trout filling
6 oz (175 g) cream cheese
1 egg
4 tbls cream
6 oz (175 g) smoked trout,
  boned and flaked
2 oz (50 g) walnuts,
  chopped
freshly ground black pepper

For the Stilton filling
melted butter
4 oz (100 g) Stilton or other
  blue cheese
4 oz (100 g) cream cheese
1 egg yolk
1 pear, peeled and cored

Smoked trout filling: Mix first three ingredients together, then fold in the last two and season with pepper.

Stilton filling: Purée all the ingredients together.

For the triangles: Unfold the filo and keep the leaves covered with plastic to keep from drying out. Remove one sheet and brush with melted butter. Cut into 5 equal strips. Place 1 tsp of filling in the centre of a strip ¾ in (1.9 cm) from the bottom. Fold a corner across the filling and continue to fold as if for a flag. Continue until all the filling is used. If you are freezing them, place on a baking sheet and freeze overnight before storing in a plastic bag.

To cook: Place on a buttered baking sheet, brush with butter and bake in a moderate oven for 25 minutes.

FIRST COURSES

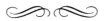

ASPARAGUS AND COURGETTE SOUP

SERVES 6

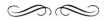

Not all soups benefit from a stock base. This water-based soup captures the special flavour of asparagus, with just a hint of courgette.

12 oz (350 g) courgettes	4 fl oz (110 ml) single cream
1 lb (450 g) asparagus	salt and pepper
3 oz (75 g) onion, very	juice of ½ lemon
finely chopped	*Garnish*
1½ oz (40 g) butter	**toasted slivered almonds**

UP TO TWO DAYS IN ADVANCE

1. Peel the courgettes and cut into thin rounds. Wash the asparagus. Cut 10 × 1-in (2.5-cm) spears from the asparagus, cover and refrigerate. Cut the rest of the asparagus into ¾-in (1.9-cm) rounds.
2. Gently sauté the onion in the butter, stirring, until soft. Add the courgettes and asparagus (except the 10 tips) and stir until coated in the butter. Add 1½ pts (900 ml) boiling water, cover and simmer for 20 minutes or until vegetables are tender.
3. Purée in a blender, food processor or vegetable mill, then rub through a sieve (this is necessary to get rid of any fibres). Cover and refrigerate.

BEFORE SERVING
(FIVE TO TEN MINUTES REHEATING TIME)

Slice the reserved asparagus tips in half lengthwise. Reheat the soup with the cream and tips. Adjust seasoning, adding lemon juice if needed. Serve garnished with the toasted almonds.

BORSCH

SERVES 6

Baked beetroot has a very good flavour and makes excellent borsch. An attractive pink, flecked with green chives, it makes an inviting start to any summer occasion.

2 lb (900 g) uncooked
    beetroot, of equal size
small bunch of spring
    onions
2 pts (1.1 L) beef stock
4 tbls tarragon vinegar

¼-pt (150-ml) carton of
    soured cream
salt and pepper

Garnish
**fresh dill or chives, very
finely chopped**

—— UP TO TWO DAYS IN ADVANCE ——

1. To keep the juices in the beetroot, cut off the leaves, leaving a bit of stalk on the beets. Rinse any dirt off carefully. The leaves can be saved and used like spinach, although the flavour is not as fine.
2. Preheat the oven to 180°C/350°F/Gas Mark 4. Wrap each beetroot individually in foil and bake on an oven sheet for about 1 hour or until cooked through.
3. Cool slightly, then slip off the skins. Chop roughly and place in a blender or food processor.
4. Cut the white parts of the spring onions into rounds and add to the beets with enough stock to blend. Purée, then scrape into a large bowl. Add the remaining stock and the tarragon vinegar. Taste for seasoning. Cover and refrigerate.

—— BEFORE SERVING ——

Stir in the soured cream, taste again and add more vinegar if necessary. Serve garnished with fresh dill or chives.

Note: Baked beetroot is excellent sliced for salads or reheated as a hot vegetable.

CALABRESE SOUP

SERVES 8

It doesn't sound very glamorous, but it is one of the nicest soups and one of the easiest to make.

1½ lb (675 g) calabrese
3 pts (1.7 L) chicken stock
½ pt (300 ml) double cream
salt and freshly ground
    black pepper

squeeze of lemon juice
Garnish
**slivered brazil nuts or
    toasted slivered almonds**

—— UP TO TWO DAYS IN ADVANCE ——

1. Peel any thick calabrese stalks. Cut the stalks and heads into small chunks.
2. Bring the stock to a simmer in a large saucepan. Add the calabrese and stalks and simmer for 30 minutes or until very soft. Purée in a blender or food processor. Cool and then cover and refrigerate.

—— BEFORE SERVING ——
(FIVE TO TEN MINUTES REHEATING TIME)

Reheat soup with the double cream to just below the boil. Taste for seasoning, adding lemon juice if needed. Garnish and serve.

Note: Any soup or sauce can have its flavour heightened by lemon juice. A small squeeze may be enough, so be cautious.

CORIANDER SOUP

SERVES 8

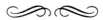

Fresh coriander makes a superb soup that is particularly good cold with added yoghurt. A different and exotic start for a summer meal.

1 medium-sized onion, very finely chopped
2 tbls butter
6 oz (175 g) courgettes, peeled and chopped
3 oz (75 g) fresh coriander leaves, chopped
salt and pepper
3 tbls semolina
1½ pts (900 ml) chicken stock

4 fl oz (110 ml) whipping cream (if serving hot)
2 egg yolks
9-oz (250-g) tub thick-set Greek yoghurt (if serving cold)

Garnish
fresh coriander leaves, chopped
toasted slivered almonds

———— UP TO THREE DAYS IN ADVANCE ————

1. Sweat the onion in the butter until soft without allowing it to colour. Add the courgettes and coriander, and stir for a few minutes. Add 1½ pts (900 ml) of water and salt, and bring to the boil. Stir in the semolina. Cover and simmer for 20 minutes or until the courgettes are tender.

2. Purée in a blender or food processor. Thin by adding the stock. Cover and refrigerate until needed.

———————— BEFORE SERVING ————————

To serve hot: Reheat soup to just below a simmer. Whisk cream and egg yolks together. Stir in two ladles of hot soup, then pour back into the soup and heat gently without allowing it to come near the boil. Garnish and serve.

To serve cold: Stir in the yoghurt, taste for seasoning and garnish with coriander and almonds.

Note: Parsley, preferably the flat-leafed variety, can be substituted for coriander to make a delicious parsley soup.

CUCUMBER AND TARRAGON SOUP

SERVES 8

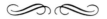

A few tablespoons of semolina gives body to this soup without detracting from the fresh cucumber flavour. It is good cold as well as hot.

1½ cucumbers
1 medium-sized onion, very finely chopped
1 tbls oil
1¾ pts (1 L) chicken stock
2 tsp tarragon vinegar
1 tbls sugar
sprig of fresh tarragon or ¼ tsp dried tarragon

2 tbls semolina
2 egg yolks
¼ pt (150 ml) double cream
salt and pepper

Garnish
cucumber slices
fresh tarragon, finely chopped

——— UP TO TWO DAYS IN ADVANCE ———

1. Peel the cucumbers. Cut 30 slices as thinly as possible. Sprinkle with salt and set aside. After 30 minutes, drain and keep refrigerated. Cut the rest of the cucumber into chunks.

2. In a large saucepan, soften the onion in the oil over low heat, stirring constantly. Add the cucumber chunks, stock, vinegar, sugar and tarragon. Bring to the boil, sprinkle in the semolina, cover and simmer for 25 minutes.

3. Purée the soup, then sieve. Return to the pan and season to taste with salt and pepper. Heat the soup to just below the boiling point. Whisk the egg yolks with the double cream in a small bowl. Whisk in a few ladlefuls of hot soup on to the eggs, then return the mixture to the pan. Stir and heat to well below the boiling point. Cool, cover and refrigerate if not using the same day.

——— BEFORE SERVING ———

To serve hot: Add the reserved cucumber slices and reheat carefully to below the boiling point. Taste for seasoning. Garnish with fresh tarragon.

To serve cold: Taste for seasoning and garnish.

LENTIL AND SORREL SOUP

SERVES 10–12

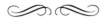

Sorrel is difficult to find in shops, but very easy to grow. Even a few plants will provide enough leaves for a lovely lemony-tasting sauce or this good soup.

1 lb (450 g) green lentils
6 oz (175 g) potatoes, peeled
  and sliced
6 oz (175 g) onions, sliced
3½ pts (2 L) chicken stock
bouquet garni
10–12 oz (275–350 g) sorrel

salt and black pepper
½ pt (300 ml) smetana or
  soured cream
squeeze of lemon juice

Garnish
a few sorrel leaves,
  shredded

TWO DAYS IN ADVANCE

1. Pick over the lentils for any stones and wash.
2. Place lentils, potatoes, onion, stock and bouquet garni in a large saucepan. Cover and simmer for at least 1¼ hours or until lentils are very soft. Check during cooking to see if there is enough liquid. Add water if needed.
3. Meanwhile, wash the sorrel, pull off the stalks and discard. Set aside a few leaves for the garnish. Wrap these in paper, then in plastic and refrigerate. Shred the rest of the sorrel coarsely.
4. Add the sorrel, salt and pepper to the lentils and cook, uncovered, for 10 minutes.
5. Purée the soup in a blender or food processor. Sieve the soup if you want a finer consistency. Cover and keep refrigerated until needed.

BEFORE SERVING
(FIVE TO TEN MINUTES REHEATING TIME)

Heat soup to the boiling point. Meanwhile, chop the sorrel for the garnish. Taste the soup for seasoning, adding lemon juice if necessary. Stir in the smetana or soured cream, garnish, and serve.

SHRIMP BISQUE

SERVES 6

Tiny shrimps in their shells are crushed, then simmered to extract all their flavour. This soup also makes a lovely sauce for baked fish.

2 oz (50 g) butter
1 carrot, very finely
   chopped
1 stalk of celery, very finely
   chopped
1 onion, very finely
   chopped
3 tbls rice
2½ pts (1.4 L) fish stock or
   water
bouquet garni
1½ lb (675 g) grey or
pink shrimps in
their shells

6 fl oz (175 ml) dry white
   wine
4 tbls Cognac
1 tbls tomato purée
3 tbls sunflower oil
3–4 slices day-old bread,
   crustless and cubed
pinch of cayenne pepper
4 fl oz (110 ml) double
   cream
salt and pepper

Garnish
**fresh mint, very finely
   chopped**

UP TO TWO DAYS IN ADVANCE

1. Heat 1 oz (25 g) butter in a large saucepan, add the vegetables and rice and stir for a few minutes to coat in the butter. Add ½ pt (300 ml) of stock or water and the bouquet garni. Cover and simmer for 15 minutes.
2. Meanwhile, peel about 24 shrimps, cover and refrigerate. Whizz the remaining shrimps and shells in a food processor with the rest of the butter until well puréed.
3. Add the wine to the saucepan and boil to reduce by half. Add the Cognac, remaining stock or water, puréed shrimp and tomato purée. Bring to the boil, cover and simmer gently for 25 minutes.
4. Work the mixture through a drum sieve with a wooden pestle or large spoon. This is an arduous task and can take 20 minutes, but it is worth the effort. Cover and refrigerate the puréed soup.

ONE TO TWO HOURS IN ADVANCE

Heat the oil in a small frying-pan until very hot. Add the croûtons and fry, shaking the pan to brown them evenly. Watch them carefully and take off the heat as they begin to brown. They will continue to darken once off the heat. Place in a sieve and leave to drain.

Bring soup to a simmer. Add cayenne and cream. Adjust seasoning and set aside off heat.

BEFORE SERVING
(FIVE TO TEN MINUTES REHEATING TIME)

Reheat the soup. Serve in warmed bowls garnished with the reserved shrimp and mint. Pass the croûtons separately.

SPINACH AND LETTUCE SOUP
SERVES 8

1 large onion, very finely chopped
1 oz (25 g) butter
1 lb (450 g) spinach
1 lb (450 g) lettuce

2½ pts (1.4 L) light chicken stock
salt and pepper
freshly grated nutmeg
¼ pt (150 ml) single cream
squeeze of lemon juice

UP TO TWO DAYS IN ADVANCE

1. Using a large saucepan, soften the onion in the butter, stirring, without allowing it to colour.
2. Carefully wash the spinach and lettuce. Remove any coarse stalks and discard. Chop both leaves coarsely. Add the greens to the onions and stir to coat in the butter. Add the stock and season if stock is not salty. Bring to the boil, cover and simmer for 20 minutes.
3. Purée in a blender or food processor. Season with some grated nutmeg and pepper. Cool, cover and refrigerate.

--------- BEFORE SERVING ---------
(FIVE TO TEN MINUTES REHEATING TIME)

Reheat the soup with the cream, season with some lemon juice if needed and serve.

Note: The lettuce can be replaced by a large bunch of watercress for another good soup.

ANCHOVY MUSHROOMS
SERVES 6

Mushrooms stuffed with an anchovy cream served on fried bread are a tasty starter or savoury.

6 croûtes (see p. 212), large enough to hold 2 mushrooms
12 mushrooms, 2½ in (6.3 cm) in diameter
2 tbls oil
squeeze of lemon juice

salt and pepper
6–8 anchovies
¼ pt (150 ml) double cream, whipped
1 tbls tomato ketchup

Garnish
mustard and cress

--------- SAME DAY AS SERVING ---------

1. Make the croûtes.
2. Cut stems from the mushrooms and use for another dish. Lightly sauté the caps in the oil, open-side down first, with a squeeze of lemon, some salt and pepper. Set aside.
3. Sieve the anchovies, then mix with the cream and ketchup.

--------- BEFORE SERVING ---------
(TWENTY MINUTES REHEATING TIME)

1. Reheat the croûtes in a low oven. Reheat the mushrooms at the same time in another dish for about 20 minutes.
2. Spoon some cream into the mushrooms, place two on each croûte and serve garnished with the mustard and cress.

STUFFED ARTICHOKE BOTTOMS

To my mind artichokes make one of the very best first courses. They can be stuffed with a variety of fillings and preparing the bottoms takes only a few minutes with a sharp knife. Buy artichokes that are a good green colour and have not started to turn black around the edges. They should still be tightly closed.

—— TO PREPARE ARTICHOKE BOTTOMS ——

1. Add the juice of half a lemon to a small bowl of cold water.
2. Break off the stems with a sharp movement.
3. Hold a very sharp knife vertically against the side of the leaves and cut off all the first few rows of bottom leaves to expose the pale centre flesh.
4. Trim the centre cone of leaves level with the top edge of the artichoke. The choke will be easily removed after cooking. Rub the

cut surfaces with lemon and place in the water.

5. To cook the artichokes make a paste with 4 tbls each of flour and water. Bring 2 pts (1.1 L) of water to the boil, add some salt, juice of half a lemon and stir in the flour paste. Simmer the bottoms for about 15 minutes or until tender. Drain. When cool enough to handle carefully ease out the chokes with the help of a spoon.

Note: Alternatively, cook artichokes whole and then pull out centre cone and choke, leaving the outer leaves to form a cup.

ARTICHOKES STUFFED WITH BROADBEANS

SERVES 6

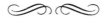

Jane Grigson's recipe and one of the best ways of serving stuffed artichokes.

6 artichoke bottoms, cooked (see above)	**4 tbls cream**
	squeeze of lemon juice
4 lb (1.8 kg) fresh broadbeans or 1½ lb (675 g) frozen broadbeans	**salt and pepper**
	1 tbls fresh sage, very finely chopped
1½ oz (40 g) butter	

─────── ONE DAY IN ADVANCE ───────

1. Prepare the artichoke bottoms. Cover and refrigerate.
2. Cook and skin the broadbeans. Sieve them into a bowl. Stir in the butter, cream and a squeeze of lemon juice. Season with salt and pepper. Cover and refrigerate.

─────── BEFORE SERVING ───────
(TEN TO FIFTEEN MINUTES REHEATING TIME)

1. Reheat the artichokes by steaming them over hot water. A drum sieve works well if you can fit it over a pan.
2. Reheat the purée in the top of a *bain-marie*.
3. Stir the herb into the purée, fill the artichokes and serve.

ARTICHOKES STUFFED
with CREAMY EGGS

SERVES 6

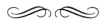

6 artichoke bottoms,
   cooked (see p. 32)
8 eggs
salt and freshly ground
   black pepper

2 oz (50 g) butter
2 tbls cream
2 tbls fresh chervil or
   chives, very finely
   chopped

UP TO ONE DAY IN ADVANCE

1. Prepare the artichoke bottoms. When cool, cover tightly in cling-film and refrigerate.

2. Whisk 7 eggs until just blended. Season lightly with salt and pepper. Over very low heat melt the butter in a heavy-based saucepan. Stir in the eggs and keep stirring with a wooden spoon until the eggs thicken. This should take about 10 minutes. If the eggs cook too fast, remove them from the heat from time to time, but keep stirring. When the eggs have thickened but are still creamy, take them off the heat and stir in the cream. Add the extra egg if you have overcooked them; save it for reheating if the eggs are nice and soft. Cover and refrigerate when cool.

BEFORE SERVING
(TEN TO FIFTEEN MINUTES REHEATING TIME)

1. Reheat the artichokes by placing over water in a steamer.

2. Reheat the eggs in a *bain-marie*, being careful not to overcook them. Add a bit more cream or the extra egg if they threaten to overcook. Check seasoning, mix in the herb and stuff the artichokes with the eggs. Serve at once.

Note: The artichokes can be reheated in a low oven if it is more convenient.

Grilled Stuffed Avocados

SERVES 6

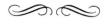

Buy prawns in their shells rather than the frozen, shelled variety. They have a better flavour and the shells make good stock.

1 shallot, very finely chopped
2 tbls oil
2 tsp curry powder
2 tsp fresh root ginger, grated
6 fl oz (175 ml) home-made mayonnaise (see p. 219)

12 oz (350 g) prawns in their shells
1 tbls fresh mint, finely chopped
Salt and pepper
3 ripe avocados

Garnish
watercress

UP TO ONE DAY IN ADVANCE

Sauté the shallot in the oil, stirring, until soft. Add the curry powder and stir for another minute. Scrape out into a bowl and mix in the ginger and mayonnaise. Cover and refrigerate.

SAME DAY AS SERVING

Peel the prawns, reserving the shells for stock. Add the prawns to the mayonnaise along with the mint. Taste for seasoning.

BEFORE SERVING
(FIVE MINUTES GRILLING TIME)

Preheat the grill. Cut avocados in half and remove stones. Stuff generously with the mayonnaise. Place about 4 in (10 cm) from the heat and grill for about 5 minutes or until the filling is a good golden colour. Garnish and serve.

Note: Pears can also be used. Peel and stuff in the same way, spooning out a bit of the centres to make a space.

Hot Mousseline of Sole with Green Peppercorn Sauce

SERVES 6

One of the best reasons for having a food processor is the ease with which you can make delicate mousselines. In this recipe a fish mousseline is poached in little moulds and served with a lemon and pepper sauce. A fish mousseline can also be used as a stuffing for baked fish or *paupiettes*.

12 oz (350 g) skinned fillets of sole, salmon, pike or brill	*For the sauce*
	2 shallots, very finely chopped
1 tsp salt	1 oz (25 g) butter
1 whole egg	1 tbls plain flour
1 egg white	¾ pt (450 ml) fish stock
pinch of cayenne pepper	small glass of white wine
pinch of white pepper	2–3 tbls of tinned green peppercorns in brine, drained
grating of nutmeg	
12 fl oz (400 ml) double cream	salt
	lemon juice
	2 tbls double cream

———— UP TO ONE DAY IN ADVANCE ————

1. Place the bowl of a food processor in the freezer. Keep fish and cream very cold.
2. *For the sauce*: Soften the shallots in the butter, stirring, over gentle heat. Add the flour and stir for 1 minute. Whisk in the fish stock and continue to whisk until it reaches a simmer. Add the wine, green peppercorns and some salt, and simmer gently for 15 minutes. Season with lemon juice. Refrigerate when cool.
3. Cut the fish into pieces and remove any bones. Purée in the cold processor for a full 4–5 minutes. Add the salt and purée again. Slowly pour in the eggs and spices and blend until very smooth. Scrape down the sides from time to time. With the machine

running, add the cream very slowly and stop the moment it is well blended. Do not over mix. Return the container to the refrigerator for 1 hour.

4. Preheat the oven to 170°C/325°F/Gas Mark 3.

5. Line 6 dariole moulds with cling-film. There are ¼-pt (150-ml) ones available for the freezer that can be used. Spoon the mixture into the moulds and smooth the tops. Place in a roasting tin and add enough hot water to come half-way up the sides of the moulds. Cover the tops with a large piece of buttered foil. Bake for about 15–20 minutes. Remove from the tin but keep in the moulds. Refrigerate when cool.

BEFORE SERVING
(TEN MINUTES BAKING TIME)

1. Preheat the oven to 200°C/400°F/Gas Mark 6.

2. Place the moulds in the roasting tin, add enough hot water to come half-way up the sides of the moulds and cover with foil. Bake for 10 minutes or until mousselines are puffed and heated through.

3. Reheat the sauce, add the cream and adjust the seasoning.

4. *To serve*: Unmould on to individual plates, remove cling-film and spoon some sauce around the edge.

Note: Although the mousselines reheat well, if you can manage to cook them before serving they will be ever better. Cling-film can be used to line moulds that are baked in a *bain-marie*. To unmould, reverse on to a plate and peel away the cling-film. Don't worry about the creases you have in the cling-film linings; they will not show when turned out.

MOULES MARINIÈRE

SERVES 6

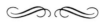

Mussels are sadly neglected in this country. Any mussel dish I have ever served has been greeted by cheers and surprise – as if it were an amazing feat. I wonder why, when they are so readily available, inexpensive and easy to prepare. This is a simple, classic way of serving them, but they are also wonderful additions to fish soups and other fish dishes.

6 lb (2.7 kg) mussels
6 tbls fresh parsley, very
   finely chopped
4 shallots, very finely
   chopped

½ pt (300 ml) dry white
   wine
1 oz (25 g) butter

SAME DAY AS SERVING

Scrub the mussels with a stiff brush, remove the beards and scrape off any barnacles with a knife. Let the mussels rest in cold salted water. Change the water at intervals if it becomes muddy. Discard any with broken shells or that are open.

ONE HOUR IN ADVANCE

Prepare parsley and shallots and keep under cling-film. Set out pans and equipment you will need. Warm a large tureen and 6 soup plates.

BEFORE SERVING
(FIVE MINUTES COOKING TIME)

1. Drain the mussels and discard any that are open.
2. Using a large saucepan with a tight-fitting lid, bring shallots with the wine to the boil. Add the mussels, cover and cook over high heat, shaking the pan occasionally, for about 5 minutes or until the mussels have just opened. Do not overcook them or they will become tough.
3. Strain the liquor through a muslin-lined sieve set over a sauce-

pan. Pour the mussels into the warmed tureen. Heat the liquor and whisk in the butter; pour over the mussels and scatter with the parsley.

Note: Although I have kept mussels overnight in cold salted water without any harm, it is best to buy them the day you intend to cook them. Always check that your guests are not allergic to shellfish.

QUENELLES
SERVES 6

Quenelles are super-light fish dumplings made from a fish mousseline and usually served in a good, creamy sauce. They can be poached the day ahead and reheated in hot water just before serving. The ingredients are the same as those used for the Hot Mousseline of Sole (see p. 36) including the Green Peppercorn Sauce.

UP TO ONE DAY IN ADVANCE

1. Follow the instructions for making Hot Mousseline of Sole to No. 3 (refrigerating the mousseline for one hour).
2. Shape the mousseline into *quenelles* using two spoons dipped in cold water. Heap the mixture on one spoon, invert it on to the second spoon and slide into a buttered roasting tin or large pan. Add enough hot water to cover the *quenelles* and bring to a simmer. Poach at a bare simmer for 10 minutes. The water should just quiver and not be bubbling. Remove with a slotted spoon and dry on paper towels. Cover and store in one layer in the refrigerator.

BEFORE SERVING
(FIVE TO EIGHT MINUTES REHEATING TIME)

1. Reheat the sauce, add the cream and adjust the seasoning.
2. Return the *quenelles* to a buttered roasting tin. Cover with hot water and poach for 5–8 minutes or until just heated through.
To serve: Arrange two *quenelles* on each plate and spoon around some sauce.

Note: Another good butter sauce can be made by reducing ½ pt (300 ml) fish stock, 4 tbls of dry white wine and 1 tbls of white wine vinegar by half. Whisk in 4 oz (100 g) of butter bit by bit over very low heat at the last minute. Add 1 tbls of double cream and season. The reduction can be done ahead, then heated before the butter is added.

RAMEKINS OF SNAILS AND MUSHROOMS

SERVES 8

This dish of snails and mushrooms in bubbling-hot garlic and parsley butter will make your guests think they are in France. Serve it with French bread to mop up the fragrant juices.

8 oz (225 g) fresh button mushrooms	**2 oz (50 g) fresh parsley leaves**
1 tbls oil	**6 oz (175 g) butter**
4 cloves garlic	**salt and pepper**
	7-oz (200-g) tin of escargots

—————— UP TO ONE DAY IN ADVANCE ——————

1. Sauté the mushrooms in the oil, stirring, until lightly cooked.
2. Process the garlic and parsley until finely chopped, add the butter, salt and pepper, and process to blend; or chop and blend by hand.
3. Drain the escargots and divide them between 8 ramekins. Add some mushrooms to each pot. Spoon in the butter and press down to cover the snails and mushrooms. Cover and refrigerate if not using the same day.

—————— BEFORE SERVING ——————
(FIFTEEN TO TWENTY MINUTES BAKING TIME)

1. Preheat the oven to 200°C/400°F/Gas Mark 6.
2. Bake the ramekins for 15–20 minutes or until bubbling hot. If

they have been in the refrigerator, place them on a baking sheet to prevent the ramekins breaking.

SEAFOOD WITH GINGER

SERVES 8

A classic idea with an Oriental touch. If there isn't enough time leave out the pastry, but the good fish stock is a must.

8 oz (225 g) puff pastry (see p. 210)
1 large carrot, cut into julienne
white part of 1 leek, cut into julienne
5 oz (125 g) celeriac, cut into julienne
3 oz (75 g) fresh root ginger, cut into julienne
8 scallops
8 oz (225 g) prawns in their shells
12 oz (350 g) brill, turbot or salmon
12 oz (350 g) monkfish
salt and pepper

1 oz (25 g) butter
1 tbls oil

For the sauce
2 shallots, very finely chopped
½ oz (15 g) butter
¼ pt (150 ml) Sauterne
½ pt (300 ml) good fish stock
1 tbls fresh root ginger, grated
4 tbls port
¼ pt (150 ml) double cream
1 tbls arrowroot (optional)

UP TO ONE DAY IN ADVANCE

1. *For the sauce*: Sauté the shallots in the butter, stirring, until soft. Add a splash of Sauterne and evaporate. Add the stock and grated ginger and simmer to reduce slightly. Add the rest of the Sauterne and simmer a few minutes. Add half the port, simmer another minute and taste for seasoning. Cool, then cover and refrigerate.
2. Make 8 puff-pastry shapes: small for a garnish; or diamond shaped, about 4 in (10 cm) each side, to be used as containers; or a fish shape if you can draw.

──── SEVERAL HOURS IN ADVANCE ────

1. Blanch the julienned vegetables and ginger in a large quantity of boiling salted water until *al dente*. Refresh under cold running water and drain. Cover with cling-film and set aside.

2. Pat the fish dry and cut into diagonal pieces. Peel the prawns. Slice the scallops into two equal discs. Season all the fish with salt and pepper. Heat ½ oz (15 g) of butter with the oil in a frying-pan. Add the fish pieces in batches and remove them before they colour, about 10 seconds each side. Place fish on a dish, cover and set aside. Set the pan aside unwashed.

──── BEFORE SERVING ────
(TEN MINUTES REHEATING TIME)

1. Preheat the oven to 180°C/350°F/Gas Mark 4.

2. Place the pastry shapes on a baking sheet and reheat for 10 minutes.

3. Reheat the sauce in the pan used for the fish. Stir in the double cream and the rest of the port if the sauce needs it. Bring to a simmer, slide all the fish in and return to a simmer. Simmer for less than 1 minute. Do not overcook.

4. Heat the vegetables and ginger in the remaining ½ oz (15 g) of butter.

To serve: Arrange a pastry container on each plate, spoon in some fish, cover with the pastry lid and garnish with the ginger and vegetables.

Note: The sauce should be thin, but can always be slightly thickened at the last minute with arrowroot. Mix the arrowroot with a few tablespoons of stock and simmer in the sauce for a few minutes.

SMOKED FISH GRATIN

SERVES 8

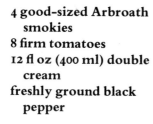

An easy and tasty starter.

4 good-sized Arbroath smokies	8 fresh basil leaves or 1 tsp fresh parsley, finely chopped
8 firm tomatoes	
12 fl oz (400 ml) double cream	6 oz (175 g) Cheddar cheese, grated
freshly ground black pepper	toast for serving

——— UP TO ONE DAY IN ADVANCE ———

1. Skin and remove all bones from the fish and discard. Flake the flesh, cover and refrigerate.
2. Peel, seed and dice the tomatoes, cover and refrigerate.

——— SEVERAL HOURS IN ADVANCE ———

Divide half the cream between 8 small ramekins or pour into one gratin dish. Layer with half the fish and grind over some pepper. Spoon the tomatoes over the fish and scatter with the basil or parsley. Add the remaining fish, more pepper and pour over the rest of the cream. Top with the cheese and set aside in a cool place.

——— BEFORE SERVING ———
(FIFTEEN MINUTES BAKING TIME)

1. Preheat the oven to 180°C/350°F/Gas Mark 4.
2. Bake on the top shelf for 15 minutes or until bubbling and brown. Serve with toast.

Note: Other smoked fish can be used. Smoked trout with some chopped cucumber is very good.

SPINACH CREAM
WITH TOMATO SAUCE

SERVES 6

An unmoulded, creamy spinach custard served on a tomato sauce is a stunning first course.

1 lb (450 g) fresh spinach	½ pt (300 ml) double cream
1 shallot, very finely chopped	salt and pepper
	few gratings of nutmeg
1 oz (25 g) butter	½ pt (300 ml) tomato sauce
½ pt (300 ml) milk	(see p. 224)
4 eggs	

--------- UP TO ONE DAY IN ADVANCE ---------

1. Wash the spinach in several changes of water. Cook with some salt and with any water left clinging to its leaves. Drain into a sieve, pressing out as much moisture as possible, then roughly chop.
2. Soften the shallot in the butter, stirring. Add the spinach and stir for about 5 minutes to evaporate all the moisture. Purée in a blender or food processor with a bit of milk.
3. Mix the eggs, milk and cream together, then stir in the spinach. Season with salt, pepper and a few gratings of nutmeg. Refrigerate unless using the same day.
4. Make the tomato sauce and keep refrigerated.

--------- BEFORE SERVING ---------
(THIRTY MINUTES BAKING TIME)

1. Preheat the oven to 170°C/325°F/Gas Mark 3.
2. Line 6 dariole or ramekin moulds with cling-film. Fill with the custard. Place some newspapers in the bottom of a roasting pan, set the moulds on the paper and pour boiling water to come just under half-way up the sides. Cover with a sheet of foil. Bake for 30 minutes or until the custards have risen and slightly shrunk from the sides. Remove from the oven and roasting tin and let stand for 5 minutes. This is important or they may collapse. Reheat the tomato

sauce, place some on 6 plates and unmould the spinach in the centres.

Note: This recipe is delicious warm or even cool, so don't let the timing worry you. You can also adapt the idea and use leeks with finely diced ham.

Spinach Soufflé

SERVES 4–5

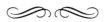

It really works, even when the whites are folded in a few hours ahead of time, as long as you are using the conventional béchamel-based soufflé. With the flourless *nouvelle cuisine* soufflé, you have to add the whites at the last minute.

12 oz (350 g) fresh spinach	¼ pt (150 ml) single cream
1 shallot, very finely chopped	4 egg yolks
	salt and pepper
1 tbls oil	grating of nutmeg
1 oz (25 g) butter	2 oz (50 g) freshly grated
2 tbls plain flour	Parmesan cheese
¼ pt (150 ml) milk	6 egg whites

—— UP TO ONE DAY IN ADVANCE ——

1. Wash the spinach in several changes of water. Blanch in a large quantity of boiling salted water for 2 minutes. Drain into a sieve, rinse under cold water, then drain again, pressing out as much moisture as possible. Sauté the shallot in the oil, stirring, until soft, but do not allow to colour. Add the spinach and stir over the heat to evaporate any moisture. Purée in a blender of food processor.
2. Make the béchamel sauce (see p. 218), using the butter, flour, milk and cream. Take the pan off the heat and beat in the egg yolks, one by one. Stir in the spinach and season well with salt, pepper and nutmeg. Cover the surface with a piece of cling-film and refrigerate.

——— ONE TO TWO HOURS IN ADVANCE ———

1. Butter a 2½-pt (1.4-L) soufflé dish or four to five ½-pt (300-ml) soufflé dishes and sprinkle with some grated cheese.
2. Reheat the spinach mixture until just hot, without allowing it to boil. Whisk the egg whites with a pinch of salt until stiff. Fold a large spoonful of whites into the spinach mixture. Fold the remaining cheese into the rest of the whites and then fold carefully into the spinach. Spoon into the prepared dish or dishes, cover with cling-film and keep in a cool place.

——— BEFORE SERVING ———
(TEN MINUTES BAKING TIME FOR INDIVIDUAL SOUFFLÉS; TWENTY-FIVE MINUTES FOR A LARGE SOUFFLÉ)

1. Preheat the oven to 200°C/400°F/Gas Mark 6.
2. Place the soufflés on a baking tray. Bake the small individual soufflés for 10 minutes; a large soufflé will need 25 minutes. Serve immediately.

SURPRISE SOUFFLÉ
SERVES 4

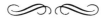

If you are fond of soufflés it is worth investing in individual soufflé dishes that hold a good ½ pt (300 ml) each. They make serving easy, and the soufflés will cook in about 10 minutes. The basic soufflé mixture can be made a day ahead and even the egg whites folded in a few hours beforehand. All you need think about is seating your guests in time.

1½ oz (40 g) butter	salt and pepper
1 oz (25 g) plain flour	extra butter for greasing
½ pt (300 ml) milk	4 artichoke bottoms,
4 egg yolks	cooked (see p. 32)
3 oz (75 g) grated cheese,	6 egg whites
half Gruyère and half	
freshly grated Parmesan	

UP TO ONE DAY IN ADVANCE

1. Prepare the artichoke bottoms. When cool, cover tightly in cling-film and refrigerate.
2. Melt the butter in a saucepan, stir in the flour and let it froth for 1 minute. Whisk in the milk and continue to whisk until the mixture comes to the boil. Simmer for a few minutes, remove from the heat and stir in the egg yolks, one by one. Stir in all the cheese and season with salt and pepper. Press a piece of cling-film on the surface to stop a skin forming and refrigerate.

TWO TO THREE HOURS IN ADVANCE

1. Butter four ½-pt (300-ml) soufflé dishes. Place an artichoke bottom in each dish.
2. Reheat the egg yolk mixture until hand hot. Do not let it get near a simmer. Remove from the heat.
3. Whisk the egg whites until stiff, adding a pinch of salt towards the end. Fold a large spoon of whites into the yolks to lighten them; then fold the yolks into the whites. Spoon into the dishes until level with the top. Cover with cling-film and keep in a cool place or refrigerate.

BEFORE SERVING
(TEN TO TWELVE MINUTES BAKING TIME FOR INDIVIDUAL SOUFFLÉS; TWENTY TO TWENTY-FIVE MINUTES FOR A LARGE SOUFFLÉ)

1. Preheat the oven to 200°C/400°F/Gas Mark 6.
2. Have a baking sheet ready for the soufflés and a tray to carry them to the table when done.
3. Remove the cling-film, place the soufflés on the baking sheet and bake for 10–12 minutes. Serve immediately.

Note: You can use a 2-pt (1.1-L) soufflé dish and arrange the artichokes on the bottom. Allow 20–25 minutes baking time.

AUBERGINE-CAVIAR SALAD

SERVES 8

Grilled aubergines have a delicious smoky flavour. Combined with walnuts they provide the focus of this salad

2 lb (900 g) very firm
   aubergines
6 tbls walnut oil
6 tbls sunflower oil
dash of tabasco
squeeze of lemon juice
salt and pepper
4 oz (100 g) walnuts, very
   finely chopped
2 tbls wine vinegar
4 oz (100 g) fresh button
   mushrooms

3 tomatoes, peeled, seeded
   and cut into strips
mixture of lettuces, such as
   curly endive, lamb's
   lettuce, watercress or
   radicchio
melba toast (see p. 212)

Garnish
fresh coriander or parsley,
   very finely chopped

UP TO TWO DAYS IN ADVANCE

1. Grill the aubergines until they are charred on all sides and soft when pierced with a fork.
2. Cool slightly, then peel off the skin with wet fingers. Purée the flesh in a blender or food processor. Scrape into a bowl and stir in 2 tbls each of walnut and sunflower oil, a dash of tabasco, lemon juice, salt and pepper. Fold in the walnuts. Cover and refrigerate.

BEFORE SERVING

1. Make a vinaigrette with the remaining oils, vinegar, salt and pepper
2. Wash and dry the lettuce, and tear into pieces.
3. Toss the mushrooms, tomatoes and lettuce with the vinaigrette.
4. Arrange some salad on each plate. Place a dollop of aubergine-caviar in the centre. Garnish with coriander or parsley and serve with melba toast.

Avocado Mousse with Yoghurt Sauce

SERVES 8

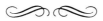

I have never liked the thick consistency of most avocado mousses. Here is a very light version, served with a fresh-tasting yoghurt sauce.

I carrot, cut into very fine julienne
I stalk of celery, cut into very fine julienne
scant ½ oz (15 g) gelatine
juice of 2 limes
4 avocados, just ripe
dash of Worcestershire sauce
salt
2 egg whites

Garnish
fresh tarragon

For the sauce
6 fl oz (175 ml) plain thick-set yoghurt
4 tbls single cream
6 fl oz (175 ml) milk
I½ tbls sugar
I½ tbls tarragon vinegar
salt

—————— UP TO ONE DAY IN ADVANCE ——————
(ALLOW FOUR HOURS MINIMUM FOR SETTING)

1. Blanch the carrot and celery for 5 seconds in boiling salted water. Refresh under cold running water; drain, dry, cover and refrigerate.
2. Soak the gelatine in the lime juice in a small cup. Place cup in hot water until gelatine is dissolved.
3. Whizz avocado flesh in a blender or food processor. Add the lime juice, salt to taste and a good dash of Worcestershire, and blend again.
4. Whisk egg whites to soft peaks and gently fold into the purée.
5. Line the ramekins you are using with cling-film. Don't worry about any creases in the cling-film. Spoon in the mousse, tap gently to settle and level tops with a spatula. Cover tops with cling-film and refrigerate.
6. Mix together the sauce ingredients and season with salt. Refrigerate.

BEFORE SERVING

1. Reverse ramekins on to plates and peel off cling-film.
2. Spoon some sauce around the mousse and swirl plates to distribute evenly. Scatter the vegetables around the sauce and garnish with a tiny bit of finely chopped tarragon.

CARPACCIO

SERVES 8

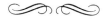

Paper-thin slices of raw beef with a dill sauce are a beautiful way to start a grand meal.

2-lb (900-g) thin piece of
   beef fillet
1 tbls oil
freshly ground black
   pepper
3 tbls fresh dill, very finely
   chopped

For the sauce
1 tbls Dijon mustard
2 tbls fresh dill, very finely
   chopped
½ tsp wine vinegar
1 tbls sugar
½ tsp salt
6 tbls cream

UP TO ONE DAY IN ADVANCE
(MINIMUM SIX HOURS)

Rub the fillet with oil, sprinkle with pepper and roll in the dill. Wrap in cling-film and refrigerate.

FOUR HOURS IN ADVANCE

Place fillet in the freezer for 2 hours.

TWO HOURS IN ADVANCE

1. Using a very sharp knife, slice the partially frozen fillet into paper-thin slices. Lay them in a single layer on each plate. If you can't get them thin enough, place between cling-film and gently pound out with a rolling pin.

2. Mix the sauce ingredients together and serve separately.

Note: The plates can be garnished with a few tiny blanched French beans. If you can't find fresh dill, us 1½ tbls dried.

CELERIAC RÉMOULADE
WITH PRAWNS
SERVES 6–8

The small leaves of a chicory make pretty containers for celeriac rémoulade. Arrange them on individual plates to resemble the spokes of a wheel, with a hub of salty prawns.

juice of ½ lemon
salt and freshly ground
    black pepper
1 good-sized celeriac root
3 tbls Dijon mustard
1 tbls wine vinegar
4 fl oz (110 ml) sunflower oil

1½ lb (675 g) prawns in
    their shells
2 small heads of chicory

Garnish
fresh basil or mint, very
    finely chopped

—— UP TO TWO DAYS IN ADVANCE ——
(MINIMUM FOUR HOURS)

1. Mix lemon juice with 1 tsp of salt in a bowl.
2. Peel the celeriac, then cut into very fine julienne. This is best done in a food processor with a julienne disc. Toss the julienne in the lemon juice and leave for 30 minutes.
3. Mix the mustard, ½ tsp of salt and vinegar together in a small bowl. Slowly whisk in the sunflower oil as for a mayonnaise (see p. 219).
4. Dry the celeriac with paper towels, then fold in the dressing. Season to taste with salt and pepper. Keep refrigerated in a covered container.

Shell the prawns (use the shells for stock).

BEFORE SERVING

Break off the chicory leaves and fill the smaller ones with the celeriac. Place some prawns in the centre of each plate and surround with the leaves like the spokes of a wheel. Garnish with basil or mint.

Note: Shelled frozen prawns have no taste to speak of. It is worth the bother of shelling your own and you have the bonus of shells for stock. Celeriac-filled leaves on a large platter are an excellent hors-d'œuvre to serve with drinks.

CHEESE ROULADE
WITH GRILLED PEPPERS
SERVES 8

Roulades always look impressive. This one is served cold and can be made a day ahead. The combination of peppers and cheese is delicious.

5 eggs, separated
3 oz (75 g) freshly grated
   Parmesan or Cheddar
   cheese
1 oz (25 g) brown
   breadcrumbs
pinch of cayenne pepper

1 tsp Dijon mustard
salt and pepper

For the filling
½ pt (300 ml) *fromage frais*
1 red pepper
1 yellow pepper

UP TO ONE DAY IN ADVANCE

1. Line a 13½ × 9½-in (33 × 24-cm) Swiss-roll tin with baking parchment. Preheat oven to 180°C/350°F/Gas Mark 4.

2. Whisk egg yolks with mustard and cayenne until light. Fold in all but 2 tbls of the cheese.

3. Whisk the egg whites with a pinch of salt until stiff. Fold into the yolk mixture, then fold in the breadcrumbs.

4. Spread over the prepared tin and bake for 15 minutes.

5. Run a knife around the edge of the tin and turn out on to a sheet of parchment paper sprinkled with the remaining 2 tbls of cheese. Cool to lukewarm, then roll up the roulade, using the paper to help. Keep rolled and when cool, cover and refrigerate.

6. Grill the peppers until they are blistered and charred on all sides. Peel off the skin with wet fingers. Cut the flesh into julienne, discarding the seeds and stalk. Cover and refrigerate.

—— TWO TO THREE HOURS IN ADVANCE ——

Unroll the roulade. Spread a layer of *fromage frais* over the surface. Scatter the peppers over the top, reroll and slide on to a serving platter. Keep in a cool place until ready to serve.

CHICKEN LIVER, BACON AND WALNUT SALAD

SERVES 6

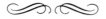

A nice way to start the meal if you are having fish as a main course.

8 oz (225 g) chicken livers
6 oz (175 g) unsmoked
   streaky bacon, thinly
   sliced
mixed salad greens
2 oz (50 g) walnut pieces,
   coarsely chopped

salt and freshly ground
   black pepper
2 oz (50 g) fresh button
   mushrooms, thinly sliced
3 tbls sherry vinegar
5 tbls sunflower oil
5 tbls walnut oil

—————— SAME DAY AS SERVING ——————

1. Remove any discoloured pieces and fat from the livers. Add the livers to a medium-sized saucepan of boiling salted water. Return to

the boil and simmer exactly 2 minutes. Drain and refresh under cold running water. When cold, cut into thin slices. Keep at room temperature under cling-film.

2. Fry the bacon until crisp, drain and crunch up into small pieces. Wrap in cling-film to keep crisp.

3. Wash and dry the lettuce, tear into pieces, wrap in a tea towel and keep refrigerated.

4. Mix salt, pepper, vinegar and oils together. Taste and adjust seasoning.

ONE TO TWO HOURS IN ADVANCE

Toss the salads with just a tiny bit of the vinaigrette. Arrange a selection on each plate and add the walnuts and chicken liver slices, which should first be lightly seasoned. Sprinkle with the mushrooms and bacon.

BEFORE SERVING
(FIVE MINUTES COOKING TIME)

Heat the remaining vinaigrette in a small saucepan. When hot, spoon some over all the plates and serve.

COOKED CRUDITÉS

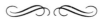

Instead of the usual platter of raw vegetables to dip and crunch on, serve a barely cooked version. Arrange them in bouquets and serve with several different sauces. It is a great way to start a meal or very nice to have with drinks.

Possible choices
asparagus
artichokes
carrots
cauliflower
courgettes
fennel
French beans

mange-tout

Sauces
aïoli (see p. 220)
caper mayonnaise (see p. 220)
curry mayonnaise (see p. 220)

Cut each vegetable into equal-sized pieces. Blanch them separately and refresh in ice water. Cover and refrigerate until you are ready to serve. Arrange a bouquet and serve with the sauces.

Cured Mackerel

SERVES 6–8

Mackerel can be cured in the same way that salmon is for gravadlax. It is excellent, easy and much less expensive. It also freezes well.

3 good-sized very fresh mackerel, filleted but not skinned
1 oz (25 g) sea salt
3/4 oz (20 g) sugar
fresh coriander or dill, roughly chopped

For the sauce
6 oz (175 g) thick-set Greek yoghurt
1 tbls fresh coriander or dill, finely chopped
squeeze of lemon juice
salt and pepper
pinch of sugar

UP TO FOUR DAYS IN ADVANCE
(MINIMUM TWO DAYS; SEVERAL WEEKS IN ADVANCE IF FROZEN)

1. Remove any bones from the fillets with tweezers. Mix the salt and sugar together. Place the fillets skin-side down and rub the cut-side with the mixture. Sprinkle with some of the coriander or dill. Sandwich the fish back together and sprinkle the skins with the rest of the herb. Wrap each fish in cling-film, then place in one layer in a dish. Place a board, then a 3-lb (1.4-kg) weight on top. Refrigerate for 1–3 days.
2. Unwrap the fish, drain off the liquid and pat dry. Wrap in fresh cling-film and place in the freezer for a few hours to facilitate slicing; or freeze up to several weeks and slice when it is semi-thawed. Cut into very thin diagonal slices and arrange on the plate in one layer. Mix the sauce ingredients together and serve separately.

DUCK BREAST SALAD WITH WALNUT DRESSING

SERVES 6

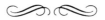

Imaginative salads inspired by *nouvelle cuisine* can be produced without any difficulty at home. They suit the trend for light, healthy dishes and look beautiful when carefully arranged on plates.

mixture of salads such as radicchio, curly endive, chicory, rugola or lamb's lettuce	2 shallots, very finely chopped
2 duck breasts, boned	6 tbls dry white wine
salt and pepper	4 tbls sherry vinegar
½ tsp dried thyme	1 tbls redcurrant jelly
8 tbls walnut oil	6 tbls sunflower oil
¼ pt (150 ml) duck stock or chicken stock	2 small peaches or ripe pears
	2 tbls walnuts, chopped

——— UP TO ONE DAY IN ADVANCE ———

Wash and dry all the salads. Refrigerate wrapped in a cloth in a plastic bag.

——— SEVERAL HOURS IN ADVANCE ———

1. Pat the breasts dry and season with salt, pepper and a little thyme. Sauté the breasts in 2 tbls of very hot walnut oil for about 5 minutes each side. They should still be springy to the touch. Cool, then slice as thinly as possible. Cover with cling-film and set aside. Deglaze the pan with some stock and set aside.

2. Using a small saucepan, simmer the shallots with the wine and vinegar until reduced to 2 tbls. Whisk in the redcurrant jelly, deglazing liquid and remaining stock. Reduce to a syrupy consistency. Remove from the heat and whisk in the remaining oils. Season to taste with salt and pepper.

————— BEFORE SERVING —————
(FIVE MINUTES REHEATING TIME)

Slice the peaches or pears. Arrange a mixture of salad, fruit slices and walnuts on 6 plates. Lay a few duck slices over the top. Reheat the vinaigrette and spoon over the salads. Serve with good hot crusty bread.

Note: Pigeon breasts can also be used and a good stock made from the rest of the birds. The breast slices can also be reheated quickly in the warm vinaigrette before arranging on the plates.

EGG MOUSSE
WITH WATERCRESS SAUCE

SERVES 8

You may feel that egg mousse has had its day, but served in small moulds with a watercress sauce it takes on a new look.

6 hard–boiled eggs	**salt and pepper**
½ pt (300 ml) mayonnaise	**dash of Worcestershire**
½ pt (300 ml) chicken stock	**sauce**
1 tbls gelatine	**¾ pt (450 ml) watercress**
1 tbls curry powder	**sauce (see p. 224)**

——— UP TO THREE DAYS IN ADVANCE ———
(MINIMUM SIX HOURS)

1. Mash the egg yolks with the mayonnaise until smooth. Chop the whites very finely and set aside.
2. Put a few tablespoons of stock in a small saucepan. Sprinkle the gelatine into the pan and leave for 5 minutes. Heat very gently, stirring, until the gelatine dissolves. Do not allow gelatine to boil. Stir into the remaining stock. (If stock is gelatinous, heat just enough to liquify.) Add the curry powder and cool until just beginning to set.
3. Fold the stock carefully into the mayonnaise, then fold in the

chopped egg whites. Season with salt, pepper and a dash of Worcestershire sauce.

4. Line 8 ramekins with cling-film. Spoon in the mixture, cover and refrigerate.

—— SAME DAY AS SERVING ——

Make the watercress sauce, cover and refrigerate.

—— BEFORE SERVING ——

Reverse moulds on to plates, peel off cling-film and surround with sauce.

FRESH FOIE GRAS SALAD

If you live in London and want to really splash out, buy a fresh foie gras. (Boucherie Lamartine, Ebury Street and Harrods are among the shops that stock this.) Lightly sautéed and served on a salad, it is quite the most delicious dish imaginable.

The foie gras usually weighs about 1 lb (450 g) and will serve 8 as a first course. There are 2 lobes that should be separated carefully. Use a small, sharp knife and scrape away any discoloured bits. Cut into ¼-in (0.6-cm) slices. There will be about 3 small slices per person. Heat a heavy frying-pan without any fat. Season the slices with salt and pepper and sear them for about 1 minute on each side (they will give off a good deal of fat). Place on a small bed of mixed salad leaves tossed with a good vinaigrette. The salad and dressing can be arranged on the plates in advance, but the liver must be cooked at the very last minute and served immediately.

GRAVAD-LAX

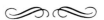

I think this is nicer than smoked salmon. It has a more delicate flavour and I love the dill sauce. Salmon is costly, but making your own gravad-lax is much less expensive than buying smoked salmon. It freezes beautifully, so make enough to freeze some for another occasion.

3 ½–4-lb (1.6–1.8-kg) middle cut of salmon, boned	*For the sauce*
	3 tbls Dijon mustard
	2 tsp caster sugar
2 oz (50 g) sea salt	3 tbls cider vinegar
1½ oz (40 g) sugar	1 tsp salt
freshly ground white pepper	¼ pt (150 ml) sunflower oil
large bunch of fresh dill	4 tbls of dill, finely chopped

Have the fishmonger bone and cut the salmon into two halves lengthwise, leaving the skin. Remove any remaining bones with tweezers. Mix the salt and sugar together and add some pepper. Roughly chop the dill, including the stalks.

Place one-third of the chopped dill in a shallow dish large enough to contain the fish. Rub the flesh side of both pieces of salmon with the sugar mixture. Place one piece of·salmon on the bed of dill, skin-side down, and cover with half the remaining dill. Place the other piece of salmon flesh-side down, on top of the dill. Spread the remaining dill over the top and cover with foil. Weigh it down with a 4-lb (1.8-kg) weight (a wrapped brick is ideal) and refrigerate for 2–3 days, turning the fish once or twice a day.

After 3 days, slice off a sliver and taste. You may wish to add more salt or leave it longer.

BEFORE SERVING

Scrape off the dill, pat dry and slice thinly across the grain.
To make the sauce: Stir the first 4 ingredients together and then gradually whisk in the oil as you would for mayonnaise. Stir in the 4 tbls of dill.

LEEK TERRINE

SERVES 8–10

This tasty and beautiful terrine is made only with leeks. Pressed in a terrine and sliced, they create a stunning mosaic of green and white rings.

5 lb (2.3 kg) leeks, young slender ones if available
salt and pepper

For the vinaigrette
8 tbls sunflower oil

8 tbls walnut oil
2 tsp Dijon mustard
3 tbls wine vinegar

Garnish
fresh chervil or dill, very finely chopped

UP TO TWO DAYS IN ADVANCE
(MINIMUM FIVE HOURS)

1. Line a 10½ × 4¼-in (26 × 10.5-cm) hinged loaf tin with cling-film. (An ordinary loaf tin can be substituted.)
2. Trim the roots and tops of the leeks and remove any withered leaves. Slit the green part in two lengthwise, and wash carefully under running water. Tie the leeks in small bundles.
3. Drop the leeks into a large quantity of boiling salted water. Cover until the water returns to the boil, then simmer, uncovered, for about 8 minutes or until the leeks are tender. Refresh in a large bowl of iced water and drain on clean tea towels.
4. Layer the leeks in the loaf tin, cutting them to fit if necessary and alternating rows of the dark and light ends. Sprinkle each layer with salt. Cover with a board that fits inside the top or with another loaf tin in which a 4-lb (1.8-kg) weight has been placed. Set on a plate and refrigerate for at least 4 hours, draining off the liquid that rises from time to time.

TWO HOURS IN ADVANCE

This is not essential but if you place the loaf tin in the freezer for 1 hour it makes it easier to cut. Do not allow it to freeze.

ONE HOUR IN ADVANCE

1. Make the vinaigrette, and chop the herb for the garnish.
2. Turn out the loaf tin carefully by pulling up the cling-film. Keep it wrapped in the cling-film and, using a very sharp, thin knife, cut into slices. With the help of a spatula, arrange in the centre of individual plates and remove the cling-film. Spoon the vinaigrette around the leeks and sprinkle the herb lightly over the vinaigrette. Leave the leeks plain.

Note: This is a beautiful dish and easy to make. The only tricky bit is the slicing. Use a very sharp knife and keep wrapped in cling-film to hold the shape.

Mackerel in White Wine

SERVES 8

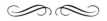

A healthy and delicious way of serving mackerel that can be prepared days ahead. Get your fishmonger to fillet the mackerel.

3–4 large fresh mackerel fillets

For the court-bouillon
1 bottle dry white wine
2 onions, very finely sliced
2 carrots, very finely sliced

1 tsp black peppercorns
bouquet garni
strip of lemon peel
pinch of salt

Garnish
fresh fennel or dill, very finely chopped

—— UP TO FIVE DAYS IN ADVANCE ——

1. Simmer all the *court-bouillon* ingredients together for 15 minutes. Leave to cool.
2. Add the fish fillets to the cool *bouillon* and bring slowly to the boil. Let it bubble 2 or 3 times, then remove from the heat and leave the fish in the liquid to cool.
3. Lift the fish from the *bouillon* and remove the skin and bones. Place in a shallow dish and strain over the *bouillon*. There should be enough to cover the fish. Pick out the best-looking carrots, onions and a few peppercorns, and place over the fish. Cover with cling-film and refrigerate. The fish will keep well for 5 days if completely covered in the liquid.

—— SEVERAL HOURS IN ADVANCE ——

Drain off some of the liquid and leave fish at room temperature.

—— BEFORE SERVING ——

Sprinkle over the herb and serve with good brown bread.

MUSSELS À L'ORANGE

SERVES 8

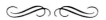

The orange-flavoured sauce is a wonderful complement to the orange mussels, and the dish can be completely prepared ahead of time.

6 lb (2.7 kg) mussels
2–3 shallots, very finely
  chopped
glass of dry white wine
2 fl oz (60 ml) double
  cream, whipped
½ pt (300 ml) mayonnaise

2 tsp *moutarde à l'orange* or
  Dijon mustard
grated rind of 1 small
  orange
salt and pepper

Garnish
watercress

─────── UP TO ONE DAY IN ADVANCE ───────

1. Scrape the mussels free of barnacles and scrub under cold running water. Pull away the beards and leave in cold salted water until ready to use. Discard any that are broken or open.
2. Using a large pan with a tight-fitting lid, heat the shallots in the wine until the wine boils. Add the mussels, cover and cook over high heat for about 5 minutes, shaking the pan a few times to cook the mussels evenly. Or better still, do the mussels in two batches. Be very careful not to overcook them, as they will become tough.
3. Strain the liquor through 2 layers of muslin. Remove the mussels from their shells and place back in the strained liquid. Cover and refrigerate if not using the same day.
4. Turn half the shells upside down to drain and reserve.

─────── SAME DAY AS SERVING ───────

1. Strain the liquor into a saucepan and boil hard to reduce to a concentrated flavour.
2. Mix the whipped cream, mayonnaise, mustard and orange rind together. Stir in 2 tbls of the mussel liquor. Taste for seasoning. Cover and refrigerate.

—— THREE TO FOUR HOURS IN ADVANCE ——

Return the mussels to their shells and top with the mayonnaise. Arrange on individual plates and keep in a cool place.

—————— BEFORE SERVING ——————

Garnish with watercress and serve.

SEVICHE MAISON

SERVES 8

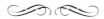

This is a lavish gala *seviche*: a border of very thin slices of scallops interlaced with watercress leaves to set off the other marinated fish. You can, of course, leave out the scallops and just increase the amount of fish. It will be very good either way. The fish must be the freshest possible. Explain to your fishmonger you are using it for a *seviche*.

16 scallops, in their shells
1½ lb (675 g) very fresh fish,
   such as sole, sea-bass,
   salmon or halibut
8 fl oz (200 ml) lime juice
salt
1 tbls fresh chervil or dill,
   very finely chopped
1 egg yolk

¼ tsp Dijon mustard
few drops of tabasco
¼ pt (150 ml) mixed olive
   oil and sunflower oil
2 tomatoes, skinned, seeded
   and diced
2 bunches of large-leafed
   watercress

—— THREE TO FOUR HOURS IN ADVANCE ——

1. Open and prepare scallops (see p. 97).
2. Cut off the small, hard muscle from the scallop. Slice the scallop into the thinnest possible discs. Use a very thin, sharp knife. Place them in a bowl and cover. Save the corals for another dish.
3. Pat the fish dry and cut into narrow strips. Place in another bowl.
4. Mix the lime juice, a pinch of salt and chervil or dill together.

Pour three-quarters of the lime juice on to the fish and toss. Cover and refrigerate.

5. Make a mayonnaise with the egg yolk, mustard, tabasco, 1 tsp of the marinade, salt and oil (see p. 219). Set aside.

ONE HOUR IN ADVANCE

1. Pour the remaining marinade over the scallops and return to the refrigerator. (They will be cooked in minutes.)
2. Drain the fish and mix with the mayonnaise. Fold in the diced tomatoes.
3. Wash and dry the watercress. Cut off the largest, round leaves (as many as you have scallop slices).
4. Drain the scallops. Arrange an outer circle of overlapping watercress leaves and scallops on each plate. Place the fish in a mound in the centre. Serve with thin slices of buttered brown bread.

SMOKED CHICKEN AND PEAR WITH WATERCRESS SAUCE

SERVES 6

12 oz (350 g) smoked
   chicken, thinly sliced
3 ripe Williams pears

For the sauce
2 bunches of watercress
1 shallot, very finely
   chopped

1 oz (25 g) butter
1 tsp fresh tarragon
2 tbls dry white wine
½ pt (300 ml) double cream
lemon juice
salt and pepper

Garnish
watercress

UP TO ONE DAY IN ADVANCE

1. Cut off the stems from the watercress and discard. Chop the leaves. Soften the shallot in the butter over gentle heat, add the watercress, very finely chopped tarragon and white wine, cover

and simmer for 1 minute. Add ¼ pt (150 ml) of cream and simmer gently, uncovered, for 10 minutes.

2. Purée the sauce and sieve if a smooth sauce is preferred. Season with lemon juice, salt and pepper to taste. Cover and refrigerate until you are ready to serve.

BEFORE SERVING

Whip the remaining cream to ribbon stage and fold into the sauce. Slice the pears. Arrange slices of chicken alternately with slices of pear in a fan-shape on each plate. Spoon a small amount of the sauce over the arrangement and garnish with the fresh watercress. Pass the remaining sauce.

SMOKED SALMON CIGARETTES

SERVES 8

Small rolls of smoked salmon filled with creamy eggs are a sumptuous first course or hors-d'œuvre. It also helps the salmon go further.

7 eggs
2 oz (50 g) unsalted butter
4 tbls double cream
salt and freshly ground
   black pepper

1 lb (450 g) thin slices of
   smoked salmon
1 tbls fresh dill, very finely
   chopped
thin slices of buttered
   brown bread for serving

UP TO ONE DAY IN ADVANCE

1. Whisk 6 eggs until just blended. Season lightly with salt and pepper.
2. Gently melt the butter in a heavy-bottomed saucepan. Stir in the eggs and over very low heat stir with a wooden spoon until the eggs thicken. This should take about 10 minutes. If the eggs cook too fast, remove them from the heat from time to time, but keep stirring. When the eggs thicken but are still creamy, take them off

the heat. Stir in the cream. The extra egg can be added at this stage if you have overcooked them. Season with pepper, but go lightly on the salt, as they will be eaten with the salmon. Cover and refrigerate.

3. If you want to get ahead you can also cut the salmon into rectangles about 4 × 3 in (10 × 8 cm). Layer them between cling-film and keep refrigerated.

SEVERAL HOURS IN ADVANCE

1. Cut the salmon into rectangles if you haven't done so already.
2. Stir up the eggs and add the dill. If they look at all set, add a bit more cream.
3. Place a spoonful of egg on each rectangle and roll up like a cigarette. Place 4–6 on each plate and leave at room temperature.
4. Serve with the buttered brown bread.

SMOKED SALMON, MUSHROOM AND AVOCADO SALAD

SERVES 6

Thin slices of raw mushrooms with strips of salmon and avocado in a lemony vinaigrette, with lots of fresh black pepper.

8 oz (225 g) fresh small button mushrooms
6 oz (175 g) shredded lettuce
8 oz (225 g) smoked salmon
2 ripe avocados
freshly ground black pepper

For the vinaigrette
4–5 tbls lemon juice
10–12 tbls mixed olive oil and sunflower oil
salt and freshly ground black pepper

Garnish
fresh dill or chervil, very finely chopped

Wipe the mushrooms clean, remove stems and keep for another use. Cut the caps into thin slices. Prepare lettuce and keep refrigerated. Cut salmon into thin strips. Prepare vinaigrette. Toss mushrooms with a few tablespoons of vinaigrette. Toss salmon with some vinaigrette in another bowl.

——————— BEFORE SERVING ———————

Place lettuce on plates, cover with slices of mushroom and avocado. Arrange the smoked salmon on top and sprinkle with a bit of vinaigrette. Grind black pepper over the salads and sprinkle with a tiny bit of herb if you are using it.

Note: You can replace the salmon with peeled prawns and add fresh mint.

SMOKED TROUT WITH MANGO

SERVES 6

Mango and smoked trout look beautiful together and taste beautiful too.

1 large bunch of watercress	**1 tbls vinegar**
3 smoked trout	**6–7 tbls oil**
2 mangoes	**2 tbls cream**
	1 tbls fresh mint, chopped
For the vinaigrette	**salt and pepper**
1 tsp mustard	

——————— SEVERAL HOURS IN ADVANCE ———————

1. Wash and dry the watercress, cut off the stems and discard.
2. Bone the trout and cut the flesh into neat strips.
3. Peel and slice the mangoes over a bowl.

4. Make the vinaigrette, seasoning to taste and add 1 tbls of mango juice.

--- BEFORE SERVING ---

Arrange some watercress on the plates. Place alternating slices of mango and trout on the watercress. Spoon over some of the vinaigrette.

Note: Vinegars differ in strength. Always start with a small amount and adjust to taste after the dressing is made. English vinegars are strong on the whole. *La Favorite* is a milder brand. Cider vinegar is often gentler than many of the wine vinegars available.

STUFFED MUSHROOMS

SERVES 8

Mushrooms stuffed with a chicken liver pâté make an attractive and tasty first course.

salt and pepper	**16 fresh mushrooms, 2½ in**
2 bay leaves	**(6.3 cm) in diameter**
8 oz (225 g) chicken livers	**3 tbls oil**
1 tbls Cognac	**2 tbls Madeira**
dash of tabasco	**toast for serving**
4 oz (125 g) melted butter	
extra melted butter for	*Garnish*
** sealing**	**watercress**

--- UP TO FIVE DAYS IN ADVANCE ---

1. Bring a small saucepan of water to the boil, add some salt and the bay leaves and simmer for 5 minutes.
2. Meanwhile, remove any discoloured bits from the livers and pat dry. Add the livers to the simmering water, bring back to the boil and simmer covered for 1½ minutes. Drain and place in a blender or food processor.
3. Purée the livers with the Cognac, tabasco, salt, pepper and

melted butter. Scrape into a bowl and adjust seasoning. Cover with a thin layer of melted butter and refrigerate if not using the same day.

SAME DAY AS SERVING

Cut the stems out of the mushrooms and save for another dish. Lightly sauté the mushrooms in the oil, open-side down first. Season with salt, pepper and the Madeira, and set aside on a dish.

BEFORE SERVING

Remove the layer of butter from the pâté. Spoon the liver into the mushrooms, place on a bed of watercress and serve with toast.

TERRINE OF SKATE AND VEGETABLES

SERVES 8–10

It is easy to extract the thin ribs of flesh from skate and they make ideal pieces for layering in terrines or arranging in salads.

1 lb (450 g) skate, thick middle-wing strip
2 pts (1.1 L) *court-bouillon* (see p. 213)
½ oz (15 g) gelatine
2 tbls white wine
8 oz (225 g) carrots, cut into matchsticks
8 oz (225 g) small French beans

For the mayonnaise
1 egg yolk
1 tsp Dijon mustard
1 tbls white wine vinegar
salt and pepper
¼ pt (150 ml) sunflower oil
2 tbls capers

Garnish
watercress

UP TO ONE DAY IN ADVANCE
(MINIMUM EIGHT HOURS)

1. Place skate in cool *court-bouillon* and bring to the boil. After one

strong bubble, remove from the heat and cool fish to tepid in the *bouillon*. If skate wings are thin, remove them as soon as the *bouillon* comes to the boil. Remove the flesh and set aside. Discard skin and bones. Strain the *bouillon* through a muslin-lined sieve into a clean pan and boil hard to reduce to 1 pt (600 ml).

2. Soak gelatine with white wine for a few minutes, then stir into the hot, but not boiling, *bouillon*. Taste for seasoning, then set pan in ice water to cool until the consistency of egg white.

3. Blanch vegetables separately in boiling salted water, refresh in cold water and drain.

4. Line a 10½ × 4¼-in (26 × 10.5-cm) hinged loaf tin with cling-film. (An ordinary loaf tin can be substituted.) Place half the fish in a layer on the bottom and cover with *bouillon*. Add the carrots and beans, and cover with *bouillon*. Top with an even layer of the remaining fish covered in *bouillon*. Set on a dish, cover and refrigerate until set and ready to serve.

5. Whisk the egg yolk, mustard, vinegar, salt and pepper together. Dribble in the oil while whisking to make a mayonnaise (see p. 219). Fold in the capers and refrigerate.

ONE HOUR IN ADVANCE

About one hour before serving turn the loaf tin out. Slice with a knife dipped in boiling water, then dried. Arrange on plates with a dollop of mayonnaise and some watercress.

Note: You can get more even layers by refrigerating each layer until it is almost set, then adding the next layer.

THREE SMOKED FISH SALAD

SERVES 6

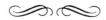

Use a variety of whatever smoked fish is available. Lightly smoked and salted fish are preferable.

mixture of salads such as
    lamb's lettuce, radicchio,
    chicory, curly endive or
    cabbage lettuce
8 quails' eggs, uncooked
6 tbls vinaigrette
½ lb (225 g) smoked salmon
½ lb (225 g) smoked eel
12 oz (350 g) smoked cod's roe

buttered brown bread for
    serving

For the dill sauce
2 tbls dill, finely chopped
1 tsp Dijon mustard
1 tsp sugar
8 fl oz (250 ml) soured
    cream

UP TO ONE DAY IN ADVANCE

Wash and dry the salads. Lightly wrap them in a cloth, place in a plastic bag and refrigerate.

SAME DAY AS SERVING

1. Bring a saucepan of water to a very gentle simmer. Using a spoon, slide the eggs into the water and simmer gently for 3 minutes. Plunge into very cold water, then peel.
2. Mix the ingredients for the dill sauce.

THIRTY MINUTES IN ADVANCE

1. Lightly toss the salad in the vinaigrette. You only want a suggestion of vinaigrette.
2. Arrange the salad on the plates. Cut the fish and roe into bite-size pieces and place over the salad. Slice eggs in half and arrange on the plates.

BEFORE SERVING

Pass the dill sauce separately and serve the salad with buttered brown bread.

MAIN COURSES

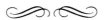

Baked Sea-bass
with Watercress Sauce

SERVES 6

Sea-bass is my favourite fish and I can think of no better treat to serve friends than baked or grilled sea-bass. The sharp watercress and lemon sauce goes very well.

3½–4-lb (1.6–1.8-kg) sea-bass, cleaned and scaled
butter
glass of white wine

For the sauce
1 shallot, very finely chopped
1 oz (25 g) butter

½ tbls plain flour
½ pt (300 ml) fish or chicken stock
½ oz (15 g) watercress leaves (no stems)
2 tbls double cream
1 tsp Dijon mustard
lemon juice
salt and pepper

—— UP TO ONE DAY IN ADVANCE ——

For the sauce: Simmer the shallot in the butter until soft. Stir in the flour, then whisk in the stock and continue to whisk until the sauce simmers. Simmer for 5 minutes. Purée the watercress with a bit of sauce in a blender or food processor, then pour back into the sauce. Add the cream and mustard, and season with quite a bit of lemon juice, salt and pepper. Cool, then cover and refrigerate.

—— SEVERAL HOURS IN ADVANCE ——

Dry the fish and season. Butter an oval flameproof dish large enough to hold the fish. Add the fish, pour over the wine and cover with an oval of buttered greaseproof paper. Set aside in a cool place. If you don't have an oval dish, use a roasting tin and make a nest for the fish out of foil.

BEFORE SERVING
(FORTY MINUTES BAKING TIME)

1. Preheat the oven to 180°C/350°F/Gas Mark 4.
2. Bake the fish for forty minutes.
3. Reheat the sauce. Place fish on a heated platter. Add some cooking juices to the sauce and serve separately.

BAKED SALMON STEAKS
SERVES 6

Baking in foil works miracles with fish or tender cuts of meat, sealing in flavour and juices. It is a great solution for busy cooks, as the parcels take only minutes to put together. They can be done in advance, but the baking should be done at the last minute. Guests enjoy opening their own fragrant parcels and eating the contents.

2 oz (50 g) butter
1 tbls fresh tarragon, very
    finely chopped
6 salmon steaks, ¾–1 in
    (1.9–2.5 cm) thick

salt and freshly ground
    black pepper
small glass of white wine

SEVERAL HOURS IN ADVANCE

1. Cut 6 heart shapes from foil, large enough to contain a steak with ease.
2. Melt the butter with the tarragon. Pat the fish dry and season with salt and pepper. Paint some butter on one side of each heart. Place one salmon steak on each heart and distribute the remaining butter equally over the fish. Sprinkle with wine, fold foil over and seal well all around. Leave at room temperature.

BEFORE SERVING
(FIFTEEN MINUTES BAKING TIME)

1. Preheat oven to 190°C/375°F/Gas Mark 5.

2. Fifteen minutes before you want the fish to be ready, place in the oven on a baking sheet.

To serve: Transfer parcels to a serving platter and let guests open their own.

Note: You can also use baking parchment to make the hearts, but crimp around the edge to seal.

BAKED TROUT WITH
TARRAGON AND ALMONDS

SERVES 6

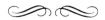

Trout baked quite simply with tarragon, butter and lemon is delicious and makes a handsome dish.

3 tbls fresh tarragon, finely
   chopped
¼ pt (150 ml) double cream
4 oz (100 g) butter
2 oz (50 g) flaked almonds

salt and pepper
6 × 8-oz (225-g) trout,
   cleaned
extra butter for greasing
juice of 1 lemon

1. Mix 1 tbls of tarragon with the cream and set aside.
2. Blend the butter with the rest of the tarragon.
3. Toast the almonds in ½ oz (15 g) butter, sprinkle with salt and set aside.
4. Wipe the trout with paper towels. Season inside and out with salt and pepper. Place a small piece of tarragon butter inside each fish and place in a buttered baking dish. Smear some butter over the fish, sprinkle with the lemon juice and cover with a piece of buttered greaseproof paper.

BEFORE SERVING
(TWENTY TO THIRTY MINUTES BAKING TIME)

1. Preheat oven to 180°C/350°F/Gas Mark 4.
2. Bake fish for 20–30 minutes.

To serve: Spoon some cream over the fish and sprinkle with the almonds.

BONED SALMON STUFFED WITH SPINACH

SERVES 10

This is a terrific party piece. A salmon is brought to the table looking quite like any other salmon, but when sliced it reveals a beautiful green stuffing. Ask the fishmonger to bone the fish from the back, keeping the fish in one piece and leaving on the head and tail. Instructions for boning the fish yourself are given below.

2½ lb (1.1 kg) fresh spinach	grated nutmeg
2 shallots, very finely chopped	8 oz (225 g) sole fillet, skinned
1 oz (25 g) butter	1 egg
1 clove garlic, crushed and finely chopped	8 fl oz (250 ml) double cream
salt and pepper	lemon juice

5–6-lb (2.3–2.7-kg) salmon, boned   ***beurre blanc* (see p. 218) or hollandaise sauce**

ONE DAY IN ADVANCE

1. Wash the spinach well. Cook with a pinch of salt and any water that clings to the leaves. Drain, pressing down in the sieve to eliminate the moisture. Chop the spinach finely.
2. Sauté the shallot in the butter until soft. Add the garlic and stir for 1 minute. Add the spinach and stir over high heat to evaporate any moisture. Season with salt, pepper and some nutmeg. Set aside to cool.
3. Purée the sole fillet in a blender or food processor for about 3 minutes or until very smooth. With the motor on, slowly add the egg and then the cream. Process only enough to blend. Season with salt, pepper and lemon juice. Mix with the spinach, cover and refrigerate.

SAME DAY AS SERVING

1. *To bone the fish*: Cut off the fins with kitchen scissors. Using a sharp-pointed knife, make an incision behind the head to one side of the backbone. Slide the knife along the backbone, down the length of the fish. Do the same on the other side to release the backbone. Snip the backbone from behind the head and in front of the tail and remove.
2. Gut the fish from the other side. Remove any extra bones with tweezers.
3. Stuff the fish with the spinach mixture, leaving room for expansion. Sew up the opening. Brush a large piece of foil with butter. Lay 2 buttered foil strips across the large piece of foil to help lift off the fish when removing later. Place the fish on top and brush with butter. Make a loose package, but seal it tightly. Place on a baking sheet and set aside.
4. Make the reduction for the *beurre blanc* if you are serving it.

1. Preheat the oven to 170°C/325°F/Gas Mark 3.
2. Allow 1 hour of baking time for a fish that weighs up to 5 lb (2.3 kg). Add 12 minutes per lb for anything over that.

To serve: Remove the thread and skin the fish if desired. Slide it on to a warm platter. Cover with foil and keep warm in a cool oven if not serving immediately. Finish off the sauce and serve separately.

COLD SALMON TROUT WITH GREEN SAUCE

SERVES 6

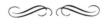

A recipe from Henrietta Green, friend and wonderful cook. The vegetables that cook with the fish are puréed and become a tasty green sauce to accompany it.

olive oil
1 large lettuce, shredded
½ cucumber, peeled and finely sliced
handful of sorrel or watercress, chopped
small bunch of mixed chervil and dill, chopped

rind and juice of 1 lemon
salt and pepper
3–4-lb (1.4–1.8-kg) salmon trout
2 glasses of dry white wine
6 oz (175 g) plain thick-set yoghurt

UP TO ONE DAY IN ADVANCE

1. Preheat the oven to 180°C/350°F/Gas Mark 4.
2. Line a roasting tin with a piece of oiled foil that is large enough to enclose the fish.
3. Mix the lettuce, cucumber, sorrel or watercress, chervil and dill, lemon juice and rind together, and season with salt and pepper. Place a layer of the mixture on the foil. Season the fish, rub with oil and stuff the cavity with some of the mixture. Place the fish in the foil, cover with the rest of the mixture and pour over the wine.

Enclose the fish in a loose but tightly sealed package. Bake for 30 minutes.

4. Remove from the oven, but leave in the package to cool and finish cooking. Remove the fish carefully and place on a platter.

5. Pour all the juices and vegetables from the foil into a blender or food processor and purée. Add just enough yoghurt to make a nice sauce and adjust seasoning. Keep sauce and fish refrigerated until serving.

Note: This dish can also be served hot. Bake for 40–50 minutes and unwrap immediately. Whizz up the sauce and serve. The idea of using the cooked vegetables for the sauce can be adapted for other dishes.

FISH CHOWDER

SERVES 6

A creamy fish soup from America that combines pork and fish in a very appetizing way. It is perfect for an informal luncheon or supper.

6 oz (175 g) salt pork or
    unsmoked bacon (rind
    removed), cut into ½-in
    (1.3-cm) cubes
1 tbls oil
1 lb (450 g) onions, thinly
    sliced
2 tbls plain flour
2 pts (1.1 L) fish stock
2 lb (900 g) potatoes, thinly
    sliced
1 tsp fresh thyme or ½ tsp
    dried thyme

1 bay leaf
2½ lb (1.1 kg) mixed fish
    fillets such as monkfish,
    cod, sole, haddock or
    other white fish, skinned
1½ pts (900 ml) milk
salt and freshly ground
    black pepper

Garnish
water biscuits, crumbled
fresh parsley, finely
    chopped

UP TO TWO DAYS IN ADVANCE

Blanch the pork or bacon in boiling water for 5 minutes. Drain and place in a large saucepan with the oil. Fry the meat until lightly browned. Add the onions and cook 10 minutes, stirring occasionally. Stir in the flour, then add the stock, potatoes, thyme and bay leaf. Season with salt and pepper. Cover and simmer until potatoes are just tender, about 20 minutes. Remove bayleaf and cool. Refrigerate if not serving the same day.

SEVERAL HOURS IN ADVANCE

Pat the fish dry. Season with salt and pepper. Cut into diagonal pieces and set aside.

BEFORE SERVING
(TEN TO TWELVE MINUTES COOKING TIME)

Simmer the soup with the milk. Add the fish, return to the boil, lower the heat and simmer gently for 4–5 minutes. Serve in large soup bowls garnished with the crumbled water biscuits and parsley.

FISH FILLETS WITH GREEN PEPPERCORN SAUCE

SERVES 6

Fish, particularly firm-fleshed fish, can be successfully poached ahead of time. A good sauce can be made in advance from the reduced poaching fumet. It only needs a minute or two of reheating before it is ready to tempt your guests.

2½ lb (1.1 kg) Dover sole, turbot, salmon or monkfish fillets, skinned
salt and pepper
1½ oz (40 g) butter
2 shallots, very finely chopped
2 pts (1.1 L) fish stock

For the sauce
¼ pt (150 ml) dry white wine
½ pt (300 ml) double cream or *crème fraîche*
3 tbls tinned green peppercorns, drained and slightly crushed
lemon juice
salt and pepper

SAME DAY AS SERVING

1. Pat the fish dry. Lightly score each fillet two or three times on the skin side to prevent curling. Season with salt and pepper. Place a tiny piece of butter on each fillet and fold over if the fillets are flat. Sprinkle the bottom of a heavy frying-pan with shallots and lay the fish on top. Pour in enough fish stock to cover the fish. Lay buttered greaseproof paper over the fillets and cover the pan with a lid. Heat gently, checking to see when the liquid boils. Let it bubble once or twice, then remove from the heat. Cover and leave for 10 minutes, then remove the fish and set aside. When fish is cold, cover with cling-film and leave in a cool place.

2. Rapidly boil down the poaching liquid until it reduces to ½ pt (300 ml). Add the wine and simmer a little. Strain into a saucepan and add the cream and peppercorns. Simmer until slightly reduced. Season with lemon juice, salt and pepper. Lay a piece of cling-film on the surface of the sauce to prevent a skin forming and set aside in a cool place.

BEFORE SERVING
(EIGHT MINUTES REHEATING TIME)

1. Place fish in a warmed, shallow flameproof serving dish.
2. Bring the sauce to a simmer. Pour over the fish and bring back to the simmer. Serve immediately.

FISH FILLETS WITH MUSSEL SAUCE

SERVES 6

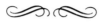

The broth from the mussels with some grainy mustard gives the sauce a very good flavour.

2 lb (900 g) mussels
1 bay leaf
fresh parsley, chopped
½ pt of dry white wine
1 shallot, very finely chopped
2 tbls butter
1 tbls plain flour
¼ pt (150 ml) cream
1 good tbls *moutarde de Meaux*

salt and pepper
2 lb (900 g) fish fillets (any one kind) such as monkfish, brill, sole or salmon trout, skinned
squeeze of lemon juice
1 tbls olive oil

Garnish
fresh parsley, very finely chopped

SAME DAY AS SERVING

1. Wash the mussels in several changes of cold water. Remove the beards and discard any broken or open ones. Place in a large pan with the bay leaf, parsley and wine. Cover and cook over high heat for 5 minutes or until mussels are open. Strain the broth through a muslin-lined sieve. Remove the mussels from their shells and set aside.

2. Sauté the shallot in the butter until soft. Add the flour and cook for 1 minute. Whisk in the mussel broth and the cream. Continue to whisk until slightly thickened. Add the *moutarde de Meaux* and season to taste.

3. Pat the fish dry and cut into diagonal pieces. Season with salt and pepper. Place in an oiled gratin dish, and add the lemon juice and oil. Cover with foil and leave at room temperature.

(FIFTEEN TO TWENTY MINUTES BAKING TIME)

1. Preheat the oven to 180°C/350°F/Gas Mark 4.
2. Bake the fish for 15–20 minutes or until just cooked.
3. Reheat the sauce with the mussels. Pour over the fish and serve garnished with the chopped parsley.

FRICASSÉE OF RED MULLET, CHICORY, GINGER AND LIME

SERVES 4

Fish with chicory is excellent, and makes an attractive and easy dish. If mullet is difficult to find, use another fish such as monkfish.

1½–2 lb (675–900 g) red mullet fillets or other fish fillets
1 shallot, very finely chopped
2 oz (50 g) butter
1-in (2.5-cm) piece of stem ginger, very finely chopped
4 heads of chicory, cut into very thin slices

2 tsp sugar
juice of 1 lime
½ pt (300 ml) fish or chicken stock
¼ pt (150 ml) double cream
salt and freshly ground black pepper

Garnish
rind of 1 orange and 1 lime, cut into julienne and blanched for 5 minutes

SEVERAL HOURS IN ADVANCE

1. Pat the fish dry and cut into small, diagonal strips.
2. Sauté the shallot in half the butter, stirring, until soft. Add the ginger and chicory, and stir until well coated in the butter. Stir in the sugar and lime juice, then add the stock and boil until reduced by half. Stir in the cream and cook until slightly thickened. Season with salt and pepper and set aside.

BEFORE SERVING
(APPROX. SEVEN MINUTES FRYING AND REHEATING TIME)

1. Season the fish. Heat the remaining butter in a frying-pan and sauté the fish for about 3 minutes each side (depending on the thickness).
2. Reheat the chicory.
To serve: Place the chicory on a heated dish. Place the fish on top and garnish with the julienne of lime and orange.

GRILLED FISH WITH MAYONNAISE

SERVES 6

It may come as a surprise that mayonnaise can be used as a coating for grilled or baked fish; it keeps the fish moist and tastes delicious.

6 × 6-oz (175-g) fish fillets	¼ pt (150 ml) home-made
salt and pepper	mayonnaise (see p. 219)
	1 tsp Dijon mustard

BEFORE SERVING
(APPROX. FIVE TO TEN MINUTES GRILLING TIME)

1. Pat the fish dry and season with salt and pepper. Place in an oiled grilling dish. Mix the mayonnaise and the mustard, and coat the fish.
2. Grill the fish (not too close to the heat) until fish is cooked and and mayonnaise is golden.

Note: The same dish can be baked. Preheat oven to 180°C/350°F/ Gas Mark 4. Bake for about 25 minutes for thick fish fillets and less for thinner ones. Caper mayonnaise (see p. 220) is also very good.

HALIBUT STEAKS AU POIVRE

SERVES 6

A peppered fish steak is a real treat and very easy to make for guests. You can sear the steaks in advance and make a little sauce. The amenable fish, as always, will only need a few minutes to cook.

2–3 tbls black peppercorns
1½ tbls plain flour
salt
2 oz (50 g) clarified butter
2 fl oz (60 ml) sherry
8 fl oz (250 ml) veal or
  chicken stock

2 fl oz (60 ml) Cognac
¼ pt (150 ml) cream
6 halibut steaks, 1 in (2.5
  cm) thick

Garnish
fresh dill, very finely
  chopped

SEVERAL HOURS IN ADVANCE

1. Place peppercorns and flour between cling-film and crush lightly with a rolling pin.
2. Pat the fish dry and season with salt. Press the pepper mixture into the fish on both sides.
3. Heat the butter in a frying-pan and quickly brown the fish on both sides. Remove to a side dish. Deglaze the pan with the sherry. Add the stock and simmer a few minutes. Add the Cognac and simmer another minute or two, then add the cream. Taste and adjust seasoning. Set aside.

BEFORE SERVING

(APPROX. EIGHT MINUTES COOKING TIME)

Bring the sauce to a simmer. Add the fish steaks to the frying pan and simmer for a few minutes on each side, until the fish is just cooked. Serve garnished with dill.

KULEBIAKA

SERVES 8–10

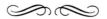

Salmon, mushrooms and rice encased in a *brioche* envelope is a very impressive dish. The preparations can be fitted in over a few days to suit your timetable. All you have to do on the day of serving is assemble the *kulebiaka*.

For the brioche dough
⅔ oz (20 g) fresh yeast
4 fl oz (110 ml) luke-warm
   milk
1 lb (450 g) plain flour
1 oz (25 g) sugar
2 tsp salt
5 eggs (at room
   temperature)
8 oz (225 g) unsalted butter

For the filling
3½–4-lb (1.6–1.8-kg)
   salmon or salmon trout

salt and pepper
4 shallots, finely chopped
8 oz (225 g) butter
8 oz (225 g) fresh
   mushrooms, sliced
juice of ½ lemon
6 oz (175 g) brown rice
¾ pt water
large bunch of fresh dill
4 hard-boiled eggs, sliced
1 egg

——— UP TO THREE DAYS IN ADVANCE ———
(MINIMUM FIVE HOURS)

For the dough: Dissolve the yeast in the milk. Mix 5 tbls of flour into the yeast mixture and leave in a warm place until doubled in volume. Sift the remaining flour into a large bowl, then add the sugar and salt. Make a well in the centre and break in the eggs. Using a wooden spoon, stir the eggs, gathering up the flour as you stir. When the mixture is blended, turn out on to a floured work surface and knead with your fingers until the dough is soft and elastic. It should be sticky, but add more flour if it is too tacky. Soften the butter by beating it with a rolling pin. Work the butter into the dough by smearing it over the dough and folding it in. The dough should be a bit sticky but soft and elastic as well. It will firm up when it rises. Place the dough in a clean bowl, cover with a plastic bag and leave to rise until doubled in volume, about 3 hours. This can also be done by refrigerating overnight. Once the dough has risen, turn it out on to a floured surface and pat into a rectangle about 16 × 9 in (40 × 23 cm). Fold the dough into three, as for a business letter. Wrap the dough in cling-film and refrigerate. This chills the dough and makes rolling out easier. If you are not using the dough the same day, place a board with weights on top over the dough. Once the butter has congealed it will not rise.

UP TO ONE DAY IN ADVANCE

1. Preheat the oven to 170°C/325°F/Gas Mark 3.
2. Season the salmon with salt and pepper and bake in a well-buttered foil parcel, slightly loose but well sealed. Bake for 40 minutes. Leave in the parcel to cool, then remove the flesh. Add flesh and all the juices to a bowl. Refrigerate if not using the same day.
3. Sauté half the shallots in 1 oz (25 g) of butter until soft. Add the mushrooms, lemon juice, salt and pepper, and sauté until soft. Scrape into a bowl and set aside. Refrigerate if not using the same day.
4. Sauté the remaining shallots in a saucepan with 1 oz (25 g) of butter. Wash the rice in several changes of water. Drain, then add to the pan and stir to coat in the butter. Add the water and bring to the boil. Lower the heat, cover and simmer very gently for 25 minutes. Turn out into a bowl and mix with a good knob of butter. Refrigerate if not using the same day.

FOUR TO FIVE HOURS IN ADVANCE

Roll the dough into a rectangle ½ in (1.3 cm) thick on a floured cloth placed on a baking sheet. Save the trimmings for decorations. Cover the middle of the dough with a layer of rice. Arrange the salmon over this and season with lots of chopped dill, salt and pepper. Spread the rest of the rice over the fish, then the hard-boiled egg slices and mushrooms. Fold the edges of the dough over the filling so they meet in the middle; moisten with water to seal. With the help of a cloth, roll the dough over on to another buttered baking sheet so the seam is on the bottom. Decorate with leaves made from the dough. Make a hole in the centre and insert a small foil funnel (made around a pencil). Mix the egg with a pinch of salt and glaze the dough. Place in the refrigerator unless baking within 1 hour.

(FORTY-FIVE MINUTES BAKING TIME)

1. Preheat oven to 200°C/400°F/Gas Mark 6.
2. Leave *kulebiaka* at room temperature while oven heats. Bake for 45 minutes. Cover the top with foil if it browns too quickly. It will stay warm in a cool oven for 20 minutes. Slide the *kulebiaka* on to a hot platter with the help of a spatula. Melt the remaining butter and pour half into the funnel. Pass the rest separately.

Note: You can bake the *kulebiaka* one day in advance, wrap it in foil and reheat in a hot oven. It isn't quite as good, and you may need additional melted butter to serve with it, but it is still a treat. You can also replace the *brioche* dough with puff pastry. It is excellent served with braised cucumbers.

LEMON SOLE
FILLETS WITH GINGER

SERVES 6

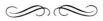

The sole is baked with a julienne of vegetables and ginger, and served with a Sauterne and ginger sauce.

3 oz (75 g) carrot	*For the sauce*
3 oz (75 g) white part of leek	1 shallot, very finely
2 oz (50 g) celeriac	chopped
¾ oz (20 g) fresh ginger	½ oz (15 g) butter
3 oz (75 g) fresh button	¼ pt (150 ml) Sauterne
mushrooms	½ pt (300 ml) fish stock
1 oz (25 g) butter	1 tsp fresh root ginger,
salt and pepper	grated
2½ lb (1.1 kg) lemon sole	¼ pt (150 ml) double cream
fillets, skinned	1 tbls arrowroot (optional)
4 tbls Sauterne	

SAME DAY AS SERVING

1. Cut the vegetables and ginger into the finest julienne you can make. Sauté the ginger in the butter, stirring, until soft. Add the

vegetables and continue to stir until they are soft, without allowing them to colour. Season with salt and pepper.

2. Pat the fish dry and season. Place a small spoonful of vegetable on each fillet and fold over to enclose the filling. Place fillets in a buttered baking dish, scatter over any remaining vegetables and sprinkle with the 4 tbls of Sauterne. Cover with foil and set aside in a cool place (not the refrigerator).

3. *For the sauce*: Soften the shallot in the butter, stirring. Add a few tablespoons of Sauterne and boil hard to evaporate. Add the stock and grated ginger and simmer until reduced by half. Add the rest of the Sauterne and the cream, and simmer a few more minutes. Adjust seasoning, place a piece of cling-film on the surface to prevent a skin forming and set aside.

BEFORE SERVING
(TWENTY-FIVE TO THIRTY MINUTES BAKING TIME)

1. Preheat the oven to 180°C/350°F/Gas Mark 4.
2. Bake the fish for 25–30 minutes.
3. Reheat the sauce. If a thicker sauce is desired, mix the arrowroot with 1 tbls of water, then stir into the sauce. Simmer a few minutes, then keep warm in a *bain-marie*.

To serve: Place a fillet on each plate and spoon over a little sauce. Serve the rest of the sauce separately.

MACKEREL
WITH CIDER AND APPLES

SERVES 6

1 large onion, sliced	salt and pepper
1 medium-sized cooking apple, diced	6 mackerel fillets
1 oz (25 g) butter	2 tbls fresh white breadcrumbs
1 tsp soft brown sugar	
2 tbls double cream	*Garnish*
½ pt (300 ml) medium-dry cider	**fresh parsley, very finely chopped**

SAME DAY AS SERVING

1. Remove all bones from the fish with tweezers.
2. Cook the onion and apple in the butter until soft, but do not allow to colour. Add the sugar and cream and cook for another minute. Remove from the heat, stir in the cider and season.
3. Place fish in a single layer in a buttered gratin dish. Season the fillets with salt and pepper, and cover each one with a little of the onion and apple mixture. Pour the remaining liquid around the fish and sprinkle with the breadcrumbs. Cover the dish with foil and set aside in a cool place.

BEFORE SERVING
(TWENTY-FIVE TO THIRTY MINUTES BAKING TIME)

1. Preheat the oven to 180°C/350°F/Gas Mark 4.
2. Bake the fish for 25–30 minutes; uncover for the last 5 minutes. Serve each fillet with some of the onion and apple mixture on top and a sprinkling of parsley.

Note: Gooseberries are delicious baked with mackerel and it is useful to freeze some when they are in season. Stew the gooseberries with a little sugar and butter, and bake on top of the fish with a bit of cider.

MARINE
'LEG OF LAMB'
SERVES 6

Monkfish is a great favourite with the French. You will find it as *lotte de mer* on many French menus and cooked in a variety of ways. When it is baked in one piece with its leg of lamb shape, it becomes a *gigot de mer*. It makes an ideal dish for entertaining.

1 carrot, very finely
  chopped
3 tbls clarified butter
2 small onions, very finely
  chopped
1 clove garlic, crushed then
  very finely chopped
8 fl oz (250 ml) dry white
  wine
6 tomatoes, peeled, seeded
  and chopped

salt and freshly ground
  black pepper
good pinch of saffron
3-lb (1.4-kg) piece of
  monkfish
4 fl oz (110 ml) double
  cream or *crème fraîche*

Garnish
**fresh parsley, chopped very
  finely**

UP TO ONE DAY IN ADVANCE

Using a saucepan, sauté the carrot in the butter, stirring, for a few minutes. Add the onions and garlic and continue to sauté until the vegetables are soft. Pour over the wine and boil hard to reduce by half. Add the tomatoes, salt and pepper, and simmer until you have a thick sauce. Cool and refrigerate unless using the same day.

SEVERAL HOURS IN ADVANCE

1. Soak the saffron in 1 tbls of warm water.
2. Pull off any grey membranes that may be left on the fish. Season the fish with salt and pepper. Place the fish in a greased flameproof dish from which you can serve. Leave in a cool place.
3. Reheat the sauce with the saffron and double cream or *crème fraîche* until it is quite thick. Season to taste then pour over the fish. Cover with foil slashed in a few places and leave in a cool place.

BEFORE SERVING
(THIRTY TO THIRTY-FIVE MINUTES BAKING TIME)

1. Preheat the oven to 180°C/350°F/Gas Mark 4.
2. Bake the fish for 20–25 minutes. Remove the foil and bake for a further 10 minutes. Garnish with the parsley and serve.

Note: Fish fillets such as cod or halibut can be cooked in the same way but will need a much shorter cooking time. The time given is for quite a thick piece of monkfish.

MONKFISH
À L'AMÉRICAINE

SERVES 6

Take advantage of monkfish, with its beautiful firm flesh and sweet flavour.

3-lb (1.4-kg) piece of
  monkfish
seasoned flour
4 tbls olive oil
1 large onion, very finely
  chopped
2 cloves garlic, crushed and
  finely chopped
3 fl oz (75 ml) Cognac

½ pt (300 ml) dry white wine
2 lb (900 g) tomatoes,
  peeled, seeded and diced
2 tbls tomato purée
1 tsp fresh tarragon,
  chopped
1 tsp sugar
salt and pepper

Garnish
fresh tarragon, chopped

SAME DAY AS SERVING

1. Pull off any grey membranes that may be left on the fish. Coat in the seasoned flour. Heat half the oil in a frying-pan and sauté the onion until soft. Add the garlic and sauté a few more minutes. Scrape out on to a dish and set aside. Add the rest of the oil and brown the fish. Pour over the Cognac and boil for a minute or two. Remove the fish, cut into pieces, cover and refrigerate.
2. Return the onion and garlic to the pan. Add the wine and simmer to reduce slightly. Add the tomatoes, tomato purée, tarragon and sugar. Simmer, uncovered, for about 15 minutes or until it is the consistency of sauce. Adjust seasoning and set aside.

BEFORE SERVING
(FIVE TO TEN MINUTES COOKING TIME)

Bring the sauce to the boil. Add the fish and simmer gently for about 5–10 minutes. Turn out on to a heated dish and garnish with the tarragon.

Note: Saffron rice would go well, and a green vegetable or salad.

MONKFISH GRATIN

SERVES 6

You can prepare this from start to finish in 5 minutes – and it is nothing to be ashamed of.

2½-lb (1.1-kg) piece of monkfish	1½ oz (40 g) freshly grated Parmesan
salt and pepper	1½ oz (40 g) freshly grated Gruyère cheese
½ pt (300 ml) double cream	

——— BEFORE SERVING ———
(FIFTEEN TO TWENTY MINUTES BAKING TIME)

1. Preheat the oven to 190°C/375°F/Gas Mark 5.
2. Pull off any grey membranes that may be left on the fish. Pat it dry, season with salt and pepper, and cut into pieces. Pour a thin film of cream over the bottom of of a gratin dish. Arrange the fish over the cream, cover with the remaining cream and sprinkle with the cheese. Bake for 15–20 minutes.

Note: You can bake the fish on a thin layer of tomatoes or cucumber for an extra touch.

Monkfish with Aubergines and Courgettes

SERVES 6

Monkfish is ideal when you haven't much time to devote to cooking: no bones to worry about and its wonderful texture gives great flexibility in cooking.

8 tomatoes
12 oz (350 g) courgettes
12 oz (350 g) firm
   aubergines
9 tbls olive oil
1 clove garlic
salt and pepper

2½-lb (1.1-kg) piece of
   monkfish
juice of ½ lemon
pinch of dried thyme

Garnish
**fresh basil, torn into small
   pieces**

SAME DAY AS SERVING

1. Peel, seed and quarter the tomatoes.
2. Wash the courgettes and aubergines, and cut into ½-in (1.3-cm) cubes.
3. Heat 6 tbls of olive oil in a frying-pan until very hot. Sauté the courgettes and aubergines, stirring, until lightly coloured. Add the tomatoes, very finely chopped garlic, salt and pepper, and cook gently for 10 minutes. Set aside.

SEVERAL HOURS IN ADVANCE

Pull off any grey membranes that may be left on the fish. Cut into pieces and pat dry. Season with salt and pepper, place in a gratin dish, and steep in the rest of the oil, lemon juice and thyme.

BEFORE SERVING
(FIFTEEN MINUTES BAKING TIME)

1. Either bake the fish, uncovered, in a preheated oven 190°C/ 375°F/Gas Mark 5 for 15 minutes or place quite low under a preheated grill for about 15 minutes.

2. Quickly reheat the vegetables. When the fish is just cooked through, cover with the vegetables, garnish and serve.

SAFFRON SCALLOPS

SERVES 4

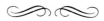

Scallops in a saffron-flavoured sauce are an exquisite dish – as glamorous as they are good. Serve with rice, which you can pack into greased ramekins and turn out on to the plates.

12 scallops, in the shell if
   possible
1 leek, cut into julienne
1 carrot, cut into julienne
pinch of saffron filaments
1 oz (25 g) butter
4 tbls French vermouth
2 shallots, very finely
   chopped
5 tbls dry white wine

½ pt (300 ml) good fish
   stock
¼ pt (150 ml) double cream
salt and pepper
12 oz (350 g) rice, cooked
1 tsp arrowroot

Garnish
fresh chervil, chopped

THE SAME DAY AS SERVING

1. Open the scallops by slipping a knife along the flat shell and severing the muscle that lies near the back. Slide a thin, flexible knife along the shell to remove the entire scallop. Alternatively, the scallops can be placed in a warm oven where they will open on their own and then can be removed with a knife. Separate the white fleshy muscle and pink coral from the other parts. The skirt can be washed and used in a stock. Wash the flesh and coral, and pat dry. Slice each scallop into two equal discs. Cover and refrigerate.
2. Blanch the leek and carrot in boiling salted water for 30 seconds. Refresh under cold water, drain and refrigerate.

SEVERAL HOURS IN ADVANCE

1. Soak the saffron in the vermouth.
2. Heat half the butter in a frying-pan. Slide the scallops and corals

into the pan and cook, stirring, for a few seconds, just until they become opaque on both sides. Season and set aside in a cool place on a plate.

3. Add the rest of the butter to the pan and sweat the shallots, stirring continually. When they are soft, add the wine and boil until evaporated. Add the stock and simmer for about 5 minutes. Add the saffron, vermouth and cream, and simmer a further few minutes. Season and set aside off the heat.

4. Pack the rice into small buttered moulds.

BEFORE SERVING
(FIFTEEN MINUTES REHEATING TIME)

1. Heat the rice in a moderate oven for about 15 minutes. Heat the vegetables at the same time in a small buttered dish, covered.

2. Mix the arrowroot with a bit of sauce, then add to the sauce. Bring sauce to a simmer, add fish and simmer 2 minutes at the very most.

To serve: Turn the rice on to the plates. Arrange the scallops and corals with some vegetables on each plate and spoon over some sauce. Garnish and serve.

SALMON FILLETS
WITH TOMATO

SERVES 4

A light, healthy dish to serve in the summer when tomatoes are in season. There isn't much to it, but if you use good oil, good fish and good tomatoes, it is excellent.

8 firm tomatoes	4 tbls extra virgin olive oil
salt and pepper	squeeze of lemon juice
1 cucumber	10 basil leaves, torn into
4 × 7-oz (200-g) wild	small pieces
salmon or salmon trout	
fillets	

SEVERAL HOURS IN ADVANCE

1. Skin, seed and chop the tomatoes. Sprinkle lightly with salt and leave in a colander to drain.
2. Peel the cucumber and slice as thinly as possible. Sprinkle with salt and allow to drain.
3. Pat the fish dry and place each fillet on a piece of foil in two Chinese steaming baskets (see p. 104).

BEFORE SERVING
(APPROX. FIVE MINUTES STEAMING AND COOKING TIME)

1. Pat the cucumber dry and arrange the slices around the edge of four plates. Warm the plates in a low oven.
2. Season the salmon with salt, pepper and a few drops of lemon juice. Place the baskets over boiling salted water. Place the lid on the top basket and steam for about 5 minutes. Do not overcook them.
3. Heat the olive oil in a saucepan and warm the tomatoes in the oil.
To serve: Place a fillet in the centre of each plate and spoon over some tomatoes. Sprinkle with basil and serve.

SEAFOOD CRÊPES WITH TARRAGON AND PERNOD

SERVES 6

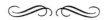

Crêpes filled with seafood in a light sauce flavoured with tarragon and Pernod are a lovely dish for a lunch party. Inexpensive fish are combined with a few scallops to enhance the flavour and texture. If the seafood is very fresh, it can be prepared a day in advance.

18 crêpes (see p. 210)
1 lb (450 g) mussels
½ pt (300 ml) dry white wine
4 oz (100 g) prawns in their shells, cooked
1 lb (450 g) monkfish, cod or haddock
1 pt (600 ml) fish stock
4–6 scallops

Garnish
bulb of fennel
fresh tarragon

For the sauce
1 shallot, very finely chopped
2 oz (50 g) butter
1½ oz (40 g) plain flour
2 tbls fresh tarragon, chopped
3 tbls Pernod
1 tbls cream
squeeze of lemon juice
salt and pepper

──────── ONE DAY IN ADVANCE ────────

1. Make the crêpes.
2. Wash the mussels in several changes of cold water. Discard any broken or open ones. Place in a saucepan with a few tablespoons of wine, cover and cook over brisk heat for a few minutes, until they just open. Strain the liquid through a muslin-lined sieve. Remove the mussels from their shells and set aside.
3. Peel the prawns and reserve the shells.
4. Cut the fish into strips. Cut each scallop into two equal discs. Bring the stock, wine, mussel liquid and prawn shells to the boil. Simmer gently for 10 minutes. Poach the fish in the simmering liquid for 1–2 minutes. Remove with a slotted spoon. Add the scallops, poach for 1–2 minutes and remove. Strain the stock through a muslin-lined sieve and set aside.
5. *For the sauce*: Sauté the shallot in the butter until soft. Add the

flour and cook gently for a few minutes. Whisk in the stock and stir until thickened. Add the tarragon and 2 tbls of Pernod and simmer 1 minute. Add the cream and taste for seasoning. It may need a bit of lemon juice or the extra tablespoon of Pernod as well as salt and pepper.

6. Place all the seafood in a bowl, cover with cling-film and refrigerate if not using the same day. Also refrigerate the sauce and crêpes.

SEVERAL HOURS IN ADVANCE

1. Peel the outer stalks of fennel and cut all the stalks into one length. Cut into thin julienne. Blanch in boiling salted water for 2–3 minutes, refresh under cold water and drain.
2. Reheat the sauce. Gently fold one-third of the sauce into the seafood. Place a good spoonful in the centre of each crêpe, good-side down, and roll up. Place in a gratin dish in one layer. Cover and leave at room temperature.

BEFORE SERVING
(FIFTEEN TO TWENTY MINUTES REHEATING TIME)

1. Preheat the oven to 180°C/350°F/Gas Mark 4.
2. Bring the sauce to a simmer and pour over the crêpes. Heat in the oven for 15–20 minutes or until hot and bubbling. If not serving immediately, keep warm in a low oven. Serve garnished with fennel and tarragon. The fennel can be reheated in a bit of butter before garnishing if desired.

SEAFOOD PILAFF

SERVES 8

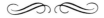

You can serve this dish hot or cold and add vegetables or different sorts of fish. It is a fine dish for a luncheon – serve with a mixed green salad.

big pinch of saffron
  filaments
2 tbls Cognac or brandy
4 pts (2.4 L) mussels
½ pt (300 ml) dry white
  wine
3 shallots, very finely
  chopped
5 tbls oil
1 lb (450 g) long-grain rice,
  unprocessed
1-lb (450-g) piece of
  monkfish

1 lb (450 g) prawns, peeled
salt and pepper
6 tbls olive oil (if serving
  cold)
2 tbls tarragon vinegar (if
  serving cold)
4 fl oz (110 ml) double
  cream (if serving hot)
2 oz (50 g) butter (if serving
  hot)

Garnish

**mixed fresh herbs, such as
  chervil, dill, tarragon or
  parsley, finely chopped**

ONE DAY IN ADVANCE

1. Soak the saffron in the Cognac.

2. Scrub the mussels with a stiff brush, remove the beards and scrape off any barnacles with a knife. Wash in cold water and discard any with broken shells or that are open.

3. Place mussels and wine in a large pot. Cover and cook over high heat, shaking the pan occasionally, for about 5 minutes or until the mussels are just open. Remove the mussels from their shells. Strain the cooking liquid through a muslin-lined sieve and add enough water to make a total of 1½ pts (900 ml).

4. Sauté the shallots in 3 tbls of oil. Wash the rice in several changes of water. Drain, then add to the shallots, stirring to coat in the oil. Pour in the mussel liquid and saffron, and bring to a quick boil. Stir, then cover and simmer over very low heat for 15 minutes. Remove from the heat, slip a tea towel under the lid, cover and leave for 10 minutes.

5. Meanwhile season the monkfish and cut into pieces. Sauté in the remaining oil for 5 minutes on each side, to just cook through.

6. Turn the rice into a large bowl. Mix with the mussels, prawns, and monkfish, and season. When cool refrigerate if not using the same day.

SEVERAL HOURS IN ADVANCE

Remove from the refrigerator if serving cold.

(TWENTY MINUTES REHEATING TIME IF SERVING HOT)

To serve hot: Reheat with the cream and butter in a *bain-marie* or in a hot oven. Garnish with the herbs and serve.
To serve cold: Make a vinaigrette with the oil and vinegar. Toss with the vinaigrette just before serving and add the fresh herbs.

Note: This dish can be made the day before, but it is better if made on the day of serving.

SMOKED HADDOCK TART

SERVES 6–8

A crisp pie crust filled with a very good kedgeree is ideal for an after-theatre supper. It is all cooked in advance and only needs a quick warm-up.

7 oz (200 g) shortcrust
  pastry (see p. 212)
3 large Finnan haddock
1 pt (600 ml) milk
2 shallots, very finely
  chopped
3 oz (75 g) butter
1 tsp curry powder
3 oz (75 g) basmati rice

1 egg yolk
¼ pt (150 ml) double cream
4 hard-boiled eggs,
  quartered
salt and freshly ground
  black pepper

Garnish
3 tbls fresh parsley, very
  finely chopped

UP TO TWO DAYS IN ADVANCE

1. Line a 10-in (26-cm) flan tin with a removable base (or six to eight 4-in (10-cm) individual tart tins) with the pastry. Refrigerate while oven heats to 200°C/400°F/Gas Mark 6. Prick the bottom, line with foil filled with dried beans and bake 15 minutes. Lower oven to 180°C/350°F/Gas Mark 4. Remove beans and foil. Cover the rim of pastry with a strip of foil if it is getting too brown and bake 20 minutes more or until done. Cool on a rack in the tin and store wrapped in cling-film.

2. Place fish in a roasting tin, cover with milk and extra water if necessary. Bring to a slow simmer and poach for 15 minutes or until cooked. Flake the fish and reserve.

3. Sauté shallots in 1 oz (25 g) of butter. Stir in curry powder, then the rice. Pour in 6 fl oz (175 ml) water. Bring to the boil, lower heat, cover and simmer gently for 15 minutes. Turn into a bowl and add remaining butter. Whisk egg yolk with cream and fold into warm, not hot, rice. Add fish and hard-boiled eggs, and season with salt and pepper. Cover and refrigerate.

—————— BEFORE SERVING ——————
(TEN MINUTES REHEATING TIME)

1. Preheat oven to 200°C/400°F/Gas Mark 6.
2. Reheat fish in a *bain-marie* over simmering water. Heat pie shell in oven for 10 minutes.

To serve: Fill shell with hot fish and garnish with the parsley.

STEAMED TROUT
FILLETS IN LETTUCE

SERVES 6–8

Inexpensive bamboo Chinese steaming baskets are perfect for entertaining. Vegetables and fish can be steamed at the same time in different basket layers and served directly from the baskets. The baskets must fit snugly on the lip of a saucepan so steam cannot escape. Enamelled aluminium saucepans with two handles are ideal. A bamboo lid on the top basket keeps the temperature constant throughout all the baskets. You will need three 12-in (30-cm) baskets plus a lid for this recipe. If you don't want to invest in steaming baskets, cook the vegetables another way and just steam the fish in a colander or vegetable steamer. It is a great recipe for any fish fillets.

2 shallots, very finely chopped
1 tbls oil

6 oz (175 g) fresh mushrooms, finely chopped

squeeze of lemon juice
salt and pepper
8 large lettuce leaves,
   Webb's Wonder or
   cabbage lettuce
4 large trout (pink fleshed if
   possible), filleted and
   skinned

8 fl oz (250 ml) *beurre blanc*
   (see p. 218)
24 small new potatoes
8 oz (225 g) mange-tout,
   stringed

SAME DAY AS SERVING

1. Sweat the shallots in the oil, stirring constantly. Add the mushrooms, lemon juice, salt and pepper. Sauté until the mushrooms give off their juices, then boil hard until all the juices have evaporated.

2. Blanch the lettuce in a large quantity of boiling salted water for a few minutes, until just limp. Refresh in a bowl of cold water, then spread out on tea towels to dry.

3. Trim the fillets and remove any bones with tweezers. By running your finger against the grain of the flesh, you can feel where they are. Pat the fillets dry and season with salt and pepper. Place a spoonful of the mushroom mixture on the fillet and roll up. Wrap in a lettuce leaf and place seam down in one of the baskets. Continue with the other fillets, filling two of the baskets.

4. Make the reduction for the *beurre blanc* and set aside.

BEFORE SERVING
(TWENTY-FIVE MINUTES STEAMING TIME)

1. Fill saucepan with 2–3 in of salted water and bring to the boil. Fill a basket with the potatoes, place on the lid, fit on the saucepan and steam for 15 minutes. Remove the lid and add the fish baskets. Cover with the lid and steam for 15 minutes. Add the mange-tout for the final 5 minutes of cooking time.

2. Finish the *beurre blanc* and keep warm over warm water.

To serve: Using oven gloves, remove baskets and place on large plates. Serve from the baskets and pass sauce separately.

Note: If you have less time (and more money) use filleted Dover soles and stuff them with a spoonful of boursin.

SQUID RISOTTO

SERVES 6

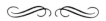

A recipe from David Pears, philosopher and cook. A ring of rice filled with squid and mushrooms and well-flavoured with chives and lemon juice.

2 lb (900 g) small squid
olive oil
6 cloves garlic, crushed then
   chopped
½ pt (300 ml) dry white
   wine
4 shallots, very finely
   chopped
8 oz (225 g) small fresh
   mushrooms
salt and pepper
1 onion, very finely
   chopped

1 lb (450 g) brown rice,
   unprocessed
good bunch of chives,
   finely chopped
2 oz (50 g) toasted flaked
   almonds

Garnish
**fresh parsley, finely
   chopped
paprika
juice of 2 lemons**

—— UP TO ONE DAY IN ADVANCE ——

1. Prepare the squid (see p. 108), but do not overwash or remove the skin. Cut into strips and pat dry.
2. Heat 3 tbls of olive oil in a frying-pan and sauté 4 cloves of the garlic with the squid for 3 minutes. Add the wine and simmer for 2 minutes. Remove the squid with a slotted spoon and place in a bowl. Boil the wine until reduced to 4–5 tbls. Add to the squid, cover and refrigerate unless using the same day.
3. Sauté the shallots in 1 tbls of olive oil, stirring, for a minute or two. Add the mushrooms and continue to sauté until softened. Season with salt and pepper, and add to the squid.
4. Sauté the onion and remaining garlic in 3 tbls of olive oil, stirring, until softened. Add the rice and stir until it is coated in the oil. Pour in 2½ pts (1.4 L) of boiling water. Bring back to the boil, add some salt, stir, then cover and simmer very gently for 45 minutes or until rice is cooked and has absorbed the water. Do not open the pan too often or the rice will not cook properly. Slip a cloth under the lid, then replace the lid and leave off the heat for 15

minutes. Alternatively, you can turn the rice into a shallow dish and dry off in a low oven for 15 minutes. Keep in a cool place overnight.

BEFORE SERVING

Add the chives and almonds to the rice and season. Add some oil if necessary. Arrange in a wall around the edge of a large dish. Fill the centre with the squid and mushrooms. Garnish the squid with the parsley and a fine sprinkling of paprika. Pour the lemon juice over both rice and squid.

Note: This can also be served hot. Reheat both rice and squid separately.

SQUID WITH TOMATOES

SERVES 6

If you haven't tackled squid before, do give it a try – the results are sweet and tender. Preparing them may sound lengthy, but after you have done it once the work goes very quickly. Serve this stew with plenty of good bread to sop up every ounce of sauce.

3 shallots, very finely
  chopped
1 carrot, very finely
  chopped
1 stalk of celery, very finely
  chopped
4 tbls olive oil
2 cloves garlic, crushed then
  finely chopped

2 tbls fresh parsley, very
  finely chopped
glass of dry white wine
1 lb (450 g) fresh tomatoes
  or a 14-oz (400-g) tin of
  chopped tomatoes
salt and pepper
3 lb (1.4 kg) small squid

Garnish
fresh parsley or coriander

UP TO THREE DAYS IN ADVANCE

1. Sauté the shallots, carrot and celery in the oil until soft. Add the garlic and parsley, and cook a further few minutes. Add the wine and boil hard to reduce. Stir in the tomatoes. Season with salt and

pepper and simmer, uncovered, for 10 minutes.

2. Meanwhile, prepare the squid. Hold the sac in one hand and pull off the head and tentacles with the other. Some of the insides will come away with the head. Cut off the tentacles in front of the eyes and reserve. You will feel a tiny hard lump at the top of the tentacles: squeeze it out and discard. Reserve the tentacles. Remove all the rest of the insides of the sac, including the long, flexible quill, and discard. Pour running water into the sac and squeeze out anything remaining inside. Dry with paper towels. Cut the sac and tentacles into thin slices.

3. Add the squid to the sauce, cover and simmer very gently for 20 minutes or until tender. Cool and refrigerate.

BEFORE SERVING
(TEN MINUTES REHEATING TIME)

Reheat the stew gently for about ten minutes. Garnish with very finely chopped parsley or coriander before serving.

Note: This goes well with bulghur, rice or pasta.

TROUT FILLETS
WITH SORREL SAUCE
SERVES 6

Sorrel has yet to find its way into the greengrocers, but it is very easy to grow. A few plants will provide enough leaves for a lovely sharp sauce.

4 large trout (pink fleshed if possible), filleted and skinned
5–6 oz (150–175 g) sorrel
2 shallots, very finely chopped
1 oz (25 g) butter
1 tbls plain flour
salt and pepper
¼ pt (150 ml) white wine
½ pt (300 ml) double cream or *crème fraîche*
squeeze of lemon juice

SAME DAY AS SERVING

1. Trim the fillets. Run your finger against the grain of the fish and remove any bones you feel with tweezers. Cover and refrigerate.
2. Wash the sorrel, pull off the coarse cenre ribs and chop the leaves. Sauté the shallots in the butter until soft. Stir in the flour. Add the sorrel, salt and pepper, and stir until sorrel is wilted. Add the wine and bring to a simmer, then stir in the cream. Simmer for a few minutes, then adjust the seasoning. It should have a nice, sharp taste. Add a bit of lemon juice if it needs it. Place a piece of cling-film over the surface to stop a skin forming and set aside.

BEFORE SERVING
(TEN TO TWELVE MINUTES STEAMING TIME)

1. Season the trout and lay on buttered pieces of foil. Place in two to three Chinese steaming baskets (see p. 104). Be sure the foil does not completely cover the bottom of the baskets or the steam will not be able to circulate. Place the lid on the top basket. Set the baskets over boiling salted water and steam for 10–12 minutes.
2. Keep the sauce warm in a *bain-marie*.
3. Serve fish from the baskets on to individual plates and spoon over some sauce.

Note: Boiled new potatoes go well with this dish. You can make a nice sauce by substituting spinach for the sorrel and adding lemon juice. It will also need to be puréed unless you chop it very finely.

TUNA ROLL

SERVES 6

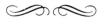

A poached tuna roll provides an inexpensive and very tasty dish for a buffet or cold lunch. It is very appetizing, studded with bits of orange carrot and garnished with capers and olives.

5–6 oz (150–175 g) potatoes
4 oz (100 g) carrots, finely diced
2 × 7-oz (200-g) tin of light-meat tuna, packed in olive oil
1 egg
1 egg white
1½ oz (40 g) freshly grated Parmesan cheese

6 tbls double cream
salt and freshly ground black pepper
½ pt (300 ml) mayonnaise for serving

Garnish
olives
capers
watercress

—————— UP TO TWO DAYS IN ADVANCE ——————

1. Peel and boil the potatoes. Pass through a vegetable mill or sieve.
2. Blanch the carrot in boiling salted water for 5 minutes, then refresh under cold water and drain.
3. Purée the tuna, egg and extra egg white in a blender or food processor. Scrape into a bowl. Stir in the cheese, potatoes, carrots and cream. Season to taste.
4. Place on a damp length of muslin and roll to form a salami-shaped roll about 3 in (7 cm) in diameter. Tie at both ends.
5. In a large saucepan bring enough water to cover the roll to the boil. Add the roll and some salt and return to the boil. Lower the heat and simmer gently for 45 minutes. Lift the roll out on to a platter and remove the muslin when cool enough to handle. Cover and refrigerate when cold.

—————— BEFORE SERVING ——————

Slice roll and place in overlapping slices on a platter. Garnish with olives, capers and watercress. Serve the mayonnaise separately.

TURBOT IN ORANGE CHAMBÉRY SAUCE

SERVES 6

Turbot is a fish to celebrate with. This lovely sauce treats it with due respect. Firm-fleshed fish such as turbot are also a great help when you are coping with guests. It should not be overcooked, but at least it takes kindly to reheating.

3 shallots, very finely chopped
1 oz (25 g) butter
extra butter for greasing
6 ×8-oz (225-g) turbot fillets, ½ in (1.3 cm) thick
fresh tarragon, chopped
6 fl oz (175 ml) Chambéry vermouth

6 fl oz (175 ml) chicken stock or fish stock
6 fl oz (300 ml) fresh orange juice
¼ pt (150 ml) double cream
salt and black pepper

Garnish
2 naval oranges
fresh tarragon, chopped

—————— SAME DAY AS SERVING ——————

1. Preheat the oven to 190°C/375°F/Gas Mark 5.
2. Sauté the shallots in the butter, stirring, until soft.
3. Pat fish dry and season. Place a large buttered piece of foil on a baking sheet. Sprinkle the centre with the shallots, set the fish on top in one layer and sprinkle with some tarragon. Enclose the fish loosely, sealing the edges carefully. Bake for 15 minutes. Remove fish to a platter and cover with cling-film when cool. Scrap the shallots and any juices from the foil into a saucepan.
4. Add the Chambéry to the pan and reduce by half. Add the stock and orange juice, and reduce by half. Add the cream, season to taste and simmer until a light coating consistency. Place a piece of cling-film on the surface of the sauce and set aside.
5. Peel the oranges and cut into segments with all pith removed.

BEFORE SERVING

(APPROX. TEN MINUTES REHEATING TIME)

1. Place orange segments in a *bain-marie* to heat.
2. Bring the sauce to a simmer. Add the fish and return to a simmer. Cover the pan, take off the heat and in 5 minutes it will be ready. Serve garnished with tarragon and the orange segments.

WHOLE BAKED COD

SERVES 8–10

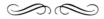

The common cod baked whole in a mock seaweed of grated courgettes and carrots is an uncommon feast – much less expensive than salmon and in its own way every bit as good. Your fishmonger may resist skinning the fish, but it can be done and more easily by him than by you.

3½ lb (1.6 kg) courgettes	3 oz (75 g) butter
salt and pepper	5–6-lb (2.3–2.7-kg) whole
1 lb (450 g) carrots	cod, skinned (but head
3 shallots, very finely	left on)
chopped	glass of Madeira

UP TO ONE DAY IN ADVANCE

1. Wash the courgettes and cut off stem and tip. Grate them (a food processor does this in seconds) and place in a colander set inside a bowl. Toss with 2 tsp of salt and leave for at least 10 minutes. Grate the carrots into another bowl.
2. Sauté the shallots in the butter in a large frying-pan. Add the carrots and sauté, stirring, for several minutes. Squeeze the courgettes by the handful to extract as much liquid as possible and add them to the pan. Continue to sauté, stirring, until courgettes soften. Season, scrape into a bowl, cover and refrigerate.

SEVERAL HOURS IN ADVANCE

1. Season the fish inside and out with salt and pepper. Butter a pan

to fit the fish. If the pan is too wide, line with foil, butter it and bunch it up to make a snug container for the fish.

2. Place half the vegetables on the foil, lay the fish on top and cover with the remaining vegetables. Pour the Madeira over the top.

BEFORE SERVING
(FORTY-FIVE TO FIFTY MINUTES BAKING TIME)

1. Preheat the oven to 180°C/350°F/Gas Mark 4.
2. Bake for 45–50 minutes. Check after 30 minutes to be sure top is not browning; cover loosely with foil if necessary.
3. *To serve*: Slide the fish on to a warmed platter and arrange the vegetables around it.

BOILED LEG OF LAMB
WITH CAPER SAUCE

SERVES 8

Boiled lamb does not sound very appealing but in fact it is absolutely delicious and gives lots of scope in timing as it can be kept hot in the cooking water for up to 1 hour. Mutton is traditionally used for boiling but it is not easy to find. Lamb adapts very nicely and the end result is beautifully flavoured tender meat.

5–5½-lb (2.3–2.5-kg) leg of lamb
salt

Garnish
watercress

For the sauce
1 shallot, very finely chopped
1½ oz (40 g) butter

¾ oz (20 g) plain flour
¾ pt (450 ml) vegetable or chicken stock, boiling
2 egg yolks
6 tbls double cream
3 tbls capers
3 tbls lemon juice
salt and freshly ground black pepper

SAME DAY AS SERVING

For the sauce: Sauté the shallot in the butter until soft, then stir in the flour. Whisk in the boiling stock and simmer, stirring, until sauce thickens slightly. Mix the egg yolks with the cream. Take sauce off the heat and stir in the egg yolk/cream mixture. Return the sauce to a very low heat and stir until the sauce thickens, without allowing it to boil. Stir in the capers and lemon juice and season. Set aside with a piece of cling-film floated over the surface to prevent a skin forming.

BEFORE SERVING
(APPROX. ONE AND A HALF HOURS BOILING AND RESTING TIME)

Placc lamb in a large saucepan and cover with enough cold water to completely submerge it. Remove the lamb, bring the water to the boil and add some salt. Put in the lamb and bring back to the boil, then lower the heat to a bare simmer, cover and allow 15 minutes per lb (450 g) of meat for medium-done. Remove from the water and leave at room temperature for 20 minutes before carving. It can also be kept in the cooking water, to which cold water should be added to make a hand-hot temperature. It will keep hot in the water for 1 hour.

2. Reheat the sauce over low heat or in a *bain-marie*.

To serve: Place on a warmed platter and garnish with watercress. Serve the sauce separately.

Note: The sauce can be made from the lamb stock but it means you have to do it much later. Onions can be cooked with the lamb and puréed to make a sauce; or, they can be added to the sauce. Serve with steamed or boiled vegetables.

BONED LEG OF LAMB WITH KIDNEYS

SERVES 10–12

If you don't have an obliging butcher, supermarkets now sell boned legs of lamb. It is a great solution for dinner parties. Carving presents no problem, and with a savoury stuffing it is almost a meal in itself.

4½-lb (2-kg) leg of lamb,
   boned (6–7 lb/2.7–3.2 kg
   before boning)
4 lamb kidneys
3 shallots, very finely
   chopped
3 oz (75 g) butter
8 oz (225 g) mushrooms,
   finely chopped
squeeze of lemon juice
salt and pepper
2 fl oz (60 ml) Cognac or
   Madeira

½ tsp dried thyme
1 tsp fresh sage, finely
   chopped
3 oz (75 g) rice, uncooked
4 oz (100 g) ham, cooked
   and diced
1 egg
oil for brushing
½ pt (300 ml) lamb stock
   for the gravy

Garnish
watercress

———— UP TO ONE DAY IN ADVANCE ————

1. Peel off my skin and fat from the kidneys and chop very finely.
2. Sauté half the shallots in half the butter until soft. Add the mushrooms, a squeeze of lemon juice, salt and pepper. Sauté, stirring, until mushrooms exude their own juices. Boil hard to evaporate. Scrape into a bowl.
3. Sauté the remaining shallots in the rest of the butter until soft. Add the kidneys and stir for a few minutes. Pour in the Cognac and reduce. Season with salt, pepper and the herbs. Scrape out and add to the mushrooms.
4. Cook the rice in a large quantity of boiling salted water until just tender. Drain and add to the mushrooms. Stir in the ham and egg. Cover and refrigerate.

───────── SAME DAY AS SERVING ─────────

Dry the lamb and season. Spoon in the stuffing. Close with skewers tied in place with string laced between them. Leave at room temperature.

───────── BEFORE SERVING ─────────
(APPROX. TWO HOURS ROASTING AND RESTING TIME)

1. Preheat the oven to 180°C/350°F/Gas Mark 4.
2. Brush the lamb with oil and set on a rack in a roasting pan. Roast for 1½–1¾ hours for pink lamb. Turn over half-way through the cooking time. Remove from the oven, place on a warmed platter, and remove skewers and string. Leave at room temperature for 20 minutes to rest before serving. If you are not ready to eat, then place in a warm oven.
3. Add the lamb stock to the pan juices to make a little gravy. Garnish the platter with watercress and serve.

Note: A light vegetable dish such as lettuce mousse (see p. 203) would go well with this recipe.

BRAISED SHOULDER
OF LAMB
WITH WALNUT STUFFING
SERVES 8

The lamb can be stuffed and braised two days in advance. It can be sliced and reheated just before serving. Ask the butcher to chop the bones for you.

shoulder of lamb, boned
1 tbls oil
bones from the shoulder of
   lamb, chopped
1 carrot chopped

1 onion, chopped
1 stalk of celery, chopped
½ pt (150 ml) French
   vermouth
1 pt (300 ml) lamb or beef
   stock

bouquet garni
sprig of rosemary or thyme

For the stuffing
2 shallots, finely chopped
1 oz (25 g) butter
8 oz (225 g) lean minced
  lamb
1 clove garlic, crushed

2 oz (50 g) fresh
  breadcrumbs
grated rind of 1 lemon
2 oz (50 g) walnuts,
  chopped
1 egg
½ tsp fresh rosemary, finely
  chopped
salt and pepper

UP TO TWO DAYS IN ADVANCE

1. Preheat the oven to 170°C/325°F/Gas Mark 3.
2. Sauté the shallots in the butter until soft. Scrape into a bowl and mix with the outer stuffing ingredients. Season well with salt and pepper.
3. Trim off any fat from the shoulder. Season the lamb, then spread the stuffing over the meat and into the pocket left by the bone. Roll up and tie at intervals.
4. In a casserole brown the lamb in the oil. Remove the lamb and add the bones and vegetables. Brown these for several minutes. Add the vermouth and boil to reduce. Season the lamb and return to the casserole. Pour in the stock and add the bouquet garni and sprig of rosemary. Bring to a simmer on top of the stove. Cover with buttered greaseproof paper and then the lid. Simmer in the oven for 2 hours. Remove the lamb from the casserole, cool, then cover and refrigerate. Strain the stock into a bowl and refrigerate.

SAME DAY AS SERVING

1. Remove fat from the stock. Bring to a simmer and adjust seasoning.
2. Slice the lamb, remove strings and lay in overlapping slices in a shallow flameproof dish. Pour over the sauce, cover with cling-film and leave at room temperature.

BEFORE SERVING
(TEN MINUTES REHEATING TIME)

Cover the lamb and reheat on top of the stove for about 10 minutes. It can also be reheated in a moderate oven for 15–20 minutes.

CASSOULET

SERVES 8–10

What could be better for a winter party than a *cassoulet*? This hearty and superb dish comes from the south-west of France. It should include some *confit d'oie* (preserved goose), which can be made at home (see p. 228) or bought in tins or jars at specialist food shops (something to bring back the next time you go to France). The *confit* can be replaced by some pieces of roast duck. The dish is substantial and only needs to be served with a salad or vegetable.

2 lb (900 g) dry white
  haricot beans
12-oz (350-g) piece of
  streaky bacon
4 cloves garlic, peeled and
  crushed
3 large onions, sliced
large bouquet garni
salt and freshly ground
  black pepper
5–6 tbls oil
4-lb (1.8-kg) shoulder of
  lamb, cut into stewing
  chunks

5 tbls tomato purée
1 pt (600 ml) dry white wine
1½ pts (900 ml) veal or beef
  stock
1 lb (450 g) chorizo sausage
1 lb (450 g) *confit d'oie* (see
  p. 228) or 4 pieces of roast
  duck
2 oz (50 g) fresh
  breadcrumbs
8 tbls fresh parsley, finely
  chopped

UP TO TWO DAYS IN ADVANCE
(MINIMUM ONE DAY)

Soak the beans overnight in enough water to cover plus a few inches.

ONE DAY IN ADVANCE

1. The next day drain the beans and place in a large saucepan. Remove the rind from the bacon and cut into small pieces. Slice the bacon into ½-in (1.3-cm) slices. Add the rind, bacon, 2 cloves of garlic, 1 sliced onion and the bouquet garni to the saucepan. Cover with water, cover and simmer slowly, for about 1½–2 hours or

until beans are tender. Towards the end of the cooking time, add some salt and pepper.

2. Meanwhile, using a frying-pan, heat the oil and brown the lamb. Remove the lamb to a heavy-based saucepan and add the rest of the sliced onions to the frying-pan. Lightly brown the onions, stirring, and add to the lamb. Add the rest of the garlic, tomato purée, wine and enough stock to cover the lamb. Season, cover and simmer gently for about 1½ hours or until lamb is tender. Spoon away any surface fat and remove the bones from the lamb. Cut the sausages into chunks. Remove the bones from the goose or duck.

3. *To assemble the cassoulet*: Place a third of the beans and bacon in the bottom of a casserole. Reserve the bean liquid. Cover with a layer of lamb, goose and sausage. Layer again with beans, then the meat and then the remaining beans. Pour over the cooking liquid from the lamb and as much bean liquid as needed to cover the beans. Spread the breadcrumbs and parsley over the top. Cover and refrigerate unless using the same day.

SEVERAL HOURS IN ADVANCE

Remove the *cassoulet* from the refrigerator and leave at room temperature.

BEFORE SERVING
(FORTY-FIVE MINUTES BAKING TIME)

1. Preheat the oven to 200°C/400°F/Gas Mark 6.
2. Bake for 30 minutes or until a crust has started to form and brown. Turn the crust into the beans with a large spoon. Reduce the oven 180°C/350°F/Gas Mark 4 and continue to cook until another crust is formed (about 15 minutes) and the *cassoulet* is bubbling. Keep warm in a low oven if not serving immediately.

FILO LAMB PARCELS

SERVES 6

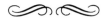

For a tasty and attractive edible parcel bake lamb chops in filo.

3 oz (75 g) butter	salt and freshly ground
3 tbls fresh mint, very finely	black pepper
chopped	1 tbls oil
6 loin lamb chops, 1½ in	6 sheets of filo pastry
(3.8 cm) thick, boned and	1 cucumber
fat removed	2 fl oz (60 ml) stock

——— SEVERAL HOURS IN ADVANCE ———

1. Mash 2 oz (50 g) of the butter with the mint and refrigerate until needed.
2. Season the chops with salt and pepper then quickly brown them on both sides in the hot oil. Leave to cool on a rack.
3. Gently melt the remaining butter. Brush a filo sheet with butter and fold in half lengthwise. Place the chop with a pat of mint butter at the bottom of the filo strip and roll up to make a parcel. Fold the ends to seal and brush with melted butter. Keep covered in clingfilm until ready to bake.
4. Peel, then cut the cucumber into batons and set aside.

——— BEFORE SERVING ———
(APPROX. TWENTY MINUTES BAKING TIME)

1. Preheat the oven to 200°C/400°F/Gas Mark 6.
2. Place the parcels on a greased baking sheet and bake for 20 minutes for medium-done meat
3. Braise the cucumber in the stock for 5 minutes.
4. Arrange a parcel and some cucumber on each plate and serve.

Note: A dab of anchovy butter (see p. 216) is a good alternative to the mint butter.

GUARDS OF HONOUR

SERVES 6

The best end-of-neck is relatively inexpensive and is an excellent small joint for a party. It looks impressive and is easy to carve into chops. The sauce is a nice extra, but not really necessary if the meat is kept juicy and pink.

2 racks of lamb, chined

Garnish
watercress

For the coating
1 clove garlic, mashed
2 tbls Dijon mustard
4 tbls oil
2 tbls breadcrumbs
salt and pepper

For the sauce
lamb bones and bits of meat
1 tbls oil
½ stalk of celery, chopped
1 small onion, chopped
1 carrot, chopped
1 tbls plain flour
4 fl oz (125 ml) dry white wine
bouquet garni

——— ONE DAY IN ADVANCE ———

1. *To prepare the racks*: Cut off the fat from the lower 3–4 in (7.6–10 cm) of rib bones. Scrape the bones clean, removing all the meat from in between the bones. Save chine bone and meat scraps for the sauce. Pull of the thicker layer of fat that covers the eye of the meat, leaving a thin layer of fat. Wrap the exposed rib bones with foil to prevent them from charring. Cover and refrigerate.
2. *For the coating*: Mix together the garlic, mustard, oil and breadcrumbs, and season well with salt and pepper. Keep covered in a cool place.
3. *For the sauce*: Chop the bones into small pieces. Heat the oil in a large saucepan and over high heat brown the bones, meat bits and vegetables. Stir in the flour, then pour over the wine and reduce. Add 1 pt (600 ml) water and bouquet garni and bring to the boil; skim, then cover and simmer gently for 2 hours. Strain, cool and refrigerate.

1. Skim the fat from the sauce, reheat and season to taste.
2. Leave lamb at room temperature.

BEFORE SERVING
(THIRTY MINUTES ROASTING TIME)

1. Place sauce in a *bain-marie* to keep warm.
2. Preheat oven to 200°C/400°F/Gas Mark 6.
3. Season racks with salt and pepper. Place in an oiled roasting pan and roast for 10 minutes. Remove them from the oven and paint with the mustard coating. Return to the oven and roast a further 20 minutes. This should give you a medium roast. Place on a serving platter with the ribs interlaced. Serve garnished with the watercress.

Note: Coating the meat before the last 20 minutes of roasting can be timed with starting the first course. The rack or loin can also be boned before it is roasted. The flap of meat from the rib bones is left on and herbs can be placed inside it before it is rolled up, tied at intervals and roasted.

LAMB KEBABS
SERVES 6

Neck fillets of lamb are ideal for kebabs. They just need to be sliced and marinated and they are ready to skewer. They can be done on an outside barbeque or inside under the grill.

4 good-sized neck fillets of lamb	6 crushed black pepper corns
6 tbls olive oil	8 crushed coriander seeds
grated rind of ½ lemon and juice	12 medium-size mushrooms
1–2 cloves garlic, crushed and chopped	6 firm tomatoes, quartered
	salt and freshly ground black pepper

HALF-DAY IN ADVANCE
(MINIMUM ONE HOUR)

1. Trim excess fat from fillets and cut into 1 inch (2.3 cm) pieces.
2. Mix olive oil, lemon juice and rind, garlic, pepper and coriander in a bowl. Add the meat and toss in the marinade. Leave in a cool place.

ONE HOUR BEFORE SERVING

1. Time your outside barbeque so it will be hot enough to cook on about 15 minutes before you serve the lamb.
2. Skewer the lamb, alternating with mushrooms and tomatoes. Season with salt and pepper.

FIFTEEN MINUTES BEFORE SERVING

Grill for 6 minutes on each side. The outside should be well browned but the inside still pink. Keep warm on the side of the barbeque or on a warmed platter under foil.

Note: You can do the grilling 30 minutes ahead of time and keep them warm, covered with foil in a low oven. Better of course to grill them at the last minute.

LEG OF LAMB
WITH HARICOT BEANS
SERVES 8–10

A favourite French bistro dish that can never be displaced. The lamb and beans can be completely cooked beforehand and reheated together. Or, if you prefer, you can roast the lamb at the last minute and serve it hot from the oven on a bed of white beans. Really delicious either way.

For the beans
1 lb (450 g) haricot beans
1 onion, stuck with 2 cloves
1 carrot, quartered
1 stalk of celery, chopped
bouquet garni
salt and pepper
1 onion, very finely
    chopped
2 tbls oil
2 cloves garlic, very finely
    chopped
2 fl oz (60 ml) French
    vermouth
14-oz (400-g) tin of
    chopped tomatoes
½ tsp dried thyme

Garnish
**fresh parsley, very finely
    chopped**

For the lamb
5–6-lb (2.3–2.7-kg) leg of
    lamb
1 clove garlic
salt and pepper
1 tsp dried oregano
1 tsp dried thyme
1 tbls olive oil
¼ pt (150 ml) dry white
    wine
¼ pt (150 ml) lamb or beef
    stock

UP TO THREE DAYS IN ADVANCE
(MINIMUM ONE DAY)

1. Soak the beans overnight in enough cold water to cover. Drain and place in a large saucepan with the onion (stuck with cloves), quartered carrot, chopped celery and bouquet garni. Add cold water to cover plus 1 in (2.5 cm). Bring slowly to the boil, lower the heat, cover and simmer gently for 1½ hours or until tender but not mushy. Discard the vegetables and bouquet garni. Season with salt and pepper.

2. Sauté the onion in the oil until soft. Add the garlic and stir for 1 minute. Pour in the vermouth and reduce by half. Add the tomatoes, thyme, salt and pepper, and simmer until the mixture thickens. Add to the beans.

3. Preheat the oven to 230°C/450°F/Gas Mark 8.

4. Trim off any fat from the lamb. Make several incisions in the lamb and insert slivers of garlic. Season with salt, pepper and the dried herbs. Rub in the olive oil. Place in a roasting tin and roast for 15 minutes. Reduce the heat to 180°C/350°F/Gas Mark 4. Allow 15 minutes per lb (450 g) including the initial searing time. Baste the meat after 30 minutes and once or twice more. Transfer the lamb to a platter and leave for at least 20 minutes before carving.

5. Deglaze the tin with the wine. Add the stock and simmer a few minutes. Skim off the fat. Season with salt and pepper. Pour the

beans into a large, shallow flameproof casserole suitable for serving. Slice the lamb and lay over the beans. Pour over the gravy, cover and refrigerate when cool.

SEVERAL HOURS IN ADVANCE

Leave casserole at room temperature.

BEFORE SERVING
(TWENTY-FIVE MINUTES REHEATING TIME)

1. Preheat the oven to 180°C/350°F/Gas Mark 4.
2. Bring casserole to a simmer on top of the stove, then place in the oven for 25 minutes to heat. Serve garnished with parsley.

MINT LAMB PARCELS
SERVES 6

Boned lamb chops are wrapped in foil and quickly baked in the oven. This easy method cooks the lamb beautifully and all the flavour is sealed in the parcel.

6 loin lamb chops, 1½ in (3.8 cm) thick, boned and fat removed	½ cucumber, peeled and sliced
3 tbls fresh mint, very finely chopped	6 small sprigs of mint
2 oz (50 g) butter	salt and freshly ground black pepper

SEVERAL HOURS IN ADVANCE

1. Mash the butter with the mint.
2. Cut 6 heart-shaped pieces of foil large enough to contain a chop.
3. Season the chops with salt and pepper. Place on the foil with a pat of mint butter, some cucumber slices and a sprig of mint. Seal the packages tightly, but leave a bit of room inside. Set aside at room temperature.

1. Preheat the oven to 180°C/350°F/Gas Mark 4.
2. Place parcels on a baking sheet and bake for 20 minutes for medium rare. Serve each guest his or her own parcel, or place them unwrapped on a heated serving platter.

MOUSSAKA

SERVES 8–10

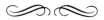

This well-known Greek dish is perfect for informal fork suppers. It can be served hot, but is even better lukewarm. It is fairly substantial and goes well with salads or rice dishes.

2 firm aubergines
salt and pepper
groundnut or sunflower oil
4 medium-sized onions, chopped
1 clove garlic, chopped
1½–2 lb (675–900 g) lean lamb, cooked or raw, minced
¼ pt (150 ml) red or white wine
8 oz (225 g) tomatoes, peeled and chopped

3 tbls fresh coriander leaves, very finely chopped
2½ oz (60 g) butter
2 oz (50 g) plain flour
1½ pts (900 ml) cold milk
1 bay leaf
8 oz (225 g) ricotta or cottage cheese
2 eggs
2 oz (50 g) breadcrumbs
2 oz (50 g) freshly grated Parmesan cheese

——————— UP TO TWO DAYS IN ADVANCE ———————

1. Wash and slice the aubergines into ½-in (1.3-cm) rounds. Place them in a colander, sprinkle generously with salt and leave for a few hours to drain. Dry with paper towels.
2. Heat a few tablespoons of oil in a frying-pan until very hot and brown the slices, adding more oil as necessary. Drain on paper towels. Add 2 tbls of oil to the pan and sauté the onions and garlic, stirring, until soft. Add the meat and brown, breaking it up at the same time with a fork. Season with salt and pepper. Pour in the

wine and boil hard to evaporate. If there is any fat on the surface, skim it off. Stir in the tomatoes and coriander and cook a further 5 minutes.

3. Melt the butter in a heavy-bottomed saucepan, stir in the flour and cook a few minutes without allowing the flour to colour. Whisk in the cold milk all in one go and continue to whisk until the sauce thickens. Add the bay leaf and simmer gently for 15 minutes, stirring occasionally. Remove the bay leaf, whisk in the ricotta or cottage cheese, then the eggs. Season to taste with salt and pepper.

4. Oil a casserole and sprinkle the bottom with breadcrumbs. Layer with meat, aubergine, breadcrumbs and Parmesan. Pour the sauce over the top and sprinkle with any remaining cheese or breadcrumbs.

5. Preheat the oven to 180°C/350°F/Gas Mark 4.

6. Bake the moussaka for 1 hour. When cool, cover and refrigerate if not using the same day.

BEFORE SERVING
(THIRTY TO FORTY-FIVE MINUTES REHEATING TIME)

Warm in a moderate oven for 30–45 minutes, depending on how hot you wish to serve it. It retains heat, so do not serve too hot.

NAVARIN D'AGNEAU
SERVES 6–7

This succulent lamb stew can be served with success even on formal occasions. It can be made from cuts of meat from the shoulder or breast, but the neck fillet is reliably tender and slices into even, round pieces. With carefully shaped vegetables, the stew looks beautiful.

3 lb (1.4 kg) boned
   lamb-neck fillets
3 tbls oil
2 tbls sugar
salt and freshly ground
   black pepper
3 tbls plain flour
1½ pts (900 ml) lamb, veal
   or beef stock
8-oz (225-g) tin of chopped
   tomatoes
2 cloves garlic, crushed and
   finely chopped

bouquet garni
12 new potatoes
12 pickling onions
6 small turnips
6 carrots
4 oz (100 g) mange-tout or
   frozen petit pois
8 oz (225 g) small French
   beans

Garnish
**fresh parsley, finely
   chopped**

UP TO TWO DAYS IN ADVANCE

1. Preheat the oven to 170°C/325°F/Gas Mark 3.
2. Cut the meat into 1-in (2.5-cm) rounds and trim off any bits of fat. Pat the meat dry with paper towels. Heat the oil in a frying-pan until very hot. Brown the meat without crowding and transfer to a large flameproof casserole. Sprinkle the sugar over the meat in the casserole and caramelize it over high heat. Season the meat with salt and pepper, and sprinkle with the flour. Stir the meat to brown the flour. Deglaze the frying-pan with some of the stock and add to the casserole; then add the rest of the stock, tomatoes, garlic and bouquet garni.
3. Peel the potatoes, onions and turnips, and shape into equal sizes. Add to the casserole and cover with a *cartouche* of paper pressed on to the surface of the ingredients; then cover with the lid. Bring to a simmer on top of the stove, then place in the oven. Keep the *navarin* just simmering gently. Regulate the temperature if necessary and simmer for 1 hour. Cool, then refrigerate if not serving the same day. Skim and blot off any fat if you are serving the same day.

SAME DAY AS SERVING

Scrape off any congealed surface fat. Leave at room temperature. Peel the carrots, cut into quarters and round the sharp edges. Cook, drain and set aside. Prepare the peas and beans. Cook the beans in a large quantity of boiling salted water until they are just *al dente*. Add the peas for the last 30 seconds of cooking time. Drain and refresh in iced water and set aside. Prepare the parsley and cover with cling-film.

──── BEFORE SERVING ────
(THIRTY MINUTES REHEATING TIME)

1. Preheat the oven to 170°C/325°F/Gas Mark 3.
2. Remove the bouquet garni, taste and adjust seasoning. Bring to a simmer on top of the stove, then place in the oven for 30 minutes.
3. Stir the beans and mange-tout or petit pois into the casserole (they will acquire enough heat from the sauce). Serve either from the casserole or turn out on to a large, heated platter and garnish. Make sure everyone receives a variety of vegetables.

NOISETTES OF LAMB

SERVES 6

Noisettes are made from a rack or loin of lamb. The meat is boned and the fat removed, but the flap is kept to wrap around the meat. It is tied at 1½-in (3.8-cm) intervals, then cut between the string into noisettes. They are great for entertaining – easy to cook, reliably tender and go with any number of sauces.

1 tbls oil	***For the Madeira sauce***
12 noisettes of lamb	**3 tbls Sercial Madeira**
salt and pepper	**8 fl oz (250 ml) double**
Garnish	**cream**
watercress	**1 oz (25 g) butter**
	1½ tbls tarragon, very
	finely chopped

──── SEVERAL HOURS IN ADVANCE ────

1. Heat the oil in a frying-pan until very hot. Sear the meat on both sides over high heat, then lower the heat and cook for about 5 minutes on each side. The meat should still be springy to the touch. Do the meat in batches to avoid crowding. Pour off all the fat from the pan and blot up any that remains with paper towels. Deglaze the

pan with the Madeira, pour in the cream and half the tarragon, and simmer a few minutes. Season to taste, then pour into a *bain-marie* and remove from the heat.

BEFORE SERVING
(TEN MINUTES REHEATING TIME)

1. Preheat the oven to 200°C/400°F/Gas Mark 6.
2. Place the noisettes in a roasting tin and warm in the oven for 10 minutes.
3. Heat the sauce with the remaining tarragon in the *bain-marie* set over low heat. Just before serving, swirl in the butter.
To serve: Place the noisettes on a serving dish, season with some salt and pepper, and garnish the dish with watercress. Pass the sauce separately.

STUFFED MOROCCAN
SHOULDER OF LAMB
SERVES 8

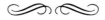

1 shoulder of lamb, boned	**8 oz (225 g) bulghur wheat**
	salt and pepper
For the stuffing	**1 egg**
4 oz (100 g) dried apricots	**2 tbls fresh coriander, finely**
1 small onion, finely	**chopped**
chopped	**3 tbls toasted pine nuts**
2 tbls oil	**1 oz (25 g) raisins**

UP TO ONE DAY IN ADVANCE

1. Pour boiling water over the apricots to cover and leave for a few hours to soften; or, simmer in a little water until soft.
2. Brown the onion in the oil. Add the bulghur and stir to coat in the oil and brown a bit. Pour over 12 fl oz (400 ml) of water and bring to the boil. Add some salt, reduce the heat and simmer gently for 15 minutes or, until water is absorbed. Turn into a bowl. Chop the softened apricots and add them together with the rest of the

ingredients to the bulghur. Mix together well and season.

3. Trim off any fat from the shoulder. Season with salt and pepper. Spread the stuffing over the meat and inside the pocket. Roll into a cylindrical shape and tie at intervals. Refrigerate wrapped in clingfilm.

SEVERAL HOURS IN ADVANCE

Leave the lamb at room temperature.

BEFORE SERVING
(ONE HOUR AND THIRTY-FIVE MINUTES ROASTING AND RESTING TIME)

1. Preheat the oven to 200°C/400°F/Gas Mark 6.
2. Roast on the top shelf of the oven for 1 hour and 20 minutes. Remove to a warm platter and allow to rest for 15 minutes before serving. It can be kept warm in a cool oven for 30 minutes.

Note: Any extra stuffing can be baked separately. If you have the time you can make a little gravy with the lamb bones.

CURLED HAM WITH MUSHROOMS

SERVES 8

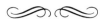

Ham steaks curl when they cook and make containers for the mushrooms. Fennel or leeks in a creamy sauce also make very good fillings.

1½ oz (40 g) dried
  mushrooms
2 shallots, finely chopped
3 tbls oil
1½ lb (675 g) fresh
  mushrooms, sliced
salt and freshly ground
  pepper
squeeze of lemon juice
1 tsp plain flour

¼ pt (150 ml) double cream
2 tbls fresh parsley, finely
  chopped
2 lb (900 g) smoked
  tenderloin of pork or
  ham steaks
2 tbls Madeira

Garnish
**fresh parsley, finely
  chopped**

SAME DAY AS SERVING

1. Soak the dried mushrooms in ¼ pt (150 ml) of water for at least 30 minutes. Drain, straining the liquid through a muslin-lined sieve.

2. Sauté the shallots in half the oil, stirring, for a minute or two. Add the fresh and dried mushrooms, salt, pepper and lemon juice, and sauté until mushrooms are cooked. Sift the flour over the mushrooms and stir in. Add the soaking water from the dried mushrooms and the cream, and boil hard until reduced to a thick sauce. Stir in the parsley and season to taste. Scrape into a bowl and set aside.

3. Cut the tenderloin into steaks about ½ in (1.3 cm) thick. Sauté the steaks in the remaining oil until lightly cooked. Remove to a shallow, greased flameproof dish. Place them in one layer, curled-side up, and spoon some mushroom mixture into the cup. Sprinkle with the Madeira and cover with foil.

(TWENTY-FIVE MINUTES BAKING TIME)

1. Preheat the oven to 180°C/350°F/Gas Mark 4.
2. Bake for about 25 minutes and serve from the dish. Garnish with a bit of parsley.

Note: Baked new potatoes and a salad of thinly sliced fennel and Gruyère cheese would go well with the ham.

PAPRIKA PORK FILLETS

SERVES 6

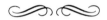

The trick with all tender cuts of meat is not to overcook them and allow them to become tough. This can easily happen when you cook in advance and reheat. The following method of cooking pork fillets keeps them beautifully tender.

3 oz (75 g) butter
2 shallots, very finely
 chopped
2 tsp paprika
1½ oz (40 g) plain flour
½ pt (300 ml) chicken stock
grated rind and juice of
 small lemon

¼ pt (150 ml) soured cream
 or *crème fraîche*
salt and black pepper
2 large pork fillets
sprig of rosemary

Garnish
**fresh parsley or celery
 leaves, very finely
 chopped**

UP TO TWO DAYS IN ADVANCE

1. Preheat oven to 200°C/400°F/Gas Mark 6.
2. Melt 1½ oz (40 g) of the butter in a small saucepan. Sauté the shallots and paprika, stirring, until tender. Stir in flour and cook a few more minutes. Whisk in the stock until it thickens, add the lemon juice and rind, and simmer 10 minutes. Pour into a bowl, add the soured cream and season to taste with salt and pepper.
3. When oven is ready, dry fillets, season and tie at intervals to keep a round shape. Place in a greased tin, smear with the remaining

butter and top with the rosemary. Bake for 15 minutes. The meat should still be quite springy to the touch and undercooked. Drain the cooking juices into the sauce. Allow meat to cool, then cover and refrigerate.

SEVERAL HOURS IN ADVANCE

Slice fillets diagonally to make larger rounds. They should be quite pink inside. Discard the rosemary. Arrange slices so that they overlap in a greased, shallow flameproof dish. Spoon over half the sauce and leave at room temperature.

BEFORE SERVING
(TWENTY MINUTES REHEATING TIME)

1. Preheat oven to 190°C/375°F/Gas Mark 5. Bake the pork, covered, for 20 minutes or until just cooked through. Do not overcook, as meat will become tough. Remove from oven and keep warm until serving.
2. Keep the remaining sauce warm in a *bain-marie*.
To serve: Spoon over the rest of the sauce and garnish.

PORK TENDERLOIN
WITH APPLES AND CALVADOS
SERVES 4–6

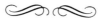

A purée of onions thickens the sauce and flavours the pork and apple slices.

2 large pork fillets	**1 oz (25 g) butter**
3 tart green apples	**1½ tbls vinegar**
2 oz sugar	**½ pt (300 ml) double cream**
	salt and pepper
For the sauce	**2½ oz (60 g) butter**
1 large onion, sliced	**6 tbls Calvados**

EST^D 1765

Hennessy
COGNAC
LICENSEE CUP

Please enter me for the Hennessy Cognac Licensee Cup 1987
(Please complete this form, IN FULL, in block capitals)

Name: _____

Club Handicap:_____or, Society Handicap_____Society Name_____

Playing Partner's Name: _____

Club Handicap:_____or, Society Handicap_____Society Name_____
(NB Maximum handicap 28; proof of handicap will be required at Regional Finals where ¾ of full handicap allowance will be given)
On Licensed Premises:

Name of Premises: _____

Road/Street: _____

Town: _____ County:_____

Post Code:_____ Tel No: _____
(NB It is most important that your premises' address is completed in full for your postal round draw)

Position held at above premises: _____

Golf Club where you are a member: _____
Did you enter the Hennessy Cognac Licensee Cup in 1986 YES/NO*
Are you a Hennessy Club member YES/NO*
Are you a) A tenanted estate*
       b) A managed estate*
       c) A free trade*   *please delete where appropriate

Name of parent brewer _____

Salesman's Name (if known) _____
We, the entrants, agree to abide by the rules of the Hennessy Cognac Licensee Cup and agree that the Tournament Director's decision, in all matters relating to the competition, shall be final and binding. I also confirm that the above premises, where I am the Licensee, is a stockist of Hennessy Cognac.

Licensee's Signature:_____ Date: _____

Please return this form to: Hennessy Cognac Licensee Cup
                          18 Park Street
                          London SE1 9EL
To arrive no later than 31st January 1987.

of the bacon rashers in half lengthwise and wrap one around each of the potatoes, securing with a cocktail stick. Place the potatoes in a roasting tray & bake on the top shelf of oven for 15 mins. Remove cocktail sticks to serve.

MUSHROOM STUFFED POTATOES

Makes 16

700g / 1½lb small new pots (or ask for 16!)
25g / 1oz butter
1 small onion, chopped
1 garlic clove, crushed
175g / 6oz button mushrooms, finely chopped
2 tblsps dry white wine
2 tblsps. double cream
S & black pepper
250g (8oz) back bacon, rind removed.

Give pots a light scrub under running H₂O, cover with cold water, add good pinch salt, bring to boil & simmer for 20 mins. Drain & cool.

To prepare filling, place butter, onion & garlic into a small saucepan & soften over a gentle heat without allowing to colour. Add mushrooms & wine. Continue to cook without a lid until nearly all the moisture has evaporated. Remove from the heat & stir in the cream. Season well with S & P, cover & put to one side until the cream is absorbed into the mixture.

When the pots have cooled, cut a small cavity in each with a vegetable peeler & spoon mushroom stuffing into it.

Heat oven to 200°C / 400°F ₤. Cut each

ESTᴰ 1765

Hennessy
COGNAC
LICENSEE CUP

Please enter me for the Hennessy Cognac Licensee Cup 1987
(Please complete this form, IN FULL, in block capitals)

Name: _____

Club Handicap:_____or, Society Handicap_____Society Name_____

Playing Partner's Name: _____

Club Handicap:_____or, Society Handicap_____Society Name_____
(NB Maximum handicap 28; proof of handicap will be required at Regional Finals where ¾ of full handicap allowance will be given)
On Licensed Premises:

Name of Premises: _____

Road/Street: _____

Town: _____ County:_____

Post Code:_____ Tel No: _____
(NB It is most important that your premises' address is completed in full for your postal round draw)

Position held at above premises: _____

Golf Club where you are a member: _____
Did you enter the Hennessy Cognac Licensee Cup in 1986 YES/NO*
Are you a Hennessy Club member YES/NO*
Are you a) A tenanted estate*
        b) A managed estate*
        c) A free trade*   *please delete where appropriate

Name of parent brewer _____

Salesman's Name (if known) _____
We, the entrants, agree to abide by the rules of the Hennessy Cognac Licensee Cup and agree that the Tournament Director's decision, in all matters relating to the competition, shall be final and binding. I also confirm that the above premises, where I am the Licensee, is a stockist of Hennessy Cognac.

Licensee's Signature:_____ Date: _____

Please return this form to: Hennessy Cognac Licensee Cup
                    18 Park Street
                    London SE1 9EL
To arrive no later than 31st January 1987.

—————— UP TO ONE DAY IN ADVANCE ——————

1. Sauté the onion in the butter until lightly coloured. Deglaze with the vinegar. Add 1 pt (600 ml) of water and cook, uncovered, until all the water has evaporated. Purée in a blender or food processor, then sieve. Heat with the cream until it will coat a spoon. Season with salt and pepper, and set aside.
2. Preheat oven to 200°C/400°F/Gas Mark 6.
3. Dry the fillets and season. Place in a greased tin, smear with ½ oz (15 g) of butter and bake for 15 minutes. The meat should still be quite springy to the touch and undercooked. Deglaze the pan with a few tablespoons of Calvados and add to the sauce. When meat has cooled, cover and refrigerate. Cover sauce and refrigerate.

—————— SEVERAL HOURS IN ADVANCE ——————

1. Slice the fillets diagonally into ½-in (1.3-cm) slices. Place the meat slices so that they overlap in a greased, shallow flameproof dish. Spoon over the sauce and leave at room temperature.
2. Peel, core and slice the apples. Heat the remaining butter in a frying-pan and sauté the apples with the sugar until soft and slightly brown. Carefully pour over the remaining Calvados and remove from the heat.

—————— BEFORE SERVING ——————
(TWENTY MINUTES BAKING TIME)

1. Preheat oven to 190°C/375°F/Gas Mark 5.
2. Cover the pork and bake for 20 minutes or until just cooked through. Keep warm until serving. Heat the apples for a few minutes and serve with the pork.

PORK WITH PRUNES AND CREAM

SERVES 6

Your friends are certain to enjoy this wonderful dish of Jane Grigson's. A happy marriage of flavours from prunes, cream and pork.

1 lb (450 g) large prunes
¾ pt (450 ml) Vouvray or other medium-sweet white wine
2 pork tenderloins
seasoned flour
1 oz (25 g) clarified butter

1 tbls redcurrant jelly
½ pt (300 ml) *crème fraîche* or double cream
salt and pepper
squeeze of lemon juice

Garnish
fresh parsley

———— UP TO ONE DAY IN ADVANCE ————

1. Soak the prunes in the wine for several hours. Place prunes and wine in a saucepan and simmer until plump, adding a little water if necessary. Strain and stone the prunes, reserving the liquid.
2. Trim the tenderloins and cut them diagonally into just under ½-in (1.3-cm) slices. Turn them in the seasoned flour and fry quickly in the clarified butter until brown on both sides. Remove with a slotted spoon to a dish. Cover and refrigerate if not using the same day.
3. Pour the prune juices in the pan and simmer a few moments. Add the jelly, whisk and boil down to a syrupy essence. Pour in the *crème fraîche* or double cream, stir and boil to a coating consistency. Season to taste, adding a little lemon juice. Pour sauce into a bowl; cover the surface with a piece of cling-film to stop a skin forming and refrigerate.

———— SEVERAL HOURS IN ADVANCE ————

Leave pork at room temperature.

(EIGHT TO TEN MINUTES REHEATING TIME)

1. Reheat the prunes in a *bain-marie*.
2. Pour the sauce into a flameproof serving dish. Bring to a simmer, add the pork and simmer for 8–10 minutes or until well heated. Arrange prunes around the edge of the dish, garnish with a tiny bit of very finely chopped parsley and serve.

PORK WITH
STILTON AND PEAR GRATIN

SERVES 8

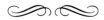

This is a simple recipe that only takes about 10 minutes working time. The pork is cooked ahead, but a quick, last-minute grilling provides a beautiful sauce.

3 pork fillets
1 oz (25 g) butter
sprig of rosemary
  (optional)
3 oz (75 g) Stilton cheese,
  weighed without rind

3 oz (75 g) cream cheese
1 egg
4 oz (100 g) ripe pear,
  peeled and cored, or
  apple sauce
Garnish
watercress

UP TO ONE DAY IN ADVANCE

1. Preheat the oven to 200°C/400°F/Gas Mark 6.
2. Pat the fillets dry and season. Place in a greased tin, smear the tops with butter and lay the rosemary over the butter. Roast for about 15 minutes. The meat should still be quite springy to the touch. Cool on a rack placed over a dish. Discard the rosemary. Refrigerate unless using the same day.
3. Purée the Stilton with the cream cheese in a blender or food processor. Add the egg and pear or apple sauce, and blend. Scrape into a bowl, cover and refrigerate.

SEVERAL HOURS IN ADVANCE

1. Slice fillets diagonally into pieces 1¼ in (3 cm) thick to make larger rounds. Smear some of the cheese mixture on the bottom of a gratin dish. Season the slices of meat and place in one layer in the dish. Spoon over the rest of the cheese. Leave at room temperature.

BEFORE SERVING
(EIGHT MINUTES GRILLING TIME)

Preheat grill to highest setting. Place pork about 6–8 in (15–20 cm) from heat and grill for about 8 minutes. Keep an eye on it to prevent too much browning. Serve garnished with watercress.

Note: You can do the same dish with boned lamb cutlets. Sauté them in a pan until just cooked. Grill them at the last minute in the same way. Another cheese such as Roquefort can be substituted.

ROAST LOIN OF PORK WITH CORIANDER AND LEMON
SERVES 8

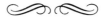

A stuffing with fresh coriander and lemon complements the pork wonderfully.

4-lb (1.8-kg) boned loin of pork
2 tbls oil
small glass of dry white wine
2–3 fl oz (60–75 ml) stock

For the stuffing
4 oz (100 g) fresh breadcrumbs
grated rind of 1 lemon

2 tbls fresh coriander, very finely chopped
1 clove garlic, crushed and finely chopped
juice of ½ lemon
1 oz (25 g) melted butter
1 egg, lightly beaten
salt and black pepper

Garnish
fresh coriander leaves
lemon slices

UP TO ONE DAY IN ADVANCE

To make the stuffing: Mix the breadcrumbs, grated lemon rind, 2 tbls of chopped coriander and garlic; then stir in the lemon juice and butter. Bind with the egg and season well with salt and pepper.

SEVERAL HOURS IN ADVANCE

Open out the meat on a board and score the rind with a sharp knife in a criss-cross pattern. Turn the meat over and cover with the stuffing. Roll up the meat to reform the loin and tie at intervals with string to keep a round shape. Leave at room temperature.

BEFORE SERVING
(TWO HOURS ROASTING AND RESTING TIME)

1. Preheat the oven to 215°C/425°F/Gas Mark 7.
2. Rub the rind with salt and place in a roasting tin with 2 tbls of oil. Roast for 15 minutes, reduce heat to 190°C/375°F/Gas Mark 5 and cook a further 1½ hours. Remove the meat from the oven and allow it to rest for 15 minutes. Pour off the fat from the tin and deglaze with a little white wine and stock to make a gravy. Carve the meat in slices and arrange them so that they overlap on a warm serving dish. Garnish with fresh coriander leaves and lemon slices.

BEEF SAUTÉ
WITH CAPERS

SERVES 6

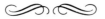

Capers taste surprisingly good with beef. With thin slices of fillet and a Madeira sauce, this dish is party fare.

2-lb (900-g) piece of beef fillet
2–3 oz (50–75 g) clarified butter
2 tbls oil
2 shallots, very finely chopped
3 fl oz (75 ml) Madeira
3 fl oz (75 ml) dry white wine

1 pt (600 ml) veal or beef stock
1 tbls arrowroot
¼ pt (150 ml) *crème fraîche* or double cream
6 oz (175 g) capers
salt and pepper

Garnish
fresh parsley, very finely chopped

——— SAME DAY AS SERVING ———

1. Slice the meat into ½-in (1.3-cm) slices. Place slices between cling-film and beat out with a rolling pin. Season with salt and pepper.
2. Heat 1 oz (25 g) of butter with the oil in a frying-pan until it sizzles. Sauté the slices on both sides to lightly brown. Remove to a platter. Add more butter as necessary and continue until all slices are done. Keep in a cool place, but do not refrigerate.
3. Sauté the shallots in a heavy-bottomed saucepan in the remaining butter. Deglaze the frying-pan with the Madeira and add to shallots. Add the wine and stock, and simmer until reduced by half.
4. Mix the arrowroot with a bit of cream, add it with the rest of the cream and the capers to the sauce. Simmer for a minute to thicken, then remove from the heat. Taste for seasoning.

——— BEFORE SERVING ———
(FIVE TO EIGHT MINUTES REHEATING TIME)

Bring sauce to a simmer in a large frying-pan. Add meat and return to a simmer. Immediately take off heat. Do not cook longer or meat will become tough. Garnish and serve on a warmed platter.

Note: Use chicken stock if you haven't any beef or veal. It will give a better result than a cube.

BEEF STEW
WITH RICE AND OLIVES
SERVES 6–8

An unusual and very good stew from the Catalan. A salad, some crusty bread and good butter are all you need to complement this dish.

3 lb (1.4 kg) chuck or blade
   steak, cubed
salt and freshly ground
   pepper
3 tbls oil
1 large onion, sliced
½ pt (300 ml) dry white
   wine
14-oz (400-g) tin of
   chopped tomatoes
1½ pts (900 ml) beef stock

½ bay leaf
½ tsp dried thyme
2 cloves garlic, peeled
8 oz (225 g) long-grained
   rice (not the easy-to-cook
   sort), uncooked
4 oz (100 g) small black
   olives, stoned
pinch of saffron filaments
2 oz (50 g) Cheddar or
   Parmesan cheese, grated

———— UP TO TWO DAYS IN ADVANCE ————

1. Preheat the oven to 170°C/325°F/Gas Mark 3.
2. Pat the meat dry and season with salt and pepper. Heat the oil in a frying-pan and brown the meat without crowding. Remove with a slotted spoon to a casserole. Add the onion and sauté, stirring, until lightly browned. Remove to the casserole. Pour off the fat and blot dry any that remains with paper towels. Deglaze the pan with the wine and pour into the casserole. Add the tomatoes and stock. With a pestle and mortar, mash the bay leaf, thyme and garlic with some salt and pepper. Scrape into the casserole.

3. Bring to a simmer on top of the stove. Cover, then simmer gently in the oven for 2 hours. Cool, then refrigerate if not serving the same day.

─────── BEFORE SERVING ───────

(APPROX. THIRTY MINUTES REHEATING TIME)

1. Preheat the oven to 170°C/325°F/Gas Mark 3.
2. Wash the rice in several changes of water.
3. Skim any fat from the stew. There should be at least 1 pt (600 ml) of liquid left. Add water if necessary. Bring to a simmer on top of the stove, add the rice, olives and saffron. Return to a simmer, cover and place in the oven for 20 minutes. Place a tea towel under the lid and keep warm in a cool oven if not serving immediately.
4. Stir in the cheese before serving.

Note: The entire stew can be prepared ahead and kept in the refrigerator for up to 3 days. Cover and reheat in a pan of boiling water for 40 minutes.

BEEF STROGANOFF

SERVES 8

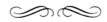

1 lb (450 g) fresh mushrooms
3 shallots, very finely chopped
2 oz (50 g) butter
2 tbls oil
squeeze of lemon juice
salt and freshly ground black pepper

2½-lb (1.1-kg) piece of beef fillet
2 fl oz (60 ml) Nouilly Prat
6 fl oz (175 ml) beef stock
1 pt (600 ml) *crème fraîche* or double cream
2 tbls Dijon mustard

Garnish
large quantity of fresh dill

─────── UP TO ONE DAY IN ADVANCE ───────

Wash and dry the mushrooms, cutting the larger ones into quarters. Sauté the shallots in ½ oz (15 g) butter and 1 tbls of oil until soft. Add the mushrooms, lemon juice, salt and pepper, and continue to sauté, stirring, until mushrooms give off their juices. Raise the heat and boil hard to evaporate most of the liquid. Transfer to a bowl, cover and refrigerate.

SEVERAL HOURS IN ADVANCE

1. Cut the meat into thin fingers 2½ in (6.3 cm) long, 1 in (2.5 cm) wide and ½ in (1.3 cm) thick. Dry with paper towels. Heat the remaining butter and oil in a frying-pan and quickly sauté the beef in batches until just lightly browned, about 2 minutes on each side. Transfer to a dish and reserve. Do not refrigerate. Deglaze with the Nouilly Prat, add the stock and reduce by half. Add the *crème fraîche* or double cream and simmer for about 10 minutes or until coating consistency. Stir in the mustard and season to taste. Place a piece of cling-film on the surface to stop a skin forming and set aside.
2. Remove mushrooms from the refrigerator.

BEFORE SERVING
(FIVE TO EIGHT MINUTES REHEATING TIME)

Bring sauce to a simmer with the mushrooms. Add beef and any juices and return to a simmer. Immediately take off the heat, garnish with very finely chopped dill and serve on warmed plates.

CAVIAR CARPACCIO

SERVES 6

This *carpaccio*, as made by the Oxford philosopher David Pears, is simply fabulous; news of it reached me through mutual friends. It is said to have originated in Harry's Bar in Venice. The idea is like *vitello tonnato* but with a caviar-flavoured mayonnaise. Serve it with the best bread you can find; a home-made loaf such as a *focaccia* would be ideal.

2-lb (900-g) piece of beef fillet	2 tbls lemon juice
2 egg yolks	8 fl oz (250 ml) olive oil or half sunflower and half olive oil
salt	
2 tbls *moutarde de Meaux*	4 oz (100 g) red salmon caviar (not lumpfish roe)

1. Wrap the fillet and place in a freezer until partially frozen.
2. Using a very sharp knife, slice the fillet into paper-thin slices.
3. Make a mayonnaise (see p. 219) with the yolks, salt, lemon juice and oil. Add the mustard and all but one-quarter of the caviar.
4. Layer a dish with the beef and mayonnaise. Cover and refrigerate. Before serving garnish with the remaining caviar.

COLD ROAST BEEF

SERVES 12

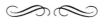

Beautifully cooked paper-thin slices of roast beef are a good solution for a summer buffet. Roast the beef the day before and take it back to the butcher so it can be extra-thinly sliced.

4½-lb (2-kg) *contre-filet* of beef, barded and tied at intervals

1. Preheat oven to 215°C/425°F/Gas Mark 7.
2. If the meat is not barded, season and smear with butter.
3. Roast for 45–50 minutes. Cool on a rack set over a platter, then refrigerate.
4. On the day of serving have your butcher slice it as thinly as possible.
5. Arrange in rolls on a platter and keep in a cool place (but not the refrigerator) until serving.

FILLET OF BEEF
WITH ANCHOVY BUTTER

SERVES 6

This is a succulent and trouble-free way of serving a beef fillet. The beef is briefly roasted ahead of time, then sliced and stuffed with anchovy butter. It is finished off in the oven during the first course. No last-minute carving and no need for a sauce with the juicy pink meat.

3-lb (1.4-kg) piece of beef
   fillet, cut from the thick
   end, trimmed and tied
salt and pepper
3 tbls oil

For the anchovy butter
4 oz (100 g) unsalted butter

6 anchovies
1 tsp lemon juice
2 tbls parsley, very finely
   chopped
black pepper

Garnish
**fresh parsley, very finely
   chopped**

—————— UP TO ONE DAY IN ADVANCE ——————

1. Preheat the oven to 230°C/450°F/Gas Mark 8.
2. Season the meat with salt and pepper. Heat the oil in a roasting tin and brown the meat on all sides. When the oven is ready roast the fillet for 10 minutes. Remove from the oven and place on a rack to cool completely.
3. *To make the anchovy butter*: Purée the butter and anchovies in a blender or food processor. Scrape out into a bowl and add the lemon juice, parsley and some pepper. Roll into a sausage shape, wrap in cling-film and refrigerate.
4. When the meat is completely cold, lay it on a piece of foil large enough to enclose the meat. Remove the string and slice into 12 × ¼-in (0.6-cm) slices, cutting almost through the meat but leaving just enough to hold the slices together. Cut the anchovy butter into slices and place between each slice of meat. Wrap the meat in foil and refrigerate unless using the same day.

──────── SEVERAL HOURS IN ADVANCE ────────

Leave meat at room temperature.

──────── BEFORE SERVING ────────
(FIFTEEN MINUTES ROASTING TIME)

1. Preheat the oven to 215°C/425°F/Gas Mark 7.
2. Roast the meat in the foil on a baking tray for 15 minutes.
To serve: Take the meat out of the foil, taking care not to lose the buttery juices. Arrange on a warm platter and scatter with some finely chopped parsley.

Note: Other savoury butters can be used or a stuffing of mushrooms and spinach. Just be sure whatever you use is moist. You can also wrap the fillet in pastry.

TONGUE WITH MUSHROOMS AND GRAPES IN PORT SAUCE

SERVES 6–8

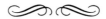

You don't automatically think of tongue for dinner parties, but it can make a welcome change. It is easy to cook, has a good flavour and goes well with any number of sauces and vegetables.

4-lb (1.8-kg) salt ox tongue
1 carrot, chopped
1 onion, chopped
1 celery stalk, chopped
2 bay leaves
2 cloves of garlic
4 sprigs of parsley
2 sprigs of thyme
6 peppercorns
6 oz (175 g) Italia grapes, peeled and pipped

For the sauce
2 shallots, very finely chopped
1 oz (25 g) butter
8 oz (225 g) fresh mushrooms, quartered
3 tbls port
½ pt (300 ml) cooking liquid or stock
2 tbls *moutarde de Meaux*
¼ pt (150 ml) cream
1 tbls arrowroot (optional)

—— UP TO THREE DAYS IN ADVANCE ——

1. If tongue is very salty, soak it in enough cold water to cover for 2 hours; then drain. Supermarket tongues do not require this, in my experience.
2. Place the tongue with the vegetables and herbs in a saucepan. Cover with fresh, cold water, bring to the boil, then cover and simmer for 3 hours.
3. Strain the cooking water and reserve it. Peel the tongue while still warm. Cover and refrigerate if not using the same day.
4. *For the sauce*: Sauté the shallots in the butter until soft. Add the mushrooms and stir for a few minutes. Pour in half the port and boil to reduce by half. Taste the cooking liquid, and if it is too salty only add a few ounces and make up the amount with stock. Add the *moutarde de Meaux* and cream, and simmer for several minutes. Add the remaining port and season if necessary. Cover and refrigerate.

—— SEVERAL HOURS IN ADVANCE ——

Slice the tongue, starting from the thick end and cutting at a slight angle. Layer in a flameproof serving dish. Pour the sauce over the tongue. Cover the dish with foil and leave at room temperature.

—— BEFORE SERVING ——
(THIRTY-FIVE TO FORTY MINUTES REHEATING TIME)

1. Preheat the oven to 170°C/325°F/Gas Mark 3.
2. Simmer the tongue in the oven for about 35–40 minutes.
3. Heat the grapes in a *bain-marie*.
To serve: Add the grapes to the tongue and serve. If a thicker sauce is desired, mix the arrowroot with water or lemon juice and stir into the sauce. Simmer for a few minutes to thicken.

STEAK AND KIDNEY
À LA DAUPHINOISE

SERVES 8

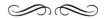

A layer of browned, sliced potatoes tops this steak and kidney stew. It is very good and gives the cook lots of flexibility with timing. Serve with a green salad or vegetable.

3 lb (1.4 kg) stewing steak	6 shallots, chopped
1 lb (450 g) ox kidney	4 sprigs of thyme
salt and freshly ground	2 lb (900 g) potatoes
black pepper	1 oz (25 g) butter
3 tbls drippings or oil	6 fl oz (175 ml) double
4 tbls plain flour	cream
1½ pts (900 ml) beef stock	

——— UP TO THREE DAYS IN ADVANCE ———

1. Trim fat from meat, cut into cubes and pat dry. Snip core from kidney and cut into pieces. Season with salt and pepper.
2. Preheat oven to 170°C/325°F/Gas Mark 3.
3. Heat fat in frying-pan and brown meat in several batches. Return all the meat to the pan, sift over the flour and stir to brown evenly. Turn meat into a casserole. Deglaze with some stock and add to the casserole. Add the remaining stock, shallots and thyme. Cover and simmer very slowly in the oven for 2½ hours or until very tender. This can also be done on top of the stove.
4. Steam the potatoes over boiling water until just tender. Peel while still warm, allow to cool, then thinly slice.
5. Place stew in a shallow flameproof dish. There should be just enough sauce to cover meat; add more if needed. Remove thyme and adjust seasoning. Layer the potatoes over the meat, seasoning each layer with salt and pepper. Cover with cling-film and refrigerate unless serving the same day.

(FORTY MINUTES REHEATING TIME)

1. Preheat oven to 180°C/350°F/Gas Mark 4.
2. Dot the potatoes with the butter and smear with the cream. Bake for about 40 minutes or until well heated and brown on top. Keep warm in a low oven.

SWEDISH MEATBALLS

SERVES 10–12

This is definitely a dinner-party meatball – moist, tender and attractively small. A good dish for large numbers. It can be made well in advance, is easy to serve and goes with just about everything.

8 shallots, very finely
   chopped
5 tbls butter
1 lb (450 g) lean minced beef
1 lb (450 g) lean minced veal
8 oz (225 g) lean minced
   pork
¼ pt (150 ml) double cream
1 tbls plain flour
2 eggs
salt and pepper

extra flour for coating
3 tbls oil
6 fl oz (175 ml) chicken or
   veal stock
1 tbls Dijon mustard
8 fl oz (250 ml) soured
   cream

Garnish
3 tbls fresh herbs such as
   dill, chervil or parsley,
   very finely chopped

UP TO THREE DAYS IN ADVANCE

1. Sauté the shallots in 2 tbls of butter until soft. Scrape them into a large bowl and add the three meats, cream, 1 tbls of flour, 2 eggs and lots of salt and pepper. Mix well, then form into balls (about the size of a ping-pong ball), using wet hands. Roll the meatballs in flour to coat very lightly.
2. Heat the remaining butter and the oil in a large frying-pan. Sauté the meatballs without crowding for about 8 minutes or until just firm and cooked. Shake the pan occasionally to brown evenly.

Remove with a slotted spoon, cool and refrigerate (cover if not serving the same day).

3. Pour off the fat from the pan and dab off any remaining fat with paper towels. Deglaze the pan with the stock, scraping up all the brown bits. Add the mustard and soured cream and simmer together until the sauce has the consistency of thin cream. Taste and adjust seasoning. Pour into a container and keep refrigerated.

SEVERAL HOURS IN ADVANCE

1. Chop herbs and cover with cling-film.
2. Place meatballs in a shallow, flameproof gratin dish, pour over the sauce and leave at room temperature.

BEFORE SERVING
(TEN MINUTES REHEATING TIME)

Cover and simmer on top of the stove for 10 minutes. Alternatively, you can cover and heat in a moderate oven for 20 minutes. Keep warm in a low oven until serving. Serve garnished with lots of fresh herbs.

BLANQUETTE DE VEAU
SERVES 6–8

3 lb (1.4 kg) veal, cut into
  2-in (5-cm) pieces
2½ pts (1.4 L) chicken stock
1 carrot, sliced
1 large onion, quartered
1 stalk of celery, sliced
2 cloves garlic, crushed
bouquet garni
32 pickling onions, peeled
2½ oz (60 g) butter

salt and freshly ground
  black pepper
2 tbls plain flour
1 lb (450 g) fresh button
  mushrooms
juice of ½ lemon
2 large egg yolks
4 fl oz (125 ml) double
  cream
Garnish
fresh parsley, very finely
  chopped

UP TO THREE DAYS IN ADVANCE

1. Using a heavy-bottomed saucepan or a flameproof casserole, place veal in cold water to cover. Bring to the boil and simmer for 2 minutes. Drain and wash quickly under cold water to remove any scum.

2. Rinse out the pan, return the meat and pour over enough stock to cover. Add the carrot, onion, celery, garlic and bouquet garni. Add some salt if stock is bland. Slowly bring to the boil, skim to remove any scum. Reduce heat to a very low simmer, cook partially covered for 1½ hours or until meat is tender. Add stock as necessary to keep meat well covered. When meat is tender, remove with a slotted spoon to a large bowl. Strain the sauce into another bowl, pressing the vegetables with the back of a spoon to extract all the juice.

3. Meanwhile, prepare the onions. Place them in a frying-pan with ½ oz (15 g) butter and 4 fl oz (110 ml) of stock from the veal. Add some salt, cover and gently simmer for 20 minutes, shaking the pan occasionally. Turn into a dish to cool, then cover and refrigerate.

4. Melt 2 oz (50 g) of butter in a heavy-based saucepan, stir in the flour and simmer for a few minutes without allowing the butter to colour. Whisk in 1¼ pts (750 ml) of veal stock and bring to a simmer, stirring. Skim if necessary. Add the mushrooms and simmer for 15 minutes. Add the lemon juice and season. Pour into the bowl with the veal and allow to cool; then cover and refrigerate.

BEFORE SERVING
(FIFTEEN TO TWENTY MINUTES REHEATING TIME)

Pour veal and onions into a flameproof casserole. Reheat slowly to a simmer, cover and simmer for 10 minutes. Mix egg yolks with cream. Whisk a ladle of hot sauce on to the yolks, then pour back into the casserole. Gently reheat to thicken, but do not allow it to boil. Adjust seasoning. Leave in a low oven until ready to serve.

To serve: Garnish with parsley and serve from the casserole.

Note: Avoid leg and loin cuts, which tend to be dry when stewed. Cuts from the breast, best end, shoulder and shin are best. If your stew does simmer by mistake after the egg yolks have been added, it should not curdle because it is a flour-based sauce.

KIDNEYS AND MUSHROOMS IN MUSTARD SAUCE

SERVES 6

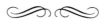

Cutting the mushrooms and kidneys into the thinnest possible slices makes this dish particularly nice. Serve it on a bed of rice and you have an easy feast.

2½ lb (1.1 kg) veal kidneys	salt and pepper
3 shallots, very finely chopped	3 fl oz (75 ml) Calvados
	½ pt (300 ml) double cream
2 oz (50 g) clarified butter	2–3 tbls Dijon mustard
1 lb (450 g) flesh mushrooms, thinly sliced	*Garnish*
squeeze of lemon juice	**fresh parsley, finely chopped**

SEVERAL HOURS IN ADVANCE

1. Peel the thin filament off the kidneys and cut out the core with scissors. Cut into very thin slices and set aside.
2. Sauté half the shallots in half the butter until soft. Add the mushrooms, a squeeze of lemon juice, salt and pepper, and sauté until the mushrooms exude their juices. Boil hard to evaporate, then scrape out on to a dish and set aside.

BEFORE SERVING
(FIVE TO EIGHT MINUTES COOKING TIME)

1. Sauté the rest of the shallots in the remaining butter in a large frying-pan. Add the kidneys and sauté briskly until browned. Season with salt and pepper, and lower the heat. Pour in the Calvados and reduce a little. Add the cream and mustard, and simmer for a minute or two. Turn out on to a heated serving dish.
2. Quickly reheat the mushrooms and place around the edge of the kidneys. Garnish with parsley and serve.

Note: Cooking the kidneys takes about 5 minutes, but it should be done at the last minute. The kidneys will lose their tenderness if they are overcooked.

OSSI BUCHI

SERVES 6

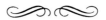

I medium-sized onion,
very finely chopped
I carrot, very finely
chopped
I stalk of celery, very finely
chopped
2 tbls butter
4 tbls oil
salt and freshly ground
pepper
flour for coating
6–8 pieces of shin of veal,
2 in (5 cm) thick
½ pt (300 ml) dry white
wine

½ pt (300 ml) veal or
chicken stock
12-oz (350-g) tin of
chopped tomatoes
2 strips of orange peel
bouquet garni

For the gremolada
2 tbls fresh parsley, finely
chopped
I small clove garlic, very
finely chopped
grated rind of ½ lemon

—— UP TO THREE DAYS IN ADVANCE ——

1. Sauté the onion, carrot and celery in 1 tbls each of butter and oil in a frying-pan. Scrape out into a flameproof casserole large enough to hold all the meat.
2. Season the meat with salt and pepper, then lightly flour. Heat the remaining butter and oil in the pan and brown the meat in batches. Place on top of the vegetables. Deglaze the pan with the wine and add to the meat. Add the stock, tomatoes, orange peel and bouquet garni. Bring to a simmer on top of the stove, then simmer very gently, covered, in a preheated oven 170°C/325°F/Gas Mark 3 for 2 hours. Cool, then refrigerate if not using the same day.

—— SEVERAL HOURS IN ADVANCE ——

1. Skim the fat from the ossi buchi and leave at room temperature.
2. Prepare the *gremolada* ingredients, mix together and cover with cling-film.

BEFORE SERVING
(FORTY MINUTES REHEATING TIME)

1. Preheat oven to 170°C/325°F/Gas Mark 3.
2. Bring stew to a simmer on top of the stove. Adjust flavouring, cover and reheat in oven for 40 minutes. Scatter the *gremolada* on top of the meat for the final 10 minutes of reheating time. Keep warm in a low oven if not serving immediately.

Note: If you prefer, the garlic can be replaced with fresh sage or rosemary. Serve with rice.

SUE'S OSSI BUCHI

SERVES 6

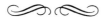

Shin of veal is an excellent stewing cut, with the succulent marrow an extra bonus. Here it combines successfully with leeks and bacon.

olive oil for browning
4 rashers of unsmoked
    streaky bacon, shredded
1 lb (450 g) tender leeks,
    finely shredded
6 pieces of shin of veal
seasoned flour
grated rind of 1 lemon
6 fresh sage leaves, shredded
2 cloves garlic, crushed

salt and pepper
½ pt (300 ml) dry white
    wine
1 pt (600 ml) veal or chicken
    stock
8 oz (225 g) fresh button
    mushrooms, finely sliced

Garnish
**2 tbls fresh parsley, finely
    chopped**

———— UP TO ONE DAY IN ADVANCE ————

1. Preheat the oven to 170°C/325°F/Gas Mark 3.
2. Heat 1 tbls of olive oil in a frying-pan and fry the bacon until cooked but not brown; add the leeks and cook until soft. Remove from the pan. Coat the veal in the seasoned flour and quickly brown in the fat, adding more oil if necessary. Remove the meat and place in a single layer in a flameproof casserole. Add the leeks, bacon, lemon rind, sage, garlic salt and pepper. Deglaze the pan with white wine and add to the veal, straining if necessary. Pour over the stock, bring to a simmer on top of the stove, then cover and simmer in the oven for 2–2½ hours or until meat is very tender. Baste a few times during the cooking time. Remove meat from dish and reduce the sauce to thicken if necessary. Refrigerate when cool.

———— SEVERAL HOURS IN ADVANCE ————

1. Remove veal from refrigerator and leave at room temperature.
2. Sauté the mushrooms in a little oil, season and add to the veal.

1. Preheat oven to 170°C/325°F/Gas Mark 3.
2. Bring casserole to a simmer on top of the stove, then place in the oven for 20–30 minutes.
To serve: Place meat on a warm serving dish. Pour over the sauce, place a pile of vegetables on each side of the meat and sprinkle with parsley.

SWEETBREADS
WITH MUSHROOMS AND CREAM
SERVES 4

Nag your butcher to get fresh rather than frozen sweetbreads. They are not expensive and are a great delicacy to share with friends.

1¼–1½ lb (600–675 g) calf's sweetbreads	1 lb (450 g) fresh mushrooms, sliced
squeeze of lemon juice	salt and pepper
2 oz (50 g) butter	4 fl oz (110 ml) Madeira
1 shallot, finely chopped	¾ pt (450 ml) double cream

UP TO ONE DAY IN ADVANCE

1. Soak the sweetbreads in cold water for 2–3 hours. Change the water a few times. Place in a pan with fresh cold water, a squeeze of lemon juice and salt. Bring to the boil and simmer for 5 minutes, skimming occasionally. Drain and rinse under cold water. Gently remove the membrane, fat and ducts. Place on a dry kitchen towel and press between two large plates with a 2-lb (900-g) weight on top. Place in the refrigerator to chill for at least 45 minutes.
2. Slice the sweetbreads diagonally into ½-in (1.3-cm) escalopes. Sauté the slices in half the butter until lightly coloured, about 3 minutes each side. Remove to a dish to cool; then cover and refrigerate.
3. Sauté the shallot in the remaining butter until soft. Add the

mushrooms, salt and pepper, and cook until tender. Scrape into a bowl and refrigerate.

4. Pour the Madeira into the pan and reduce by half. Add the cream and reduce to a thin coating consistency. Pour into a bowl, place a piece of cling-film on the surface and refrigerate.

SEVERAL HOURS IN ADVANCE

Leave all the ingredients at room temperature

BEFORE SERVING
(APPROX. SEVEN MINUTES)

Reheat the mushrooms in a saucepan. Reheat the sweetbreads in the sauce until just heated through, about 7 minutes.

To serve: Serve the sweetbreads on a warm platter surrounded by mushrooms.

VEAL STEW
WITH OLIVES AND TOMATOES
SERVES 7–8

3 lb (1.4 kg) stewing veal, cubed	grated rind of ½ lemon
3 tbls butter	bouquet garni
2 tbls oil	6 tomatoes
3 tbls plain flour	salt and pepper
wine glass of dry white wine	4 oz (100 g) black olives, stoned
1½ pts (900 ml) chicken or veal stock	*Garnish*
	fresh basil or parsley, very finely chopped

UP TO THREE DAYS IN ADVANCE

1. Pat the meat dry and season with salt and pepper. Heat the butter and oil in a frying-pan until foaming, then brown the meat in batches. Transfer to a flameproof casserole. Sprinkle the flour over the last batch of meat and toss to distribute evenly. Add to the

casserole, then deglaze the pan with the wine. Pour this into the casserole along with the stock, rind and bouquet garni. Cover with a *cartouche* of baking parchment pressed on top of the ingredients and a tight-fitting lid.

2. Preheat the oven to 170°C/325°F/Gas Mark 3.

3. Bring the stew to a simmer on top of the stove, then place in the oven and simmer gently for 1½ hours or until veal is just tender. Refrigerate unless using the same day.

SAME DAY AS SERVING

1. Peel, skin and seed the tomatoes, then cut in strips. Sprinkle with salt and leave in a sieve to drain.

2. Leave stew at room temperature.

BEFORE SERVING
(TWENTY MINUTES REHEATING TIME)

1. Preheat oven to 170°C/325°F/Gas Mark 3.

2. Bring veal to a simmer on top of the stove. Discard bouquet garni, add tomatoes and olives, and season. Cover and heat in the oven for about 20 minutes. Keep warm in a low oven if not serving immediately. Garnish with the herb before serving.

VEAL WITH CHERRIES AND CARDAMOM

SERVES 6–8

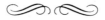

Although this is a fairly old Russian dish, it might have been invented by a *nouvelle cuisine* chef. Morello cherries with a hint of cardamom give a unique and wonderful flavour to this stew. Polish morello cherries in jars are good alternatives if fresh cherries are not available.

3 lb (1.4 kg) veal, cut into
   1-in (2.5-cm) cubes
3 oz (75 g) butter
2 tbls plain flour
sugar to taste
1 pt (600 ml) veal or chicken
   stock
1¼ lbs (550 g) fresh or
   tinned morello cherries,
   stoned

6 spring onions, finely
   chopped
3 oz (75 g) sultanas
small glass of tawny port
4–6 green cardamom pods,
   slightly crushed
salt and pepper

Garnish
fresh chives, finely snipped

UP TO TWO DAYS IN ADVANCE

1. Pat the veal dry and season with salt and pepper. Heat the butter in a frying-pan and brown the meat. Reduce the heat, sprinkle the meat with the flour and stir to coat evenly without browning. Season and remove the meat to a casserole.

2. Deglaze the pan with some stock and add to the meat. If you are using tinned cherries, drain them and reserve the juice. Add the cherries, spring onions, sultanas, port, cardamom and the remaining stock to the casserole. Press a covering of greaseproof paper down on to the meat and cover the casserole with a lid.

3. Preheat the oven to 170°C/325°F/Gas Mark 3. Simmer the veal in the oven for 1½ hours or until veal is tender. Adjust the oven so it simmers very gently. When tender, remove from the oven and strain the sauce into a saucepan. Boil to reduce if too thin. Taste for seasoning, adding cherry syrup or sugar (if cherries were fresh) to taste. Return the sauce to the casserole and refrigerate.

SEVERAL HOURS IN ADVANCE

Leave stew at room temperature.

BEFORE SERVING
(TEN TO FIFTEEN MINUTES REHEATING TIME)

Reheat gently on top of the stove or in a warm oven for about 10–15 minutes. Serve garnished with chives.

Note: Although stews are flexible, be careful to simmer very gently and not to overcook the meat. Veal can become very dry.

BASIL STUFFED POUSSIN

SERVES 8

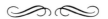

By placing a stuffing under the skin of the poussin, the meat stays beautifully moist and the skin goes crisp and brown. Poussins cut in half easily and make just the right portion for a serving.

4 poussins

For the stuffing
8 oz (225 g) ricotta cheese
   (as fresh as possible)
2 oz (50 g) freshly grated
   Parmesan cheese

4 tbls double cream
1 egg yolk
2 tbls *pesto* (see p. 223) or 3
   tbls fresh basil or parsley,
   very finely chopped
salt and pepper

—— UP TO ONE DAY IN ADVANCE ——

1. Mix all the stuffing ingredients together and season with salt and pepper.
2. Place a poussin on its breast. Remove the backbone by cutting down each side with kitchen scissors. Remove any small bones that may have broken. Turn the bird over, breast up, and flatten the bird with your hand. Slip your fingers between the flesh and the skin to create a pocket. Spoon in the stuffing and spread it evenly over the legs and breast in a thin layer. Repeat for each bird. Refrigerate if not using the same day.

—— SEVERAL HOURS IN ADVANCE ——

Leave the poussins at room temperature.

—— BEFORE SERVING ——
(THIRTY MINUTES ROASTING TIME)

1. Preheat the oven to 200°C/400°F/Gas Mark 6.
2. Place the flattened poussins side by side in a lightly oiled roasting pan. Sprinkle with salt and pepper and roast for 30 minutes.

Note: You can do exactly the same thing with a chicken. Roast it for about 1 hour and carve it into 4 pieces. A stuffing made from parsley, finely chopped garlic and butter is good too.

BEAUJOLAIS CHICKEN

SERVES 4–6

20 small pickling onions, peeled	1 bottle red Beaujolais
2 oz (50 g) butter	3 fl oz (75 ml) Cognac
¾ pt (450 ml) chicken stock	1 tbls tomato purée
1 tbls sugar	2 cloves garlic, crushed
1 tbls oil	bouquet garni
8-oz (225-g) piece of streaky bacon, cut into lardons	1 lb (450 g) fresh small mushrooms
3 lb (1.4 kg) chicken pieces	1 oz (25 g) plain flour
salt and black pepper	*Garnish*
	fresh parsley, very finely chopped

—————— UP TO FOUR DAYS IN ADVANCE ——————

1. Place the peeled onions in a frying-pan with 1 oz (25 g) of butter, ¼ pt (150 ml) stock and the sugar. Cover and simmer for 15 minutes; then uncover and continue to simmer until liquid has almost evaporated. Swirl the pan to glaze the onions at the end of the reduction. Remove onions from pan and set aside.

2. Add the oil to the pan and sauté bacon until lightly browned; remove and set aside. Pour out all but 1 tbls of fat. Pat chicken pieces dry and season with salt and pepper. Brown the chicken on all sides and remove to a heavy flameproof casserole. Deglaze the frying-pan with some wine and add to the chicken. Add the Cognac and boil to reduce by half. Add the wine and just enough stock to cover the chicken. Stir in the tomato purée, garlic and bouquet garni. Cover and simmer very gently for 25 minutes. Add the mushrooms for the last 15 minutes of cooking time.

3. Remove the chicken to a side plate. Blend 1 oz (25 g) each of butter and flour together to make a paste and stir into the hot liquid. Simmer a few minutes to thicken, then taste for seasoning. Return the chicken and onions to the casserole, cool, cover and refrigerate.

—— THREE TO FOUR HOURS IN ADVANCE ——

Remove any coagulated fat. Leave at room temperature.

—————— BEFORE SERVING ——————
(FIFTEEN MINUTES REHEATING TIME)

Bring to a simmer, basting with the sauce. Cover and simmer for 15 minutes to heat. Alternatively, reheat by first bringing to a simmer on the top of the stove, then place in a moderate oven for 20 minutes. Garnish with parsley and serve.

Note: Serve with steamed potatoes and a chilled bottle of Beaujolais.

BONED CHICKEN STUFFED WITH COURGETTES AND CORIANDER

SERVES 10–12

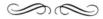

Boning a chicken may seem a daunting task but it really isn't difficult, and the benefits are great: a good sauce can be made in advance with the bones; carving is easy; and the final result is a delicious and impressive dish. It reheats beautifully and is good cold too. Try to find free-range chickens. They are much leaner and perfect for boning.

2 × 3½-lb (1.8-kg) chickens
4 oz (100 g) brown rice, uncooked
1½ lb (675 g) courgettes
2 shallots
1 tbls oil
1 oz (25 g) butter
2 tbls fresh coriander, very finely chopped

2 oz (50 g) pistachio nuts, very finely chopped
1 egg
salt and pepper
1½ times recipe of sauce for Chicken Breasts Stuffed with Crab (see p. 164)

—————— UP TO ONE DAY IN ADVANCE ——————

1. *To bone a chicken*: Cut off the wings at the elbow, leaving the largest wing bone on. Cut off the ankle joint on the legs if necessary. Place the bird on its breast, slit the skin down the backbone from neck to tail. With a fairly short, sharp knife, using short strokes, scrape the flesh away from the carcass, easing the skin and flesh back as you go. Work on one side at a time. Cut the flesh from the sabre-shaped bone near the wing. Wiggle the wing to find the ball-and-socket joint and sever it where it meets the carcass. Do the same with the thigh bone, so that the wing and thigh are separated from the carcass but still attached to the skin. Repeat on the other side. Cut against the ridge of the breastbone to free the skin, being careful not to pierce it. Hold the end of the wing bone in one hand, cut through the tendons and scrape the meat from the bone, drawing the skin inside out and using the knife to cut the bone free. Repeat the process with the thigh and drumstick bones, then do the other side. It is easier to find the joints if you wiggle the bones. Push the skin from the legs and wings right-side out. Tidy up the chicken by cutting away any excess fat and sinews. Refrigerate unless using the same day.
2. Using the bones, make chicken stock for the sauce (see p. 214). Make the sauce and refrigerate when cold.
3. Cook the rice in a large quantity of boiling salted water for 25 minutes or until tender. Drain and place in a bowl. Refrigerate unless using the same day.

—————— SAME DAY AS SERVING ——————

1. Wash the courgettes but do not peel. Grate them and leave in a colander with a sprinkling of salt for 10 minutes. Squeeze the courgettes by the handful and discard the juice.
2. Sauté the shallots in the oil until soft. Add the butter and sauté the coriander and nuts for a minute or two. Stir in the courgettes and cook, stirring, for several minutes. Turn into the bowl. Stir in the rice and egg, and season.
3. Place the chickens skin-side down and season the flesh with salt and pepper. Heap the stuffing down the centre of the chicken. Bring the side edges together so they meet and sew up with black thread (black is easy to see for removal). Fold the neck skin over and stitch across. Mould into a sausage shape.

1. Preheat the oven to 190°C/375°F/Gas Mark 5.
2. Roast the chickens on a rack in a roasting tin for 1 hour. Turn the chicken after 30 minutes.
3. Reheat the sauce in a *bain-marie*, keeping it well below simmering point.
4. Place the chickens on a serving platter and keep warm in a cool oven until you are ready to serve. Pass the sauce separately.

Note: The chicken can be cooked a day ahead, then sliced and reheated in the sauce. This works very successfully. If you are using a sauce with egg yolks, add them to only half the sauce and use the other half to reheat the chicken slices. Keep the egged half warm over warm water and add to the chicken before serving.

CHICKEN BREASTS STUFFED WITH CRAB

SERVES 6

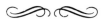

A lovely dish devised by my catering friend Sue Oury.

6 chicken breasts, skinned
   and boned
salt and pepper
1 pt (600 ml) chicken stock
½ pt (300 ml) dry white
   wine
2 spring onions
1 slice of lemon
1 bay leaf
1 slice of onion

For the mousse
9 oz (250 g) well-chilled
   crab meat, mostly white

1 egg white
3 tbls double cream
salt and pepper
1 tsp tarragon, chopped

For the sauce
1 oz (25 g) butter
¾ oz (20 g) flour
¾ pt (450 ml) chicken stock
4 tbls double cream
1 tbls tarragon, chopped
salt and pepper
2 egg yolks
2 tbls lemon juice

ONE DAY IN ADVANCE

1. Place cold crabmeat in a food processor and blend for 30 seconds. Slowly add egg white and cream and process just long enough to blend. Add salt, pepper and 1 tsp of tarragon and blend for a few seconds. Chill in the refrigerator for 30 minutes.
2. Meanwhile, detatch the small, feather-shaped fillet from the breasts. Flatten the breasts and fillets by beating lightly with a wet rolling pin. Season the breasts with salt and pepper. Place a spoonful of the mousse on the breast, lay the fillet over the top and tuck in all the ends to make a parcel. Fold the edges together to enclose filling. Cover and refrigerate.
3. *For the sauce*: Stir the butter and flour together until foaming, whisk in the stock and continue to whisk until the sauce comes to a simmer and thickens. Stir in the cream and tarragon, and season with salt and pepper. Refrigerate when cool.

BEFORE SERVING
(THIRTY MINUTES COOKING TIME)

1. Preheat the oven to 170°C/325°F/Gas Mark 3.
2. Pack the breasts tightly in a flameproof dish. Cover the chicken with the stock, wine, spring onions, lemon slice, bay leaf and slice of onion. Bring to a simmer on top of the stove, then cover and simmer in the oven for 30 minutes.
3. Reheat the sauce, whisk the egg yolks with the lemon juice and add to the hot, but not boiling, sauce. Season to taste, adding more lemon juice if necessary and keep warm in a *bain-marie*.
4. Remove breasts with a slotted spoon and place on a warm platter (keep poaching liquid for stock). Spoon over some sauce and serve.

CHICKEN BREASTS
WITH GARLIC CREAM SAUCE

SERVES 6

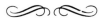

Garlic with cream is incredibly good as a sauce for chicken or pasta. It takes only minutes to prepare.

6 small chicken breasts,
    skinned and boned
seasoned flour
4 oz (100 g) clarified butter
¼ pt (150 ml) chicken stock
2 cloves garlic, crushed then
    very finely chopped

½ pt (300 ml) cream
salt and pepper

Garnish
**parsley, very finely
    chopped**

SAME DAY AS SERVING

1. Dust the chicken in seasoned flour. Heat 2 oz (50 g) of clarified butter in a frying-pan and quickly sauté the breasts about 5–7 minutes on each side. They should be quite springy to the touch. Remove them and set aside. Deglaze the pan with the stock and reserve.
2. Using a small saucepan, gently sauté the garlic in 1 oz (25 g) of butter, stirring, until soft. Do not allow garlic or butter to colour. Add the deglazing liquid and the cream. Simmer until slightly thickened. Season to taste and set aside.

BEFORE SERVING
(THREE TO FOUR MINUTES REHEATING TIME)

1. Reheat the chicken in the remaining 1 oz (25 g) of butter to just heat through, about 1 minute each side. Do not overcook. Keep warm in a cool oven.
2. Keep sauce warm in a *bain-marie*.

To serve: Place a breast on each plate, spoon over some sauce and garnish with the parsley.

Note: Garlic varies in strength – you may need to increase the amount.

Chicken Breasts with Red Wine and Onions

SERVES 4

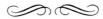

The braising liquid from the onions provides the sauce for this tasty chicken dish. It goes well with rice.

24 pickling onions, peeled
¾ pt (450 ml) chicken stock
¾ pt (450 ml) red wine
3 oz (75 g) butter
1 tbls sugar
salt and pepper
1½ tbls plain flour

4 chicken breasts, skinned
and boned
1 tbls oil
10 oz (275 g) frozen petits
pois

Garnish
fresh parsley, very finely
chopped

———— UP TO TWO DAYS IN ADVANCE ————

1. Place the onions in a frying-pan large enough so they fit in one layer. Pour over the stock, wine, ½ oz (15 g) of butter, sugar, salt and pepper. Bring to the boil, then simmer, uncovered, until the onions are tender and the liquid reduced. Remove the onions with a slotted spoon and reserve. Blend the flour with 1 oz (25 g) of butter. Whisk into the liquid and simmer until slightly thickened.

2. Dry the chicken and season with salt and pepper. Using another frying-pan, heat the remaining butter with the oil until foaming. Sauté the breasts about 3–4 minutes on each side. They should still be springy to the touch. Remove from the pan. Pour away the fat. Deglaze with some of the onion sauce.

3. Place the chicken in a small flameproof casserole, cover with the onions and pour over the sauce and the deglazing liquid. Refrigerate if not serving the same day.

———— SEVERAL HOURS IN ADVANCE ————

Remove chicken from the refrigerator and leave at room temperature.

BEFORE SERVING
(TWENTY MINUTES REHEATING TIME)

1. Preheat the oven to 170°C/325°F/Gas Mark 3.
2. Add the peas to the casserole, breaking them up if in a block. Bring the casserole to a simmer on top of the stove then cover and place in oven. Heat for about 20 minutes or until just heated through. Keep warm in a low oven until you are ready to serve. *To serve*: Garnish with parsley and serve from the casserole.

CHICKEN PROVENÇAL

SERVES 6

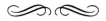

Golden-browned chicken pieces braised with red, green and yellow peppers and black olives look as appetizing as they taste. Serve with rice and you have a handsome main course.

3 peppers, mixed colours
3 tbls olive oil
salt and pepper
3½ lb (1.6 kg) chicken pieces
½ oz (15 g) butter
3 onions, sliced
2 cloves garlic, crushed then chopped

¼ pt (150 ml) dry white wine
1 pt (600 ml) chicken stock
1 tbls fresh thyme, chopped or ½ tbls dried thyme
2 oz (50 g) black olives

Garnish
fresh parsley, finely chopped

UP TO TWO DAYS IN ADVANCE

1. Grill the peppers until the skins are charred on all sides. Place them in a paper bag for a few minutes, then peel off the skins with wet fingers. Discard the seeds and core, cut the flesh into strips. Toss with 2 tbls of olive oil and season. Refrigerate unless using the same day.
2. Wipe the chicken dry and season. Heat 1 tbls of oil in a frying-pan just large enough for the pieces to fit snugly. Sauté the chicken until golden on all sides. Remove chicken and set aside. Pour off any fat from the pan. Add the butter and sauté the onions

and garlic, stirring, for a few minutes. Return the chicken to the pan, pour in the wine and boil hard to evaporate. Add the stock and thyme, bring to a simmer, cover and simmer for 10–15 minutes. Transfer the chicken to a flameproof casserole. Reduce the stock, adjust seasoning and pour over the chicken. Cool and refrigerate unless using the same day.

SEVERAL HOURS IN ADVANCE

Leave casserole at room temperature.

BEFORE SERVING
(TWENTY-FIVE MINUTES REHEATING TIME)

1. Preheat the oven to 180°C/350°F/Gas Mark 4.
2. Add the peppers and olives to the casserole. Bring to a simmer on top of the stove, then cover and heat in the oven for about 25 minutes.
3. Garnish with the fresh parsley.

Note: The onions keep the chicken moist and a sauce is not necessary, but you can thicken the liquid with a bit of arrowroot before serving if you wish.

COLD TUNA CHICKEN
SERVES 6

A variation on the Italian *vitello tonnato* – just as good and a lot less expensive. An ideal summer dish.

2 lb (900 g) boned rolled chicken
1 carrot
1 stalk of celery
1 small onion
few sprigs of parsley

1 bay leaf

Garnish
lemon slices
fresh parsley
capers

For the tuna sauce
7-oz (200-g) tin of white-
meat tuna in olive oil
2 tbls capers
5 anchovy fillets

2 tbls lemon juice
8 tbls olive oil
5 fl oz (150 ml) home-made
mayonnaise (see p. 219)

UP TO THREE DAYS IN ADVANCE
(MINIMUM ONE DAY)

1. In a pot just large enough to contain the chicken, add the chicken, vegetables, herbs and just enough water to cover. Remove the chicken and set aside. Bring the water and vegetables to the boil, add the chicken, cover and simmer very gently until tender, about 1 hour. Allow the chicken to cool in the liquid, then cover and refrigerate.
2. Blend or process the tuna, capers, anchovies, lemon juice and olive oil. Scrape out into a bowl and add the mayonnaise. Cover and refrigerate.

SEVERAL HOURS IN ADVANCE

Smear the bottom of a serving dish with some sauce. Arrange slices of chicken over this, edge to edge. Cover the layer with sauce and over this another layer of chicken. Continue until you have used all the chicken, and finish with a layer of sauce. Cover with cling-film and refrigerate.

BEFORE SERVING

Garnish with lemon slices, parsley and capers.

FILO CHICKEN BREASTS
SERVES 8

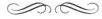

Chicken breasts stay beautifully moist baked in filo and have the added advantage of good looking and tasting pastry.

8 small chicken breasts,
  skinned and boned
salt and freshly ground
  black pepper
3½ oz (85 g) butter
2 tbls Cognac
2 shallots, very finely
  chopped

1 lb (450 g) fresh
  mushrooms, finely
  chopped
squeeze of lemon juice
1 tbls fresh parsley, finely
  chopped
8 paper-thin slices Parma
  ham
8 sheets of filo pastry

SAME DAY AS SERVING

1. Pat the chicken dry and season with salt and pepper. Heat 1 oz (25 g) of butter in a frying-pan and lightly seal the chicken on both sides, about 30 seconds each side. Remove the chicken from the pan and deglaze with the Cognac. Add ½ oz (15 g) of butter to the pan and sauté the shallots, stirring, for a few minutes. Add the mushrooms, lemon juice, salt and pepper, and sauté, stirring, until the mushrooms give off their juices. Boil hard to evaporate, stir in the parsley and scrape into a bowl.

2. Spread some mushrooms over the breasts and wrap with the ham.

3. Melt the remaining butter. Cut the filo in half, making 16 sheets. Brush a sheet with butter, place a second on top and brush with butter. Place breast at narrow end and fold to make a rectangular package. Fold ends under to seal. Place packages in a greased roasting tin, cover with cling-film and refrigerate.

BEFORE SERVING
(THIRTY MINUTES BAKING TIME)

1. Preheat the oven to 200°C/400°F/Gas Mark 6.

2. Brush melted butter over the packages and bake for about 30 minutes. Place on a warmed serving dish and serve.

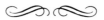

FILO CHICKEN PIE

SERVES 10–12

Filo leaves are easy to use and much lighter than other pastries. An ordinary chicken pie is transformed into a many-layered wonder. This dish freezes very successfully.

2 × 4½-lb (2-kg) chickens	salt and pepper
2 onions, halved	1½ lb (675 g) calabrese
2 carrots, chopped	11 sheets of filo pastry
1 stalk of celery, chopped	melted butter
1 bay leaf	3 oz (75 g) freshly grated
bouquet garni	Parmesan or Cheddar
3 oz (75 g) butter	cheese
3 oz (75 g) plain flour	

UP TO THREE DAYS IN ADVANCE

1. Place the chickens in enough water to cover. Add onions, carrots, celery, bay leaf and bouquet garni. Bring to the boil, then cover and simmer very gently for 50 minutes. Lift the chickens out of the liquid and cool. Remove the flesh and set aside. Place bones and skin back in the liquid and simmer gently for 1½ hours. Strain stock and leave overnight in the refrigerator if possible, so congealed fat can be easily removed; or, skim off fat with a spoon, then blot the surface with paper towels.
2. *To make the sauce*: Whisk the butter and flour over low heat for a few minutes, add 2 pts (1.1 L) of stock and whisk until sauce thickens. Simmer gently for 10 minutes and season. Place a piece of cling-film over the surface to stop a skin forming. Refrigerate when cool.

UP TO ONE DAY IN ADVANCE

1. Heat the sauce and mix with the chicken.
2. Peel any coarse stalks of calabrese and slice in half. Cook heads and stalks in a large quantity of boiling salted water for about 5 minutes, or until *al dente*. Lift out with a sieve, refresh in ice water and drain. Chop coarsely.

3. Carefully unfold the filo leaves. Keep the leaves covered with a sheet of plastic. Lift off one sheet, brush with melted butter and line a large rectangular flameproof dish. Add 2 more filo layers, brushing each with butter before placing in dish. Spread the calabrese over the filo, cover with the sauce and chicken, and sprinkle over the cheese. Cover the top with 8 buttered layers of filo. Cover with cling-film and refrigerate.

BEFORE SERVING
(FORTY MINUTES BAKING TIME)

1. Preheat the oven to 190°C/375°F/Gas Mark 5.
2. Lightly score the top few layers of filo in a diamond pattern. Brush with melted butter. Bake for 40 minutes or until the pastry is crisp and the chicken bubbling hot. Serve immediately if possible. It can be kept warm in a low oven for 20 minutes.

Note: For freezing cook all the ingredients for the pie in one day, layer with filo and freeze. Bake from frozen, adding 10 minutes to the cooking time. For an equally good dish substitute leeks for the calabrese and add about 8 oz (225 g) of cooked ham, cut into batons.

HASSAN'S CHICKEN WITH ORANGE TAGINE
SERVES 8–10

Hassan is the Moroccan cook of a friend who lives in Tangiers and who is known for her delicious food. This *tagine* has a very fresh taste of oranges and spices. The chicken turns a golden colour from the tumeric, and with the vivid orange slices the dish is exotic and beautiful.

4 thin-skinned eating oranges, washed	6 tbls oil
2 × 2½-lb (1.1-kg) chickens, cut into serving pieces	2 medium-sized onions, very finely chopped
salt	3–4 cloves garlic, crushed then finely chopped

½ whole nutmeg, grated
1 tsp ground pepper
1 tsp cinnamon
1 tsp ginger
1 tsp tumeric
3 tbls fresh parsley, very
finely chopped
3 tbls fresh coriander, very
finely chopped

1 pt (600 ml) freshly
squeezed orange juice
4 oz (100 g) sugar

Garnish

toasted sesame seeds
fresh coriander leaves,
finely chopped

UP TO ONE DAY IN ADVANCE

1. Cut the oranges lengthwise into 8 wedges. Remove seeds but leave the skins.

2. Trim off any extra skin and fat from the chicken and pat dry. Heat half the oil in a frying-pan and brown the chicken without crowding. Drain on paper towels. Season with salt.

3. Heat the remaining oil in a large flameproof casserole. Add the onions, garlic and dried spices. Cook, stirring, for a few minutes. Stir in the parsley and coriander, and cook a few more minutes. Add the orange juice and bring to a simmer. Add the orange segments and return to a simmer, then place the chicken carefully on top of the oranges. Cover and simmer gently for 30 minutes. Add the sugar in a heap on the edge of the chicken. It will slowly mix itself into the sauce, so there is no need to stir. Simmer a further 30 minutes. Taste and adjust seasoning. Refrigerate if not using the same day.

BEFORE SERVING

(TWENTY MINUTES REHEATING TIME)

Simmer very gently on top of the stove for 20 minutes, half covered.

To serve: Serve from the casserole or arrange on a heated serving platter. Scatter over the sesame seeds and coriander.

Note: The sauce is supposed to be very thin. If you like, thicken it with 1 tbls of arrowroot mixed with a bit of juice. Simmer in the sauce for a few minutes.

LEMON CHICKEN SLICES

SERVES 4–6

This is a great dish when you have no time for advance preparation. All there is to it is a quick sauté of thin chicken slices and an instant butter and lemon sauce. It is incredibly tender and good, and would go well with calabrese and rice.

3 large chicken breasts, boned	4 tbls chicken stock
salt and freshly ground black pepper	juice of 1 lemon
2 tbls oil	3 tbls fresh parsley, very finely chopped
4 oz (100 g) clarified butter	*Garnish*
	1 lemon, very thinly sliced

———— UP TO ONE DAY IN ADVANCE ————

Pull off the skin from the chicken. It can be fried and added to salads. Detach the small feather-shaped fillet and set aside. Place the breast skin-side up on a board. Hold the breast down with one hand and, with a sharp, thin knife, slice the breast lengthwise into two equal halves. Place the pieces between cling-film and gently hammer out the fillets and thicker slices using a rolling pin. Remove any tendons and trim off any jagged pieces. Layer with cling-film and refrigerate unless using the same day.

———— BEFORE SERVING ————
(APPROX. TEN MINUTES COOKING TIME)

Season the chicken with salt and pepper. Heat the oil and half the butter in a large frying-pan until bubbling. Quickly sauté the chicken, a few pieces at a time, about 1 minute each side. Remove to a warm platter. When all the pieces are cooked, deglaze with the stock, stir in the lemon juice, remaining butter and parsley. Simmer for 1 minute, then pour over the chicken. Garnish with the lemon slices and serve immediately.

WATERCRESS CHICKEN THIGHS

SERVES 8

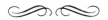

Chicken thighs can be bought already boned. With a food processor a lovely light mousseline stuffing can be made in minutes.

16 chicken thighs, skinned
  and boned
1½ pts (900 ml) chicken
  stock
2 shallots, very finely
  chopped
1 tbls oil
½ pt (300 ml) dry white
  wine
3 fl oz (75 ml) double cream
1 tsp fresh tarragon, very
  finely chopped
lemon juice

salt and pepper
2 tomatoes, skinned, seeded
  and finely chopped

For the stuffing
2 oz (50 g) watercress leaves
5 oz (150 g) cold chicken
  breast (about 1 small
  breast), boned
½ pt (300 ml) very cold
  double cream
salt and pepper

UP TO TWO DAYS IN ADVANCE

1. Place processor bowl and blade in freezer while you prepare the stuffing ingredients. Blanch the watercress in boiling salted water for 1 minute. Drain, refresh under cold water and drain again, squeezing as much water out as you can. Chop leaves and discard the stems. Remove the sinews and any fat from the chicken and chop. Process the chicken breast for 4–5 minutes. Slowly pour in the cream, with the motor on, and process only long enough to blend. Add watercress and blend. Season with salt and lots of pepper.

2. Dry the chicken thighs and season. Place a spoonful of stuffing on the inside of the thigh and roll up. Wrap with a piece of cling-film and twist the ends to help keep a round shape.

3. Pour the stock into a frying-pan large enough to hold the chicken in one layer and bring to a simmer. Add the chicken, cover and simmer very gently for 30 minutes, turning the thighs over once during cooking time. (Don't worry if they expand and even come out of the cling-film.) Lift them out after the 30 minutes with a slotted spoon, remove the cling-film when cool and refrigerate.

4. Soften the shallots in the oil, stirring. Add the wine and reduce by half. Strain the chicken liquid into the pan and reduce further. Add the cream and tarragon, and simmer a few more minutes. Season to taste with lemon juice, salt and pepper.

BEFORE SERVING
(FIFTEEN MINUTES REHEATING TIME)

1. Preheat the oven to 180°C/350°F/Gas Mark 4.

2. Place chicken in a shallow flameproof dish. Spoon over half of the sauce, bring to a simmer on top of the stove, then cover and heat in the oven for 15 minutes. Reheat the rest of the sauce with the tomatoes. Place 2 thighs on each plate and spoon over some of the sauce.

Braised Guinea Fowl with Chicory

SERVES 4–6

Guinea fowl has a very good flavour and makes a nice change from chicken. It is delicious in this creamy chicory sauce and is a fine dish to share with friends.

1 guinea fowl, cut into 8
   pieces
½ oz (15 g) butter
4 oz (100 g) streaky bacon,
   chopped
small glass of sweet muscat
   wine
6 firm heads of chicory,
   sliced

2 green cardamom pods,
   lightly crushed (optional)
½ tsp lemon rind, grated
¼ pt (150 ml) chicken stock
¼ pt (150 ml) double cream
salt and black pepper
1 tbls lemon juice

Garnish
**fresh parsley, very finely
chopped**

———— SAME DAY AS SERVING ————

1. Season the guinea fowl. Heat the butter in a frying-pan and brown the guinea fowl on all sides. Remove the guinea fowl from the pan, add the bacon and stir until lightly browned. Pour off any fat from the pan and return the guinea fowl. Pour in the wine and reduce by half. Add the chicory, cardamom, lemon rind and stock, and bring to the boil. Cover and simmer for 20 minutes.
2. Remove the guinea fowl, add the cream to the pan and boil to thicken slightly. Season with salt, pepper and the lemon juice. Scrape into a shallow flameproof dish. Place the guinea fowl on top and set aside.

———— BEFORE SERVING ————
(TWENTY MINUTES REHEATING TIME)

1. Preheat the oven to 170°C/325°F/Gas Mark 3.
2. Bring to a simmer on top of the stove; then cover and heat in the oven for about 20 minutes. Garnish with parsley and serve from the dish.

DUCK BREASTS
WITH CIDER AND APPLES

SERVES 6

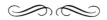

Duck breasts are excellent for parties and are becoming easier to find boned. The sauce is made from cider and Calvados and is served with glazed apple slices.

2 tart eating apples	**1 tbls vegetable oil**
2 oz (50 g) butter	**½ oz (15 g) butter**
2 tbls sugar	**4 fl oz (110 ml) Calvados**
6 duck breasts	**½ pt (300 ml) French or**
salt and pepper	**English dry cider**
	a few parsley stalks
For the sauce	**¾ pt (450 ml) duck or**
4 shallots	**chicken stock**
1 carrot	**1 tbls arrowroot (optional)**
1 stalk of celery	

—— UP TO ONE DAY IN ADVANCE ——

1. *For the sauce*: Chop the vegetables as finely as possible. Sauté them in the oil and butter, stirring, until they begin to soften. Pour in half the Calvados and boil to evaporate. Add the cider and parsley stalks and reduce by half. Add the stock and reduce by half. Add the rest of the Calvados and season to taste.
2. Strain the sauce, pressing out as much of the liquid as possible. Refrigerate unless using the same day.

—— SEVERAL HOURS IN ADVANCE ——

1. Peel, core and slice the apples. Fry them in 1½ oz (40 g) of the butter and sugar until tender and glazed. Set aside.
2. If you want a thicker sauce, mix the arrowroot with 1 tbls of water, then whisk into the sauce until it thickens slightly.

(FIFTEEN MINUTES ROASTING TIME)

1. Preheat the oven to 215°C/425°F/Gas Mark 7.
2. Heat the remaining butter in a roasting tin. Pat the breasts dry, prick the skin all over and season with salt and pepper. Place skin-side up in the pan and roast for 15 minutes.
3. Reheat the sauce in a *bain-marie* and heat the apple slices.
To serve: Place breasts in the centre of a warm platter, garnish with apple slices and spoon over the sauce.

Note: If you prefer to cook the breasts before your guests arrive, roast them several hours in advance, slice them and reheat in the sauce. Duck with Rosemary Sauce (see p. 181) gives the exact timing.

DUCK BREASTS WITH GINGER

SERVES 4

This dish is the creation of Sue Oury, a friend and a very talented cook.

¾ oz (20 g) fresh root ginger, peeled and cut into very fine julienne
4 duck breasts, boned
salt and pepper
1 tbls oil
3 raspberry vinegar

8 fl oz (250 ml) duck or chicken stock
8 fl oz (250 ml) green ginger wine
piece of stem ginger, cut into julienne

SAME DAY AS SERVING

1. Blanch the julienne of fresh ginger in boiling water for 30 seconds, then drain.
2. Season the duck breasts and sauté in the oil, skin-side down, for about 8 minutes; then turn over and sauté for a further 6 minutes. They should still be springy to the touch. Remove breasts and deglaze with the vinegar. Add the fresh ginger, stock and ginger

wine, and reduce by half. Season to taste. When cool, remove skin from breasts (see note below) and cover with cling-film.

BEFORE SERVING
(APPROX. FIVE MINUTES REHEATING TIME)

Reheat the sauce with the stem ginger until it simmers. Add the breasts, bring back to a simmer, and simmer 1–2 minutes. Remove the breasts to a warmed platter and spoon with some sauce. Serve immediately.

Note: The skin can be cut into matchsticks and baked until crisp. Use as a garnish over the breasts or in a salad.

DUCK BREASTS
WITH ROSEMARY SAUCE
SERVES 6

An easy way of cooking duck breasts for parties: briefly roast them in advance, slice them when they are cool and warm them quickly in a sauce before serving. They will still be pink and tender. Four breasts can be sliced to provide 6 servings.

4 duck breasts
sprig of rosemary
1 tbls fresh rosemary, very finely chopped
½ oz (15 g) butter
1 shallot, very finely chopped
½ carrot, very finely chopped
½ stalk of celery, very finely chopped

small glass of French vermouth or dry white wine
½ pt (300 ml) duck or chicken stock
salt and pepper
squeeze of lemon juice
1 tsp arrowroot
1 tbls port

SEVERAL HOURS IN ADVANCE

1. Preheat the oven to 215°C/425°F/Gas Mark 7.
2. Score the duck skin and rub with salt and pepper; then place in an oiled baking tin and place a sprig of rosemary on top. Roast for 10 minutes. Remove to a dish and leave to cool.
3. Sauté the vegetables in the butter, stirring, until softened. Pour off any fat from the roasting tin and deglaze with the vermouth or white wine. Add to the vegetables and simmer until reduced to a few tablespoons. Add the stock and chopped rosemary, and simmer until slightly reduced. Taste for seasoning, adding lemon juice as necessary. Pour the sauce into a frying-pan and set aside.
4. Remove the skin from the ducks (this can be fried until crisp and served cut into strips with the duck or in a salad). Add any juices from the duck to the sauce. Cut the duck into thin slices, cover and set aside.

BEFORE SERVING
(THREE TO FIVE MINUTES REHEATING TIME)

Mix the arrowroot with the port and add to the sauce. Bring to a simmer, add the duck and heat for only about 15 seconds. Serve immediately.

Note: A purée of celeriac or swedes goes well with the duck. The purée can be baked in greased ramekins and turned out on to individual plates.

BREASTS OF WILD DUCK
WITH HONEY

SERVES 4

This dish only uses the breasts but the legs can be used for a salad or rice dish to accompany it. The carcass makes the stock for the sauce.

4 tbls lime-blossom honey
½ tsp dried thyme
3 tbls tarragon vinegar
4 wild duck breasts
salt and pepper
1 tbls oil
honey for glazing

Garnish
fresh thyme leaves,
 chopped

For the stock
½ oz (15 g) butter
1 tbls oil
carcasses of 2 wild ducks,
 chopped
1 carrot, very finely chopped

1 onion, very finely
 chopped
½ stalk of celery, very
 finely chopped
4 oz (100 g) fresh
 mushrooms, chopped
¾ lb (350 g) tomatoes,
 chopped
1 clove garlic, crushed
bouquet garni
salt and pepper
6 fl oz (175 ml) red wine

For the beurre manié
¾ oz (20 g) butter
¾ oz (20 g) plain flour

UP TO ONE DAY IN ADVANCE

For the stock: Heat butter and oil in a large frying-pan and brown the chopped carcasses (do not burn). Pour off the fat and add the carrot, onion, celery and mushrooms. Cook the vegetables, stirring occasionally, until lightly coloured. Add the tomatoes, garlic and bouquet garni, and season with salt and pepper. Cook a little more, then add the wine and reduce completely. The browning of bones and vegetables can also be done in a hot oven in a roasting tin. Add 1¾ pts (1 L) water and simmer gently, skimming off the fat from the surface a few times, for 1 hour. Strain into a clean saucepan and reduce to ¾ pt (450 ml). Season and refrigerate when cool.

SAME DAY AS SERVING

1. Skin fat from the stock and bring to a simmer.
2. Simmer the honey with the thyme for a few minutes. Add the vinegar, then strain into the stock. Taste and add more honey or vinegar as needed. Set aside.

ONE HOUR IN ADVANCE

Season the breasts with salt and pepper. Heat the oil in a saucepan and place breasts skin-side down. Cook for 8 minutes or until lightly browned. Turn them over and cook another 6 minutes. They should still be springy to the touch. Remove from the pan and set aside. Set the pan aside.

BEFORE SERVING
(APPROX. THREE MINUTES REHEATING TIME)

1. Reheat the sauce. Blend the butter and flour together for *beurre manié* and add to the sauce if you want it thicker. Keep sauce warm over hot water.
2. Add a bit more butter to the frying-pan if needed, and quickly sauté the breasts just enough to reheat, a minute or two at most. Glaze the breasts with a thin coating of honey. Place on individual plates with some sauce and garnish with a fine sprinkling of fresh thyme.

GROUSE À LA CRÈME
SERVES 4

Straightforward roasted grouse with a quick boil-up of red wine, cream and pan juices at the end of the roasting. There couldn't be a better way to enjoy grouse.

4 grouse (not barded)	**salt and freshly ground**
1 tbls oil	**black pepper**
1 oz (25 g) clarified butter	**2 fl oz (60 ml) red wine**
	1 pt (600 ml) double cream

SEVERAL HOURS IN ADVANCE
Brown the grouse in the oil and butter, and season well.

BEFORE SERVING
(TWENTY MINUTES ROASTING TIME)

1. Preheat the oven to 215°C/425°F/Gas Mark 7.
2. Place grouse breast-side down in a roasting pan and roast for 20

minutes. Turn them on to the other side half-way through the cooking time.

3. Remove the birds to a warm platter. Deglaze the pan with the red wine; then add the cream and boil hard until it thickens. Season to taste and serve immediately.

PARTRIDGE WITH RED CABBAGE

SERVES 6

Partridge served on a bed of red cabbage with raisins and pine nuts.

I oz (25 g) raisins
2 tbls brandy
salt and pepper
4 partridges
I tbls oil
I tbls butter
I small onion, chopped
I carrot, chopped
I stalk of celery, chopped
I clove garlic, chopped
small glass of port
¼ pt (150 ml) double cream

For the cabbage
2 lb (900 g) red cabbage

I onion, finely chopped
I tsp cumin seeds
2 small cooking apples, peeled, cored and chopped
I oz (25 g) butter
3 tbls cider vinegar
1½ tbls brown sugar
salt and pepper

Garnish
I oz (25 g) pine nuts
fresh parsley, very finely chopped

ONE DAY IN ADVANCE

1. Wash, quarter and cut out the stalk from the cabbage. Shred the cabbage finely. Sauté the onion, cumin seeds and apple in the butter, stirring, until soft. Add the cabbage, vinegar and sugar, and mix well. Add 4 tbls of water, salt and pepper. Cover and simmer very gently for 1½ hours. Check occasionally and add extra water if necessary.

2. Soak the raisins in the brandy.

3. Preheat the oven to 190°C/375°F/Gas Mark 5.

4. Using a casserole, brown the well-seasoned birds in the oil and butter. Remove from the casserole and add the vegetables, including the garlic. Stir to soften slightly. Return the birds to the casserole, pour in the port and bring to a simmer. Tuck a piece of greaseproof paper over the birds, then cover and roast in the oven for 35 minutes. When the partridges are cool, split them in half. Strain the sauce into a small saucepan, then add cream, raisins and brandy. Simmer a few minutes, then season to taste. Refrigerate the partridges and sauce separately.

BEFORE SERVING
(THIRTY MINUTES REHEATING TIME)

1. Preheat the oven to 170°C/325°F/Gas Mark 3.
2. Spread the cabbage in the bottom of a shallow flameproof dish. Place the partridge on top and spoon over the sauce. Cover with foil and reheat in the oven for about 30 minutes.
To serve: Garnish with the pine nuts and parsley and serve.

ROAST HAUNCH
OF VENISON
SERVES 12

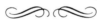

Until quite recently I felt daunted by the idea of roasting a large piece of venison. I suspected it would be too complicated or taste too gamey or dry. When I finally did try, I was proved very wrong. It was no more complicated than any other roast and the meat was tender, with a delicate, mild flavour. It has been a terrific hit with my guests. Although I do suggest larding a haunch to be on the safe side, the one time I didn't bother it was fine. Cover it with a layer of caul or pork-back fat if you are not larding. It is delicious served with a parsley purée and a potato and celeriac gratin – both can be made in advance (see p. 197 and p. 201).

8–9-lb (3.6–4.1-kg) haunch
of venison

For the larding
pork-back fat, cut into ¼-in
(5-mm) strips (if not
larding, caul or
pork-back fat to
cover haunch)

For the marinade
2 fl oz (60 ml) olive oil
3 fl oz (75 ml) dry white
wine
2 tbls dried herbs (thyme,
oregano and savory)

For the sauce
1 shallot, very finely
chopped
1 tbls oil
1 carrot, very finely
chopped
5 fresh mushrooms, very
finely chopped
3 fl oz (75 ml) Cognac
4 fl oz (110 ml) Madeira
1 pt (600 ml) good game
stock (see p. 215)
salt and pepper
1 tbls arrowroot

UP TO TWO DAYS IN ADVANCE
(MINIMUM EIGHT HOURS)

To lard the haunch: Thread the needle with a strip of the fat. Lard the round side of the meat by taking single, shallow stitches about 1½ in (3.8 cm) long. Cut the ends of the lard slightly larger than the stitch. Cover the surface with stitches about 1 in (2.5 cm) apart.
2. Place the meat on a large piece of foil. Pour over the marinade; rub in the herbs. Cover with foil and leave for at least 6 hours or overnight.
3. Sauté the shallot in the oil, stirring, for a couple of minutes. Add the carrot and mushrooms, and sauté a few more minutes. Pour in the Cognac and reduce by half. Add the Madeira and stock, and simmer gently for 5 minutes. Strain into a bowl, season to taste and refrigerate when cool.

SAME DAY AS SERVING

Leave meat at room temperature.

BEFORE SERVING
(APPROX. ONE AND A HALF HOURS ROASTING
AND RESTING TIME)

1. Preheat the oven to 215°C/425°F/Gas Mark 7.

2. Place meat in a roasting tin and pour over the marinade. Roast for 20 minutes in the hot oven. Reduce the oven to 180°C/350°F/Gas Mark 4. Allow 10 minutes per lb (450 g), including the initial searing time. Baste a few times with olive oil. Remove from the oven and rest for 15 minutes before serving.

3. Reheat the sauce. Deglaze the roasting tin with some sauce, then strain into the rest of the sauce. Mix the arrowroot with 1 tbls of water, add to the sauce and simmer a few minutes. Check seasoning and serve.

Note: If you buy dry-salted caul, soak it in warm water for 30 minutes; then rinse and drain. Fresh caul should be rinsed, spread out and blotted dry with paper towels.

VENISON STEW

SERVES 8

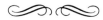

A rich and flavourful stew for a cold winter night's gathering.

3 lb (1.4 kg) venison, boned
  and cubed
6-oz (175-g) piece of
  unsmoked streaky bacon,
  diced
1 tbls oil
½ oz (15 g) plain flour
1 tbls sugar
salt and pepper
1 lb (450 g) fresh
  mushrooms, cleaned and
  quartered
2 oz (50 g) butter
squeeze of lemon juice

16 shallots

Garnish
8 croutons, fried in clarified
  butter
fresh parsley, finely chopped

For the marinade
1 large onion, sliced
2 carrots, sliced
3 tbls oil
8 juniper berries
sprig of thyme
1 bay leaf
1 pt (600 ml) red wine

UP TO FIVE DAYS IN ADVANCE
(MINIMUM THREE DAYS)

Mix the meat with the marinade ingredients in a bowl. Cover and refrigerate for 2–3 days, stirring occasionally.

UP TO TWO DAYS IN ADVANCE

1. Remove meat from the marinade and dry with paper towels. Reserve the marinade.
2. Using a large frying-pan, sauté the bacon in the oil until lightly browned. Remove bacon to a flameproof casserole. Add the venison to the pan and brown without crowding. Transfer to the casserole. Add the marinade vegetables to the pan and stir until soft. Stir in the flour and sugar. Pour in the rest of the marinade and bring to a simmer, stirring. Add to the casserole with extra water if needed so meat is just covered. Place a disc of greaseproof paper on top of the stew and cover with the lid. Simmer on top of the stove or in a low oven for 1½–2 hours. Regulate the heat so it simmers very gently. Cool, then refrigerate.

SAME DAY AS SERVING

1. Skim the fat from the stew, then bring to a simmer. Strain the sauce, pressing as many of the vegetables through as possible. Season to taste.
2. Sauté the mushrooms in ½ oz (15 g) of butter. Season with lemon juice, salt and pepper. Add to the stew.
3. Peel the shallots. Place them in cold water to cover and simmer for 5 minutes. Drain and add 1½ oz of butter. Cover and simmer for about 5 minutes or until tender. Pour into the casserole.

BEFORE SERVING
(FIFTEEN TO TWENTY MINUTES REHEATING TIME)

1. Fry the croûtons in clarified butter until golden. Drain on paper towels. Keep warm in a low oven.
2. Reheat the stew on top of the stove, simmering gently for 15–20 minutes. Alternatively, bring the stew to a simmer on top of the stove and place in a moderate oven for about 25 minutes. Serve with the croûtons and some parsley sprinkled over the top.

RABBIT WITH APRICOTS

SERVES 6

The flavour of dried apricots and a light wine sauce goes beautifully with rabbit. It is my favourite rabbit dish and one I am happy to serve at any time.

4 lb (1.8 kg) rabbit pieces
8 oz (225 g) dried apricots
salt and pepper
1 oz (25 g) butter
2 tbls olive oil
½ small carrot, finely
   chopped
½ stalk of celery, finely
   chopped
2 shallots, finely chopped

1 clove garlic, finely
   chopped
2 tbls plain flour
3 heaped tbls apricot jam
bouquet garni

For the marinade
1 bottle dry white wine
1 onion, sliced
1 carrot, sliced
2 cloves garlic, sliced

UP TO FOUR DAYS IN ADVANCE
(MINIMUM ONE DAY)

1. Place the rabbit with all the marinade ingredients, cover and refrigerate for 24 hours.
2. Soak the apricots overnight in enough boiling water to cover.

UP TO THREE DAYS IN ADVANCE

1. Remove rabbit from marinade and dry. Season with salt and pepper. Place marinade ingredients in a saucepan, bring to the boil and skim off any scum that comes to the surface. Strain and set aside. Discard the vegetables.
2. Heat the butter and oil in a frying-pan and lightly brown the meat. Remove and set aside. Add the carrot, celery, shallots and garlic, and cook, stirring, until vegetables are soft. Stir in the flour and cook a few minutes more. Deglaze the pan with some of the marinade. Pour the contents of the pan into a flameproof casserole. Stir in 2 tbls of jam and place the meat on top. Add the rest of the marinade and the bouquet garni. Cover with a disc of greaseproof

paper laid over the stew and the lid. Bring to a simmer on top of the stove, then simmer in the oven for 30 minutes.

3. Remove rabbit from casserole. Discard the bouquet garni. Strain the liquid, pressing as many of the vegetables through as you can. Season to taste with salt and pepper, and add the rest of the jam if it needs it. Wash the casserole; return the meat and sauce. Cover and refrigerate.

SEVERAL HOURS IN ADVANCE

Leave casserole at room temperature.

BEFORE SERVING
(TWENTY-FIVE MINUTES REHEATING TIME)

1. Preheat the oven to 170°C/325°F/Gas Mark 3.
2. Bring casserole to a simmer on top of the stove, then place in the oven for 25 minutes or until heated. Keep warm in a low oven if not serving immediately.
3. Heat apricots in a *bain-marie* over barely simmering water.
To serve: Arrange some meat on each plate, spoon over the sauce and place a few apricots on one side.

RABBIT WITH PRUNES
SERVES 6

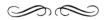

Farmed rabbit has a mild flavour and I find it preferable for entertaining. Its firm texture stands up beautifully in stews.

4 lb (1.8 kg) rabbit pieces
8 oz (225 g) prunes
½ oz (15 g) butter
1 tbls oil
½ oz (15 g) flour
½ pt (300 ml) chicken stock
bouquet garni

2 cloves garlic, crushed
salt and pepper
Garnish
6 triangles of white bread, fried in clarified butter
fresh parsley, very finely chopped

For the marinade
¾ pt (450 ml) red wine such
   as Côtes du Rhône or
   Mâcon
bouquet garni

4 juniper berries
4 peppercorns, crushed
2 tbls olive oil
1 carrot, chopped
1 onion, chopped

UP TO FOUR DAYS IN ADVANCE
(MINIMUM ONE DAY)

1. Place the rabbit with all the marinade ingredients. Cover and refrigerate for 24 hours.
2. Soak the prunes overnight in boiling tea or water.

UP TO THREE DAYS IN ADVANCE

1. Dry the rabbit with paper towels. Heat the butter and oil in a large frying-pan and lightly brown the rabbit pieces. Remove from the pan. Add the carrot and onion from the marinade and sauté until soft. Stir in the flour, then whisk in the rest of the marinade. Return the rabbit, add the stock, bouquet garni and garlic. Bring to the boil, cover and simmer gently for 25 minutes.
2. Remove the rabbit from the frying-pan. Discard the bouquet garni. Strain the sauce into a flameproof casserole, pressing as many of the vegetables through as you can. Adjust the sauce, reducing it if it is too thin or sieving a few prunes into the sauce to thicken it. Adjust seasoning, adding salt and pepper if necessary. Add the rabbit and prunes. Cover and refrigerate unless using the same day.

SEVERAL HOURS IN ADVANCE

1. Leave casserole at room temperature.
2. Fry bread until golden in clarified butter.

BEFORE SERVING
(TWENTY-FIVE MINUTES REHEATING TIME)

1. Preheat the oven to 180°C/350°F/Gas Mark 4.
2. Bring casserole to a simmer on top of the stove, then heat in the oven for about 25 minutes. Heat bread for about 10 minutes in oven.
3. Garnish with parsley and the fried bread.

VEGETABLES AND SALADS

BLANCHED VEGETABLES

Blanched vegetables retain their bright colour and texture. They can be blanched several hours ahead and reheated quickly in butter at the last minute.

Drop them into a large quantity of boiling salted water. Do them in small amounts so that the water will return to the boil as quickly as possible. Have a large bowl at hand filled with iced water. When they are at the *al dente* stage, scoop them out (a long-handled Chinese flat sieve is perfect) and drop into the water. Drain and keep sealed in cling-film until needed.

SWEET AND SOUR VEGETABLES

Prepare a selection of vegetables weighing about 2½ lb (1.1 kg), cutting them into equal-sized pieces if possible. Blanch each separately, following the instructions for Blanched Vegetables (see above). Before serving, heat 3 tbls of wine vinegar, 4 tbls of white wine and 3 tbls of sugar together in a large frying-pan or wok. Toss the vegetables in the sweet and sour sauce, season and serve.

VEGETABLE PURÉES

Vegetable purées can be made one day in advance, if kept covered in the refrigerator.

Cut vegetables into small pieces and blanch, following the instructions for Blanched Vegetables (see above). Purée in a blender or food processor and refrigerate. Before serving, melt about 1 oz (25 g) of butter per lb (450 g) of vegetables in a saucepan. Add the purée, season and stir until heated. Cream can also be added.

Celeriac Purée

SERVES 6

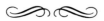

2 eating apples	3 oz (75 g) butter
1 potato	¼–½ pt (150–300 ml) cream
1 large celeriac	salt and pepper

Peel, core and slice the apples. Peel the potato and celeriac, and cut both into thick slices. Cook the apple, celeriac and potato in boiling salted water for about 20 minutes or until tender. Drain, then purée through a vegetable mill or potato ricer. Whisk in the butter and enough cream to make a light, fluffy purée. Season with salt and pepper.

To reheat: Place in a *bain-marie*, stirring occasionally, until hot.

Lentil Purée

SERVES 8

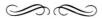

12 oz (350 g) brown or green lentils	bouquet garni
	salt and pepper
1 onion, stuck with a clove	2 oz (50 g) butter
1 carrot, chopped	fresh coriander, very finely
1 stalk of celery, chopped	chopped (optional)

Pick over the lentils and remove any grit. Combine the lentils with the vegetables, bouquet garni and 2½ pts (1.4 L) of water in a saucepan. Cover and simmer until lentils are tender, about 45 minutes. Add some salt the last 10 minutes of cooking time. Remove the onion, then rub the lentils and vegetables through a sieve. Before serving add butter and seasoning to lentils and stir over brisk heat until purée is the right consistency. Keep warm in a *bain-marie*. Add the coriander just before serving.

ONION PURÉE (SOUBISE)

SERVES 4–6

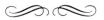

May be cooked several hours in advance and then reheated.

1½ oz (40 g) butter	2 oz (50 g) long-grain rice,
1½ lb (675 g) onions,	cooked
sliced	salt and pepper

Melt the butter in a casserole and stir in the onions and rice. Add some salt, cover and bake in a low oven, 150°C/300°F/Gas Mark 2, for about 45 minutes or until onions are tender. Purée in a blender or food processor. Before serving reheat in the oven with a bit more butter or in a *bain-marie*.

PARSLEY PURÉE

SERVES 6

12 oz (350 g) parsley leaves	½ oz (15 g) butter
4 fl oz (110 ml) double	salt and pepper
cream	

Wash and drain the parsley. Remove the stalks before weighing. Simmer in ¾ pt (450 ml) boiling salted water for 10 minutes. Drain, then purée in a blender or food processor with the cream. Reheat with the butter and season.

Braised Celeriac

SERVES 6

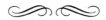

1 large celeriac	1 oz (25 g) butter
3 fl oz (75 ml) good chicken stock	salt and pepper

─────── UP TO ONE DAY IN ADVANCE ───────

1. Peel the celeriac, cut into ½-in (1.3-cm) slices, then cut the slices into ½-in (1.3-cm) sticks.

2. Simmer celeriac, stock and butter with some salt and pepper, covered, about 20 minutes or until tender. Cool, then refrigerate.

─────── BEFORE SERVING ───────

(APPROX. FIVE MINUTES REHEATING TIME)

Reheat in the braising liquid, boiling hard to evaporate if there is a surplus of liquid.

Baked Fennel Gratin

SERVES 8

Delicious with almost anything. You can replace the bacon with a few ounces of grated Parmesan if you want to keep it vegetarian.

6 bulbs of fennel	butter
¾ pt (450 ml) béchamel sauce (see p. 218)	6 oz (175 g) streaky bacon
salt and pepper	2 oz (50 g) breadcrumbs

─────── UP TO ONE DAY IN ADVANCE ───────

1. Cut off the root ends and feathery tops from the fennel and discard. Peel the coarse outer stalks. Slice the fennel into julienne on a mandolin grater or with a food processor.

2. Blanch the fennel in a large quantity of boiling salted water for a few minutes; it must be kept *al dente*. Drain, refresh under cold water and drain again. Mix with the béchamel sauce and season.

3. Butter a gratin dish, pour in the fennel, cover and refrigerate.

SEVERAL HOURS IN ADVANCE

Fry the bacon until very crisp. Drain, then chop into small bits. Mix with the breadcrumbs and sprinkle over the fennel. Dot the top with butter and leave at room temperature.

BEFORE SERVING
(TWENTY-FIVE MINUTES BAKING TIME)

1. Preheat the oven to 200°C/400°F/Gas Mark 6.
2. Bake for about 25 minutes or until top is brown and fennel is bubbling hot.

BAKED PARSNIPS
AND TOMATOES
SERVES 6–8

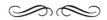

Parsnips baked with tomatoes and cream go particularly well with beef. Prepare well in advance and bake alongside the joint.

2 lb (900 g) parsnips
1½ oz (40 g) butter
1 lb (450 g) tomatoes
3 oz (75 g) Gruyère cheese,
  grated

1 oz (25 g) breadcrumbs
2–3 tbls brown sugar
½ pt (300 ml) single cream
salt and pepper

——— UP TO ONE DAY IN ADVANCE ———

1. Peel the parsnips and cut into strips. Sauté in the butter until slightly softened and coloured.
2. Peel the tomatoes and slice.
3. Mix the cheese with the breadcrumbs.
4. Grease an oven dish and layer with: parsnips, sprinkling of sugar, a few spoons of cream, tomatoes, salt, pepper, cream and the breadcrumb mixture. Repeat these layers, ending with the breadcrumbs. Pour over any cream that remains, cover and refrigerate.

——— BEFORE SERVING ———
(ONE HOUR BAKING TIME)

1. Preheat the oven to 180°C/350°F/Gas Mark 4.
2. Bake for a good hour; cover the top if it browns too much.

POTATO AND CELERIAC GRATIN

SERVES 6–8

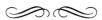

Particularly good with game.

2½ lb (1.1 kg) waxy
   potatoes
1 celeriac
4 oz (100 g) butter

salt and freshly ground
   black pepper
1 pt (600 ml) single cream
   or half cream and half
   stock

——— SEVERAL HOURS IN ADVANCE ———

1. Peel and cut the potatoes into thin slices. Place in a bowl of cold water.
2. Peel and slice the celeriac. Heat half the butter in a frying-pan and sauté the celeriac just long enough to coat the slices in the butter.
3. Butter a gratin dish. Layer with the potatoes and celeriac, seasoning each layer and dotting with butter. End with a good layer of potatoes. Pour over the cream (and stock if used) and dot with butter. Cover with cling-film and set aside in a cool place.

——— BEFORE SERVING ———
(ONE HOUR BAKING TIME)

1. Preheat the oven to 190°C/375°F/Gas Mark 5.
2. Bake for about 1 hour. Cover the top with foil if it browns too much. Keep warm in a low oven until ready to serve.

HOT POTATOES VINAIGRETTE

Steam or boil new potatoes in the usual way until cooked. Drain. Pour a good vinaigrette over the potatoes and then toss with a fork, breaking the potatoes up slightly. Season with salt, pepper and dill (if available).

MOUSSELINE POTATOES
SERVES 6

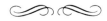

2 lb (900 g) potatoes	salt and pepper
2½ oz (60 g) butter	1 egg (if reheating)
¼ pt (150 ml) hot milk	

Peel and quarter the potatoes. Drop into boiling salted water to cover and boil until tender. Drain well, then pass through a vegetable mill or sieve. Whisk in the butter. Add just enough hot milk to make a light, fluffy mixture. Season well.

To keep hot: Place in a warm oven with a thin layer of milk covering the top.

To reheat: Add an egg to the potatoes and place in a moderate oven for about 30 minutes.

Variation: Blanch 2 heads of garlic, separated into cloves, in boiling water for 3 minutes. Drain. Peel the cloves, cover and simmer in 2 tbls of oil and 1 oz (25 g) of butter until soft, about 15 minutes. Sieve and whisk into purée just before serving.

SAUTÉED NEW POTATOES

2 oz (50 g) clarified butter	salt and pepper
2 lb (900 g) equal-sized new potatoes, peeled	fresh parsley, very finely chopped

Heat butter in a pan large enough for the potatoes to fit in one layer. Add potatoes and shake pan gently to coat the potatoes in the butter. Cover the pan and cook over low heat until potatoes are cooked inside and browned outside, about 20 minutes. Season with salt, pepper and parsley. Reheat in a bit more butter, uncovered.

VEGETABLE MOUSSES

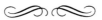

Whisked egg whites can be added to warm, not hot, vegetable purées and baked in a water bath or kept warm in a *bain-marie*. They can be turned out of small ramekins on to serving plates. The amount of egg white depends on the vegetable and how light you want it, but try 2 egg whites to about 12 oz (350 g) of vegetable.

LETTUCE MOUSSE

SERVES 6

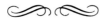

4 heads of lettuce
2 tbls cream
salt and pepper

2 oz (50 g) butter
2 egg whites

——— SEVERAL HOURS IN ADVANCE ———

Wash the lettuce and remove any coarse stalks. Blanch the leaves in boiling salted water for 1 or 2 minutes or until just wilted. Drain, pressing out as much moisture as possible. Purée in a blender or food processor. Cover and refrigerate.

——— BEFORE SERVING ———

Whisk the egg whites with a pinch of salt until stiff. Stir the lettuce with the butter over brisk heat to evaporate any moisture. Remove from the heat and when lettuce is no longer hot but still warm, fold in the whites and cream. Season with salt and pepper. Keep warm in a *bain-marie* or bake in greased ramekins in a roasting pan filled with hot water in a moderate oven for 30 minutes.

BULGHUR

SERVES 4–6

Bulghur (also called cracked wheat) comes in two textures. You want the coarser type for this recipe.

2 shallots, finely chopped	**salt and pepper**
1 oz (25 g) butter	*Garnish*
8 oz (225 g) coarse bulghur	**fresh herbs, chopped**

Sauté the shallots in the butter until soft. Add the bulghur and sauté, stirring, until it absorbs the butter. Pour ¾ pt (450 ml) of water over the bulghur and bring to the boil. Add some salt, cover and simmer gently for about 20 minutes. Slip a cloth under the lid and replace the lid. Leave off heat and serve within 20 minutes. Reheat in the oven or on top of the stove with a bit more butter. Season and serve with fresh herbs. It can also be toasted in a dry pan (stir continuously) before the water is added.

SAFFRON RICE

SERVES 6

good pinch of saffron	**1 tbls oil**
filaments	**12 oz (350 g) basmati or**
2 shallots, very finely	**long-grain rice**
chopped	**½ tsp tumeric**
1 oz (25 g) butter	**salt and pepper**

Soak the saffron in 2 tbls of hot water. Sauté the shallots in the butter and oil until soft. Wash the rice in several changes of cold water, then drain in a sieve. Stir the tumeric into the shallots and then stir in the rice. Sauté until rice is coated in the fat. Add the saffron and soaking water, pour over ¾ pt (450 ml) water and a pinch of salt, and bring quickly to the boil. Stir once, lower heat to a bare simmer, cover and simmer for 20 minutes. Remove from the heat. Slip a tea towel under the lid, replace the lid and leave until ready to serve. It will stay hot for about 30 minutes. Season with salt and pepper before serving.

Note: To cook rice well ahead of time, turn out into a bowl the moment it is cooked. Reheat in a moderate oven before serving.

SAUTÉED CHERRY TOMATOES

SERVES 8

It may seem a daunting job to skin these tiny tomatoes, but it goes quite quickly and they usually have such a good flavour and look attractive too.

**1½ lb (700 g) cherry
tomatoes
1 oz (25 g) butter**

salt and pepper
Garnish
basil leaves, snipped

——————— SAME DAY AS SERVING ———————

Bring a small saucepan of water to the boil. Drop 4 or 5 tomatoes into the water and leave for only 3 seconds. Remove with a slotted spoon and peel. Pick off a bit from the stem; the rest will slide off easily. Leave in a large, shallow dish in one layer.

——————— BEFORE SERVING ———————
(APPROX. FIVE MINUTES REHEATING TIME)

Melt the butter in a large frying-pan, slide in the tomatoes and gently heat in the butter. Season well with salt and pepper and serve garnished with the basil.

PROVENÇAL TOMATOES

SERVES 6

6 firm tomatoes	5 tbls olive oil
salt and pepper	3 tbls fresh parsley, very
2 cloves garlic, crushed	finely chopped
4 tbls fresh breadcrumbs	pinch of dried thyme

Cut the tomatoes in half crosswise. Gently squeeze out the seeds and discard. Spoon out the pulp and set aside. Season the tomatoes with salt and pepper, and leave to drain upside down. Mix all the other ingredients together and add the tomato pulp. Spoon into the tomatoes. Place in an oiled tin and bake for 15 minutes in the top of a hot oven.

TOMATOES STUFFED WITH COURGETTES

SERVES 6

6 firm tomatoes	2 shallots, very finely
1½ lb (675 g) courgettes	chopped
salt and pepper	1 tbls oil
	1 oz (25 g) butter

Prepare the shells as for Provençal Tomatoes (see above). Wash and trim the ends of the courgettes. Grate them, toss with 1 scant tsp of salt and leave in a colander for 10 minutes. Sauté the shallots in the oil and butter until soft. Squeeze the courgettes by the handful to extract as much liquid as possible. Add the dry courgettes to the pan and sauté, stirring, for a few minutes. Season with salt and pepper. Spoon into the tomato shells. Place in an oiled tin and bake for 15 minutes in a hot oven. Grated Parmesan cheese can also be added, depending on the dish that will accompany them.

Lentil and Chutney Salad

SERVES 8–10

1 lb (450 g) green lentils
1 onion, stuck with 2 cloves
1 carrot, quartered
bouquet garni
4 tbls mango chutney
lots of fresh coriander, very
  finely chopped

For the vinaigrette
4 fl oz (110 ml) sunflower oil
  or olive oil
4–5 tbls balsamic or
  tarragon vinegar
lemon juice
salt and pepper

—————— UP TO ONE DAY IN ADVANCE ——————

1. Pick over the lentils for any grit, then rinse in a few changes of cold water. Place in a large saucepan with 3 pts (1.7 L) water, onion, carrot and bouquet garni. Bring to the boil and skim if necessary. Lower the heat, cover and simmer for about 25 minutes or until lentils are tender but still hold their shape. It is important not to overcook them. Drain and discard the vegetables and bouquet garni. Pour into a bowl.
2. Mix the vinaigrette ingredients together and add to the lentils. Add the chutney and most of the coriander and toss all together. Season well with salt and pepper. Refrigerate until you are ready to serve. Keep the rest of the coriander wrapped in cling-film and add just before serving.

Wilted Cabbage Salad

SERVES 8–10

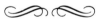

It is useful to have a few cabbage salads up your sleeve for the winter when hot-house lettuce is feeble. Wilting the cabbage with boiling water gives it a softer taste, but it still has some bite.

1 small white cabbage

8 oz (225 g) unsmoked
  streaky bacon, shredded

For the dressing	¼ pt (150 ml) cream
3 oz (75 g) Roquefort cheese	¼ pt (150 ml) plain thick-set
1 tbls Cognac	yoghurt
1 tbls vinegar	salt and pepper

SAME DAY AS SERVING

1. Shred the cabbage and place in a bowl. Pour boiling water over the cabbage to cover. Place a plate with a weight on top over the cabbage to keep it submerged and leave for 10 minutes. Drain in a colander, pressing out as much water as you can with your hands.
2. Meanwhile, fry the bacon until crisp and drain.
3. Mix the dressing ingredients together. Season lightly with salt, as the cheese and bacon are both salty.
4. Toss the cabbage with the dressing.

BEFORE SERVING

Add the bacon to the salad and serve.

Note: Croutons can be fried in olive oil or clarified butter and added.

BASICS

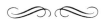

CRÊPES
MAKES 18 CRÊPES

Layered with cling-film, crêpes will keep for three days in the refrigerator or for four weeks in the freezer.

4 oz (100 g) plain flour
pinch of salt
6 fl oz (175 ml) milk

3 eggs
3 tbls unsalted butter, melted
oil for greasing

1. Sift flour with salt into a bowl. Make a well in the centre and fill with half the milk. Whisk the milk into the flour gradually, then whisk in the eggs. Stir in the melted butter, 3 fl oz (75 ml) of water and the remaining milk. Whisk only enough to blend or crêpes will be tough. Leave to rest for at least 30 minutes.
2. Oil a 9-in (23-cm) crêpe pan and heat until very hot. The batter should have the consistency of thin cream. Add more milk or water if necessary. Add a serving spoon of batter to the pan, then tilt the pan so bottom is evenly coated. Pour out any excess batter and next time add less. Cook over high heat for about 30 seconds, flip over and cook the second side for only 10 seconds. It will take a few crêpes before the consistency, amount of batter and heat are just right. Pile them on a plate and when cool layer with cling-film or greaseproof paper. Refrigerate for up to three days.

PUFF PASTRY
MAKES 8 OZ (225 G) PASTRY

8 oz (225 g) unsalted butter
8 oz (225 g) strong flour

1 tsp salt

1. It is important to work on a cold surface: smooth Formica or stainless steel surfaces are good, but marble is ideal. Melt 2 tbls of the butter. Sift the flour on to the working surface, add the salt and make a well in the centre. Add a scant ¼ pt (150 ml) of cold water and the butter. Gradually work in the flour to form a dough, adding more water when necessary. Wrap in cling-film and chill for 15 minutes.
2. Lightly flour the dough and roll out into a 12-in (30-cm) square. Flour the butter and hit it with a rolling pin to soften. It should be about the same consistency as the dough. Shape it into a 6-in (15-cm) square.
3. Set the butter in the centre of the dough and fold in the corners to cover the butter and form an envelope. Flour the surface and turn over, seam-side down. Roll out to a rectangle 20 × 8 in (50 × 20 cm). Fold the rectangle into three, as if folding a business letter. Turn the dough 90° clockwise – this is called a turn. Roll out again and fold in three, making a second turn. Wrap in cling-film and refrigerate for 15 minutes. Make a

note of the time and how many turns you have done. Make 2 more turns and refrigerate again for 15 minutes. Repeat again, making a total of 6 turns. Chill at least 15 minutes before using.

4. The dough can be frozen or kept tightly wrapped in the refrigerator for 4 days. Let the dough come to room temperature before rolling out. Get ahead by making double quantities and freezing half. Puff pastry can be baked 1–2 days in advance if stored in an airtight container. Give the pastry a quick reheat before serving.

PUFF PASTRY SHAPES

A buttery and many-layered (729 to be exact!) puff pastry crescent or other shape is a delicious garnish to creamy dishes, particularly seafood. Larger round or diamond shapes can be used as containers for chicken, fish or vegetables.

puff pastry
1 egg for glaze

1. Preheat the oven to 215°C/425°F/Gas Mark 7.
2. Roll the dough into a large rectangle. Cut into shapes and transfer to a damp baking sheet. Add a pinch of salt to the egg if you are using the shapes for a savoury dish. Brush the surface of the shapes, being careful not to get any on the edges. Chill for 15 minutes. Bake for 15–20 minutes or until puffed and brown.
3. If you are making shapes to fill, use a sharp knife and trace a line about ¼ in (.6 cm) from the edge. This will form a 'hat' that can be cut off after baking.
4. Cool the pastry on racks and store in airtight containers when cold. Save all the scraps of dough, pile them one on top of another and use for biscuits, *palmiers* (see p. 212) or tarts.

PUFF PASTRY FOR TARTS

Puff pastry makes a superb pie crust, but it must be partially baked first. Roll it out as you would any pastry and line the tin. Refrigerate for 30 minutes. Prick the bottom all over with a fork and line with a piece of crumpled greaseproof paper and enough beans to fill the tin three-quarters full. Bake in a preheated oven 215°C/425°F/Gas Mark 7 for 12–15 minutes. Remove the paper and beans, and bake a further 5–6 minutes. A fully baked 'blind' pie shell would need about 25 minutes in all.

PALMIERS

These can be made with the scrapes of dough and can be any size. Small ones are particularly nice to serve with ices or coffee. Sprinkle a work surface with sugar and roll the dough out to a rectangle. Use sugar as you would flour. Sprinkle the surface of the rectangle with sugar and roll the sides to the centre so they meet. Press lightly to seal, then fold one rolled section on top of the other. Cut slices using a sharp knife. Place on a baking sheet, cut-side down, and refrigerate for 15 minutes. Then bake in a hot oven for about 8 minutes.

SHORTCRUST PASTRY
MAKES 6 OZ (175 G) PASTRY

6 oz (175 g) flour
½ tsp salt
1 tbls sugar
1 tsp baking powder

3 oz (75 g) very cold unsalted butter
1 egg yolk
3–4 tbls double cream

Sift the flour, salt, sugar and baking powder into a mixing bowl. Cut the butter into small pieces and rub into the mixture with the tips of your fingers until the mixture acquires the texture of oatmeal. Blend the egg yolk and cream together and, using a fork, stir into the flour mixture. Turn the dough out on to a lightly floured surface and knead for 10 seconds with the heel of your hand. Wrap the dough in cling-film and refrigerate for at least 30 minutes before using.

Note: If the pastry is being used for a savoury filling, omit the sugar.

MELBA TOAST

Remove the crust from white sliced bread. Toast in a toaster. While still warm, insert knife in the centre and split into two. Crisp up the thin slices in a moderate oven until pale golden. Store in an airtight container.

CROÛTONS AND CROÛTES

Croûtons are cubes or triangles of fried bread. Croûtes are larger pieces usually served with something on them.

To make either, remove the crusts from thick slices of white bread and cut to desired shapes. Heat clarified butter or equal quantities of butter and oil in a frying-pan until very hot. Fry until lightly browned on both sides.

Drain on crumpled paper towels. Store in an airtight container. Reheat in a low oven.

CRÈME FRAÎCHE
MAKES 14 FL OZ (425 ML)

Crème fraîche has a lovely nutty flavour and is excellent for sauces. It does not separate when cooked as yoghurt and soured cream do. A coating on grilled meat or fish seals in the natural juices.

Gently heat 1 pt (600 ml) whipping cream with 4 fl oz (110 ml) buttermilk or soured cream to 24–29°C/75–85°F. Do not let it heat above 29°C/85°F. Remove from the heat and pour into a warm bowl. Cover loosely and leave at room temperature (not below 15°C/60°F for 5–8 hours or until thickened. Alternatively, pour into a warmed wide-necked thermos. Screw on the top and leave for the same time. It will keep for 10 days in the refrigerator.

COURT-BOUILLON

This is used to poach fish. It can then in turn be used in place of the water to make fish stock.

1 small onion, sliced	bouquet garni
1 small carrot, sliced	2 tbls white wine vinegar
6 peppercorns	2 tsp salt

Add all the ingredients to 2 pts (1.1 L) of water and bring to the boil. Reduce heat and simmer gently, uncovered, for 15 minutes.

WHITE VEAL STOCK

4–5 lb (1.8–2.3 kg) veal bones, sawn into small pieces	2 stalks of celery, cut into chunks
2 onions, quartered	8 peppercorns
2 carrots, cut into chunks	bouquet garni
	8 cloves garlic, unpeeled

Place bones in enough cold water to cover, bring to the boil and simmer for 5 minutes. Drain and rinse the bones under cold running water. Wash out the pan, add the bones and all the other ingredients. Bring slowly to the boil, then simmer for 4–5 hours, skimming occasionally at first. Strain, then reduce by boiling hard if flavour is not concentrated enough. Chill and skim off any fat. Stock will keep for 3 days in the refrigerator or it can be frozen.

BROWN VEAL STOCK

The same ingredients are used for brown as for white veal stock, plus 1 tbls tomato purée. Preheat the oven to a very high heat. Place bones in a roasting tin and roast them, stirring occasionally, for about 25 minutes. Add the chopped vegetables and continue to roast until they are also brown. Be careful not to char the bones. Pour bones and vegetables into a large saucepan, add tomato purée, bouquet garni, garlic, peppercorns and enough water to cover, and simmer as for white veal stock. The colour can be enhanced by adding onion skins.

CHICKEN STOCK

Chicken stock is invaluable to have on hand. Leftover cooked carcasses can be used, but make stock with them as soon as possible. Inexpensive uncooked pieces such as necks or wings, or a boiling fowl, will vastly improve the flavour.

3–4 lb (1.4–1.8 kg) chicken carcasses and scraps, cooked or uncooked	½ pt (300 ml) dry white wine
2 onions, unpeeled and quartered	parsley stalks
2 carrots, quartered	1 bay leaf
1 stalk of celery with leaves, sliced	pinch of salt
	sprig of thyme
	8 peppercorns

Place the chicken in a large saucepan. Add the vegetables and wine, and boil until the wine has almost evaporated. Add remaining ingredients except the peppercorns, cover with cold water and bring to the boil. Reduce heat and simmer very gently for 2–2½ hours. Add the peppercorns for the final half hour of cooking time. Strain the stock and taste – if flavour is too weak, boil until reduced. Cool, then refrigerate. Skim off the fat when it has congealed. Any remaining fat can be removed when stock is reheated by drawing a piece of paper towel over the surface.

To keep: Boil stock every 2–3 days for 5 minutes if stored in the refrigerator. Stock freezes well and small amounts of reduced stock can be frozen in ice-cube trays for use in sauces.

Note: If you do not intend to reduce the stock, add more salt during cooking. By simmering the stock very gently it should be clear enough to use as a bouillon without further clarification.

FISH STOCK

With any luck you should be able to charm your fishmonger into wonderful free fish bones and heads. Only white fish can be used, but you can always add some inexpensive fish such as whiting. Fish stock can be the basis for fish soup or for poaching fish. When reduced, it can be used in making fish sauces.

1 large onion, sliced	3 lb (1.4 kg) white fish bones
2 carrots, sliced	and heads, gills removed
½ stalk of celery, sliced	bouquet garni
white part of 1 leek, sliced	½ pt (300 ml) white wine
3 tbls olive oil	8 peppercorns

In a large saucepan sauté the vegetables in the oil, stirring, for several minutes. Rinse the fish, add to the pan and stir a few more minutes. Add 5 pts (3 L) of water and the bouquet garni. Salt lightly and bring to the boil. Skim well and simmer for 15 minutes. Add the wine and peppercorns, and simmer a further 15 minutes. Strain through a muslin-lined sieve. Cool, then skim and blot off any surface fat.

Note: Never simmer fish bones longer than 30 minutes or the stock will be bitter. Reduce stock to desired strength after removing all solids. For a clear bouillon, do not press fish or vegetables when straining.

GAME STOCK

1 tbls oil	mushroom trimmings
3 lb (1.4 kg) trimmings and	5 juniper berries
bones from rabbit, hare,	sprig of thyme
venison or game birds,	sprig of sage
chopped	1 bay leaf
1 carrot, very finely	½ pt (300 ml) white or
chopped	red wine
1 onion, very finely chopped	1½ pts (900 ml) veal stock
1 stalk of celery, very finely	or water
chopped	

Heat the oil in a large saucepan and brown the trimmings and bones, stirring occasionally. Add the vegetables and the juniper berries and sauté for a few minutes. Add the herbs and wine, and reduce by half. Add the stock or water and bring to the boil. Lower the heat and simmer gently for 2 hours, skimming occasionally. Strain through a muslin-lined sieve. Refrigerate when cool. Remove the fat from the surface when cold.

HERB BUTTERS

Herb butters are very useful to have on hand to serve on grilled meats, steamed fish, or vegetables. They are also good on rice or pasta, and can be smeared under the skin of chicken before roasting. Layer some between slices of French bread and bake in foil to make not only garlic bread but also other herb breads. All kinds of fresh herbs can be used – whatever is in season. The amount to add depends on the herb, but a guide is 4–5 tbls of a finely chopped herb to 6 oz (175 g) of butter. Blend them together, roll into a sausage shape and cover tightly in cling-film. Refrigerate or place in your freezer, where it will keep well for a month.

GARLIC BUTTER

> 2 cloves garlic, very finely
>   chopped
> 6 oz (175 g) butter, softened

ANCHOVY BUTTER

> 2-oz (50-g) tin of anchovy
>   fillets, drained and sieved
> 4 oz (125 g) butter
> freshly ground black pepper

GREEN PEPPERCORN BUTTER

> 3 tbls green peppercorns,
>   drained and crushed
> 1 tbls Dijon mustard
> 1 tbls lemon juice
> 6 oz (175 g) butter

CORIANDER BUTTER

> 5 tbls fresh coriander, very
>   finely chopped
> 6 oz (175 g) butter

SAUCES

Beurre Blanc
MAKES ABOUT ½ PT (300 ML)

Beurre blanc should be made at the last minute, but the reduction of wine and vinegar can be done in advance. The final whisking in of butter takes no more than a minute or two. It can also be kept warm in a *bain-marie* filled with warm, not hot, water or in a wide-necked thermos for about 30 minutes. The sauce is never very hot; otherwise the butter would become oily.

1 shallot, very finely chopped	8 oz (225 g) cold unsalted
3 tbls mild wine or tarragon	butter
vinegar	salt and pepper
3 tbls dry white wine	

SEVERAL HOURS IN ADVANCE

In a small, heavy saucepan (not aluminium) boil the shallot, vinegar and wine together until reduced to 1½ tbls. Set aside. Cut the butter into ½-oz (15-g) chunks and keep refrigerated.

BEFORE SERVING

Bring the reduction back to the boil. Lower the heat and whisk in the pieces of butter gradually, sometimes off the heat or over very low heat. The butter must only soften without melting. Season with salt and pepper, and serve immediately. Alternatively, make 30 minutes in advance and keep in a thermos or over warm water.

Variations: Add fresh herbs; or ½ tsp tomato purée; or ½ tsp anchovy paste. You can also replace the vinegar with lime or lemon juice and add some peel. Cold herb butters can replace the plain butter.

Béchamel Sauce
MAKES ABOUT 1 PT (600 ML)

1 pt (600 ml) milk	8 peppercorns
1 slice of onion	2 oz (50 g) butter
2-in (5-cm) piece of celery	3 tbls plain flour
stalk	salt and freshly ground black
1 bay leaf	pepper
1 blade of mace	gratings of nutmeg

Bring the milk slowly to the boil with the vegetables and spices. Remove from the heat the moment it reaches the boil, cover and leave to infuse for

15 minutes. Melt the butter in a heavy-based saucepan, whisk in the flour and cook for a minute or until foaming – do not allow to colour. Strain in the hot milk while whisking and continue to whisk until it simmers and thickens. Simmer for at least 5 minutes. Season to taste with salt, pepper and a few gratings of nutmeg if desired.

HOLLANDAISE SAUCE
MAKES ABOUT ½ PT (300 ML)

6 oz (175 g) unsalted butter
3 egg yolks
2 tbls water
1 tbls lemon juice

salt and freshly ground white
pepper
lemon juice to taste

Melt the butter and set aside to cool to tepid. Whisk the egg yolks, water, 1 tbls of lemon juice, salt and pepper in a basin until light. Set the basin over a pan of barely simmering water and continue to whisk until the mixture leaves a ribbon trail when the whisk is lifted. Take off the heat and whisk in the butter a few dribbles at a time. As sauce thickens, the butter can be added more quickly. If you are making the sauce in advance, stop when the sauce thickens and before all the butter is added; beat in hot melted butter in dribbles to heat sauce just before serving. Season to taste with lemon juice, salt and pepper.

Note: A pinch of cornflour whisked into the egg yolks will help to stabilize the sauce; this is very useful if you are planning to make it in advance and reheat. Press a piece of cling-film on to the surface of the sauce to prevent the formation of a skin.

MAYONNAISE
MAKES ABOUT 1 PT (600 ML)

A good home-made mayonnaise is very versatile. Apart from using with cold dishes, it can be used to coat meat and fish for grilling and baking. Herbs, vegetables and fruit can be added to mayonnaise and it can be lightened with yoghurt or soured cream. It will keep for 2–3 days in the bottom of the refrigerator.

3 egg yolks, at room
temperature
1 tsp Dijon mustard

2 tbls white wine vinegar
salt and pepper
¾ pt (450 ml) oil

Whisk the egg yolks, mustard, 1 tbls of vinegar, salt and pepper until thick. Whisk in the oil drop by drop. After a few tbls of oil have been added, the yolks will thicken and the oil can be added in a slow stream; whisk continually. When all the oil has been added, season to taste with vinegar, salt and pepper.

AÏOLI
MAKES ABOUT 1 PT (600 ML)

1 slice white bread, crusts removed	3 egg yolks
2 fl oz (60 ml) milk	¾ pt (450 ml) mixed olive oil and sunflower oil
6 cloves garlic	juice of ½ lemon
pinch of salt	

1. Soak the bread in the milk, then squeeze dry.
2. Purée garlic, salt and bread in a blender or food processor. Add the yolks and blend. With the machine on, pour the oil slowly into the mixture to obtain a firm sauce. Scrape into a bowl and add lemon juice to taste. Season and store in the refrigerator.

CAPER MAYONNAISE
MAKES ABOUT ½ PT (300 ML)

½ small onion, very finely chopped	1 tbls oil
1 clove garlic, very finely chopped	3 tbls capers
	¼ pt (150 ml) mayonnaise
	¼ pt (150 ml) *fromage frais*

Sauté the onion and garlic in the oil, stirring, until soft. Scrape into a bowl and mix with the other ingredients.

CURRY MAYONNAISE
MAKES ABOUT ½ PT (300 ML)

1 shallot, very finely chopped	pinch of sugar
1 tbls oil	¼ pt (150 ml) mayonnaise
2 tbls curry powder	¼ pt (150 ml) soured cream
1 tsp cumin	

Sauté the shallot in the oil until soft. Stir in the curry powder and cumin, and stir a few minutes. Scrape into a bowl and mix with the other ingredients.

GREEN MAYONNAISE
MAKES ABOUT I PT (600 ML)

3 oz (75 g) watercress leaves
I oz (25 g) parsley leaves
½ oz (15 g) fresh chives or dill,
   finely chopped

½ pt (300 ml) mayonnaise or
  ¼ pt (150 ml) mayonnaise
  and ¼ pt plain thick-set
  yoghurt
lemon juice
salt and pepper

Process or blend the greens, fold into the mayonnaise and season.

MANGO MAYONNAISE
MAKES ABOUT I PT (600 ML)

This is an amazingly good mayonnaise, particularly with cold salmon.
Purée the flesh from one mango. Add to ¾ pt (450 ml) of mayonnaise,
along with I tbls of very finely chopped fresh mint.

SPINACH MAYONNAISE
MAKES ABOUT ½ PT (300 ML)

8 oz (225 g) spinach
¼ pt (150 ml) mayonnaise

lemon juice
salt and pepper

Wash the spinach well. Cook it in any water that is left clinging to the
leaves, plus a pinch of salt. Drain and press out excess moisture. Chop
finely and fold into mayonnaise. Season with lemon juice, salt and pepper.

ASPARAGUS SAUCE
MAKES ABOUT I PT (600 ML)

For chicken and fish.

I lb (450 g) asparagus
2 oz (50 g) butter

juice of ½ lemon
salt and pepper

Snap off the tough ends of the asparagus and save for soup. Cut the asparagus into ½-in (1.3-cm) lengths. Cook in boiling salted water until tender. Drain, saving the water, and purée in a blender or food processor. Add the butter, lemon juice, salt and pepper and blend again, adding enough cooking water to make a sauce of coating consistency. Refrigerate and reheat when needed. If serving cold, replace the butter with oil.

CORIANDER SAUCE
MAKES ABOUT ½ PT (300 ML)

I shallot or small onion, very
  finely chopped
I tbls oil
3 oz (75 g) coriander leaves,
  chopped

salt and pepper
4 oz (100 g) *fromage frais*
4 fl oz (110 ml) double cream

Sauté the shallot or onion in the oil until soft. Scrape into a blender or food processor and blend with the coriander leaves, salt and pepper. Add the *fromage frais* and cream. Can be served hot as well as cold. Keep below simmering point if heating.

GOOSEBERRY SAUCE
MAKES ABOUT I PT (600 ML)

I lb (450 g) gooseberries
I oz (25 g) butter
I egg

sugar
pinch of salt

Simmer gooseberries with the butter and I tbls of water until soft. Strain the berries or pass them through a vegetable mill; then beat in the egg. Season to taste with sugar and a pinch of salt. Keep the sauce on the tart side.

HORSERADISH WALNUT SAUCE
MAKES ABOUT ¾ PT (450 ML)

4 oz (100 g) walnut halves

1 tbls lemon juice
1½ tsp caster sugar
1 tbls walnut oil

½ pt (300 ml) double cream
salt and pepper
3 oz (75 g) grated horseradish

Soak the walnuts in boiling water for few minutes. Peel off as much skin as you can while they are still warm. Grind the nuts in a blender or food processor. Scrape into a bowl and add the lemon juice, sugar, oil, cream, salt and pepper. Add horseradish gradually to the cream and stop when the taste is right.

PESTO

Pesto is very useful to have on hand. It is well known for its magic as a sauce for pasta, but it is also delicious mixed in rice or in baked potatoes. It can add great flavour to a stuffing or can pep up a bland sauce. Freeze basil in the summer when it is available. It is easy to grow your own supply in a sunny window. Use it in small amounts, as the flavour is very concentrated.

2 oz (50 g) fresh basil leaves,
   coarse stalks removed
4 fl oz (100 ml) olive oil
3 oz (75 g) pine nuts
2 cloves garlic, peeled

pinch of salt
2 oz (50 g) butter
4 oz (100 g) freshly grated
   Parmesan cheese

Purée the basil, oil, nuts, garlic and salt in a blender or food processor. Scrape into a bowl and fold in the butter and cheese.
To freeze: Purée basil, oil, nuts and salt. Freeze; add the garlic, butter and cheese when thawed. Label it so that you remember to add the missing ingredients.

PRAWN SAUCE
MAKES ABOUT 1 PT (600 ML)

1 lb (450 g) prawns in their
   shells
1 carrot, very finely chopped
½ stalk of celery, very finely
   chopped
1 small onion, very finely
   chopped
3 tomatoes
1 tbls tomato purée

1 shallot, very finely chopped
2 tbls oil
1 clove garlic, crushed then
   chopped
3 tbls port
2 tbls brandy
½ pt (300 ml) white wine
salt and pepper
¼ pt (150 ml) double cream

1. Shell the prawns. Set the prawns aside and place the shells in a food processor and purée.

2. Using a heavy-bottomed saucepan, sauté the carrot, celery, onion and shallot in the oil until soft. Add the crushed shells and garlic, and stir for a few minutes. Add the port and brandy, and reduce by half. Add the wine, ½ pt (300 ml) water, tomatoes, tomato purée, salt and pepper. Cover and simmer for 15 minutes. Strain the sauce through a sieve, extracting as much juice as possible. Process some of the juice with one-third of the prawns (save the rest of the prawns for another dish). Add this to the remaining sauce and reduce over brisk heat to desired consistency. Add the cream and taste for seasoning.

TOMATO SAUCE
MAKES ABOUT 1½ PTS (900 ML)

2 shallots	1½ lb (675 g) ripe tomatoes
1 carrot	salt and pepper
1 stalk of celery	pinch of sugar
2 tbls olive oil	fresh basil or parsley, chopped

Chop the shallots, carrot and celery. Sauté in the oil for a few minutes. Chop the tomatoes roughly and add to the vegetables. Cover and simmer until the vegetables are soft. Purée and then sieve. Season with salt, pepper and a pinch of sugar to taste. Before serving add the fresh herb and thin with cream if desired.

WATERCRESS SAUCE
MAKES ABOUT ¾ PT (450 ML)
For chicken or fish.

8 oz (225 g) watercress, thick stems removed	¼ pt (150 ml) chicken stock
1 shallot, very finely chopped	¼ pt (150 ml) double cream
½ oz (15 g) butter	squeeze of lemon juice
	salt and pepper

Blanch the watercress in a large quantity of boiling salted water for 1 minute. Refresh under cold running water, drain and squeeze out excess moisture. Place in a blender or food processor. Sauté the shallot in the butter until soft. Add the stock and reduce by half. Add to the blender or food processor and purée. Add the cream and season with lemon juice, salt and pepper.

YOGHURT AND CARDAMOM SAUCE
MAKES ABOUT ½ PT (300 ML)

6 cardamom pods	8½-oz (240-g) carton of

1 tbls fresh parsley, finely	thick-set Greek yoghurt
chopped	salt and freshly ground black
1 tsp caster sugar	pepper

Remove the black seeds from the cardamom pods and grind to a powder with a pestle and mortar. Stir the ground cardamom, parsley and sugar into the yoghurt. Season with salt and pepper.

YOGHURT AND CORIANDER SAUCE
MAKES ABOUT ½ PT (300 ML)

4 tbls fresh coriander leaves,	8½-oz (240-g) carton of
very finely chopped	thick-set Greek yoghurt
1 tsp caster sugar	salt and freshly ground black
squeeze of lemon juice	pepper

Mix the coriander, sugar and some lemon juice into the yoghurt. Season with salt and pepper.

CARAMEL SAUCE
MAKES ABOUT 8 FL OZ (250 ML)

Caramel Sauce is delicious served with baked apples or bananas, or fresh fruit and yoghurt. It can also be used with ice creams and puddings.

Combine 6 oz (175 g) sugar with 4 tbls of water in a small, heavy-bottomed saucepan. Cook gently until sugar dissolves, then increase heat, rotating the pan occasionally until sugar is a rich brown caramel. Remove from the heat and add 6 fl oz (175 ml) warm water (stand back, as the caramel may spit). Stir over gentle heat until caramel is melted. Will keep in a covered jar for several weeks.

For a Caramel Cream Sauce, substitute 6 fl oz (175 ml) of whipping cream for the warm water. Will keep for a week if refrigerated.

RASPBERRY SAUCE

Sieve fresh or frozen raspberries and mix with sieved icing sugar and 1 tbls of Kirsch. Thin with lemon or orange juice if necessary. The sauce will keep for a week in the refrigerator or can be frozen.

HOT FUDGE SAUCE
MAKES ABOUT 8 FL OZ (250 ML)

2½ oz (60 g) unsalted butter
6 tbls cocoa powder
5 tbls water

6 oz (175 g) sugar
2 tbls golden syrup
1 tsp vanilla essence

Melt the butter with the cocoa. Add the water, sugar and syrup, and boil together for 3 minutes. Keep refrigerated. Before serving reheat in a *bain-marie* and stir in the vanilla.

LEMON SAUCE FOR DESSERTS
MAKES ABOUT 8 FL OZ (250 ML)

2 oz (50 g) sugar
pared rind and juice of 2 lemons

2 egg yolks

1. Bring ¼ pt (150 ml) water, 1 oz (25 g) sugar, lemon juice and pared rind to the boil. Take off heat, cover and leave to infuse for 5 minutes.
2. Strain the lemon water into the top of a double saucepan set over barely simmering water. Whisk in the egg yolks and the rest of the sugar. Stir until sauce thickens slightly, without allowing it to boil. Taste and add more sugar or lemon juice if needed. Sieve and cool. Will keep for 4 days in the refrigerator.

PISTACHIO SAUCE
MAKES ABOUT 1 PT (600 ML)

2½ oz (60 g) pistachio nuts,
   shelled
1 oz (25 g) blanched almonds

4½ oz (135 g) caster sugar
1 pt (600 ml) milk
4 egg yolks

1. Preheat the oven to 180°C/350°F/Gas Mark 4.
2. Toast nuts on an oven sheet for 5 minutes.
3. Rub between a tea towel to remove as much of the skin as possible.
4. Blend the nuts in a blender or food processor with half of the sugar to a paste. Scrape into a saucepan, add the milk and bring to the boil. Remove from the heat, cover and leave for 30 minutes. Strain into a clean pan.
5. Whisk the yolks and remaining sugar together until light and thick. Reheat the milk to just below the boil. Pour some of the milk over the yolks while whisking, then pour the mixture back into the saucepan and stir over low heat until the custard thickens. Do not allow it to come near the boil. Whisk off heat for a minute or two, then place cling-film on the surface to stop a skin forming and cool. Refrigerate and use within 3 days.

EXTRAS

CONFIT D'OIE
MAKES ENOUGH TO FILL 2 × 2-PT (1.1-L) JARS

Confit d'oie is goose that is cooked and then stored in fat. Although it may seem an archaic method of preservation, it produces succulent results that are not in the least fatty. It is used in *cassoulet* and is delicious eaten on its own, heated in a bit of the fat.

3 tbls coarse sea salt	1 large bay leaf
½ tsp dried thyme	5–6-lb (2.3–2.7-kg) goose or
½ tsp coriander seeds	duck
½ tsp juniper berries	2 lb (900 g) goose fat or fresh
¼ tsp black peppercorns	pork fat or lard
½ tsp allspice berries	

———— UP TO TWO TO THREE MONTHS ————
IN ADVANCE

1. Grind the salt, herbs and spices together in a coffee grinder or blender. Cut the meat into small joints. Save all the extra bits of fat and skin (the carcass can be used for stock). Rub the spice mixture all over the pieces of meat. Place in a bowl and weigh down with a plate and weights or large cans. Leave for 24 hours.

2. Meanwhile, render the fat. Place the extra skin and fat (and pork fat if you are using it) with 4 fl oz (110 ml) water in a saucepan. Cover and boil over moderate heat for about 20 minutes or until the fat has melted and the water evaporated. Remove the skin with a slotted spoon and save as crackling for a savoury nibble.

3. The next day rub the spices off the meat with paper towels and place the meat with the fat in a saucepan. The meat must be completely covered by fat. Cover and simmer gently for about 1¼ hours or until meat is tender when pierced with a fork. Remove meat with a slotted spoon to clean jars, strain the fat through a double layer of muslin and pour over the meat to cover. Shake the jars to distribute the fat, cover and refrigerate when cool. To remove the meat set the jar in a bowl of hot water until the fat has softened. If you are not using all the *confit d'oie*, cover what remains in fat and store as before.

Note: If you are keeping the preserved goose for several weeks, place a twig in the bottom of each jar, so the goose will not rest on the bottom and can be surrounded by fat.

SPICED KUMQUATS
MAKES ABOUT 3 LB (1.4 KG)

These are particularly good with ham, tongue or turkey. Store for about 6 weeks before using.

3 lb (1.4 kg) kumquats
2 lb (900 g) sugar
1 stick cinnamon
¼ oz (7 g) cloves

6 blades of mace
4 cardamom pods
1 pt (600 ml) cider vinegar

1. Place the kumquats in a saucepan, barely cover with water, cover and simmer for 20 minutes. Meanwhile, dissolve the sugar with the spices in the vinegar over gentle heat. Bring to the boil and boil for 5 minutes.
2. Drain the kumquats, reserving the liquid. Place the kunquats in the syrup, adding the reserved liquid to cover the fruit if necessary. Simmer for 30 minutes. Remove pan from the heat and leave uncovered for 24 hours, turning the fruit occasionally in the syrup.
3. The next day bring the kumquats and syrup to the boil, drain the fruit and pack in sterilized jars. Bring the syrup back to the boil and boil hard to thicken slightly. Pour over the kumquats, distributing the spices between the jars and seal.

ITALIAN FLAT BREAD WITH SAGE
(*Focaccia*)

A different bread, such as this lovely, crusty Italian one, takes very little extra effort to make and gives quite a boost to almost any meal.

**1 oz (25 g) fresh yeast or ½ oz
    (15 g) dried yeast**
2 tsp salt
**1 lb (450 g) plain or strong
    white flour**

**5 tbls Italian extra virgin olive
    oil**
12 fresh sage leaves, chopped

—— UP TO TWO DAYS IN ADVANCE ——
(MINIMUM FOUR HOURS)

1. Dissolve the yeast in a scant ½ pt (300 ml) of lukewarm water. Mix the salt into the flour, make a well in the centre and add the yeasty water and 4 tbls of olive oil. Knead until the dough is smooth and elastic. This can also be done in a food processor. Place the dough in a lightly oiled bowl, cover with a plastic bag and leave to rise in a warm place until doubled in volume.

2. Knock the dough down and knead it again, this time adding the sage and distributing it evenly.

3. Place a heavy metal baking sheet in the oven and preheat to 200°C/400°F/Gas Mark 6.

4. On a floured surface, shape and roll the dough out in a circle 12 in (30 cm) in diameter and ½ in (1.3 cm) thick. Dimple the surface with your finger and dribble the remaining oil over it. Either slide a floured board under the bread and then quickly slide it off on to the hot baking sheet, or pick it up with your hands and toss it on to the sheet. It doesn't matter if the shape becomes irregular. Bake for about 35 minutes or until a deep golden colour. Cool on a rack, then wrap and keep in a bread bin.

To serve: Reheat in a hot oven for 10 minutes or serve as it is.

Note: You can make this bread using other herbs.

CORN BREAD
MAKES 14 MUFFINS

An American speciality that is always enjoyed by guests. It can be baked in the morning and reheated with butter in foil.

9 oz (250 g) cornmeal (*polenta*)	2 oz (50 g) butter, melted and
5 oz (150 g) self-raising flour	cooled
1 tbls sugar	2 oz (50 g) margarine, melted
1 tbls baking powder	and cooled
1 tsp salt	½ pt (300 ml) warm milk
2 eggs	extra butter for greasing and
	buttering

SAME DAY AS SERVING

1. Preheat the oven to 200°C/400°F/Gas Mark 6. Grease a bun tin with wells 1½ in (3.8 cm) deep or a 9 × 5 × 4-in (23 × 12 × 10-cm) loaf tin.

2. Sift all the dry ingredients together into a large bowl.

3. Beat the eggs, then stir in the melted fats and warm milk. Pour into the centre of the dry ingredients. Using a large spoon, fold together until just blended. Spoon into the prepared tin. Bake buns 20 minutes; a loaf should be baked for 35 minutes. Leave in the tin for a few minutes, then turn out on to a rack.

BEFORE SERVING
(FIFTEEN MINUTES BAKING TIME)

1. Preheat the oven to 200°C/400°F/Gas Mark 6.
2. Slice muffins in half, spread butter on one half, sandwich together and wrap loosely in foil. Bake about 15 minutes. Serve hot or warm.

PRALINE
MAKES 6 OZ (175 G)

Ground praline is very useful to have on hand as a flavouring for yoghurt, ice creams, cakes and fruit salads. It will keep for weeks in a sealed container. It also can be kept in bite-size pieces to serve as a sweet with coffee.

4 oz (100 g) unblanched almonds or peeled hazelnuts	**4 oz (100 g) sugar**

1. Oil a marble surface or baking sheet.
2. Place nuts and sugar in a heavy-bottomed saucepan and heat gently until sugar starts to melt. Continue to heat, stirring occasionally, until the sugar goes a dark brown. The sugar may go lumpy at first, but it will dissolve as it caramelizes. When the syrup is a good caramel colour, pour quickly on to the prepared surface. Leave until cold, then grind in a food processor or rotary cheese grater.

BRANDY-SNAP CUPS
MAKES ABOUT 12 LARGE CUPS

A brandy-snap dough is easier to shape into cups than other *tuile* mixtures. It takes minutes to make the mixture and you have more time when they come out of the oven to remove them and place in bowls or cups to shape – other *tuile* mixtures set in seconds. They are incredibly impressive. Even ordinary fruit salad is glamorous served in a fragile-looking brandy-snap cup.

4 oz (100 g) butter	**1½ tsp around ginger**
4 oz (100 g) demerara sugar	**4 oz (100 g) plain flour**
4 oz (100 g) golden syrup	**1 tbls lemon juice**

UP TO SIX DAYS IN ADVANCE

1. Preheat the oven to 170°C/325°F/Gas Mark 3. Line a baking sheet with baking parchment.

2. Place the butter, sugar and syrup in a saucepan and melt over gentle heat. Sift the ginger and flour together and stir into the syrup. Add the lemon juice.

3. Place large tablespoons of the mixture on the baking parchment, leaving room for them to spread. Bake for 8 minutes or until golden brown and bubbling. Remove from the oven and cool for a minute or two. Lift off with a spatula and place in small bowls or large cups.

4. Store in an airtight container when cold.

TUILES

Tuiles shaped into cups for serving sorbets or fruit are always appreciated. They are not difficult to make and can be stored in airtight containers days in advance. This recipe makes about 10 *tuiles* 6 in (15 cm) in diameter.

2 oz (50 g) unsalted butter	**whites of 2 large eggs**
3 oz (75 g) caster sugar	**1½ oz (40 g) plain flour**
pinch of salt	**1 tbls lemon juice**
grated rind of ½ lemon	**butter for greasing**
2 tbls double cream	

———— UP TO SIX DAYS IN ADVANCE ————

1. Preheat the oven to 215°C/425°F/Gas Mark 7.

2. Butter and flour a baking sheet. Lightly draw 10 circles 6 in (15 cm) in diameter about 1½ in (3.8 cm) apart. A bowl turned upside down and gently rotated can be used.

3. Cream the butter with a wooden spoon, then blend in the sugar, salt, lemon rind and cream. Add the egg whites, stirring only enough to blend. Sift, then fold in the flour and lastly the lemon juice.

4. Place 1 tbls of the batter in the centre of each circle and spread it out with the back of a metal spoon to cover the circle. Bake for about 5 minutes or until the edges are just beginning to darken. One at a time remove the *tuiles* with a spatula and place in a large cup or small bowl, or shape around a rolling pin or metal horn. Set the baking sheet on the open oven door to keep the *tuiles* warm and pliable. Work quickly, as they became crisp in seconds. Wait for the oven to reach the correct temperature before baking the next batch. Store carefully in an airtight container.

CHOCOLATE TRUFFLES
MAKES I LB (450 G)

Almost everyone finds chocolate truffles irresistible, particularly if they melt in the mouth as these do. The flavour can be varied by adding a liqueur or some praline.

For the truffles
7 fl oz (200 ml) single cream
I oz (25 g) butter
I vanilla pod
I lb (450 g) good plain
   chocolate
2 tbls rum or brandy (optional)
I oz (25 g) praline, coarsely
   ground (see p. 231; optional)

For the coverings
4 tbls cocoa
2 tbls icing sugar
chocolate vermicelli or finely
   chopped nuts

——— UP TO EIGHT DAYS IN ADVANCE ———
(MINIMUM ONE DAY)

1. Heat the cream with the butter and vanilla pod until it reaches a rolling boil. Remove from the heat and take out the pod (which can be rinsed, dried and placed in a jar with sugar to make vanilla sugar if desired).
2. Meanwhile, break the chocolate into small pieces and melt in a double boiler set over hot, but not boiling, water. Mix the chocolate into the cream and add the alcohol if you are using it. Pour into a shallow tin lined with parchment paper and spread out. Leave in a cool place overnight.
3. Pull off small pieces of chocolate and roll into balls on the palms on your hands. At this stage incorporate the praline into the balls if you wish. Mix the cocoa and icing sugar together and roll the truffles to coat evenly. Alternatively, roll in either the nuts or vermicelli. Cover and store in the refrigerator until ready to serve.

DESSERTS

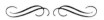

APPLE-AMARETTI STRUDEL

SERVES 10–12

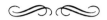

Packaged filo leaves are the answer for light, easy and delicious strudels. This apple filling with some crushed, fragrant *amaretti* biscuits is very, very good.

12 sheets of filo pastry
6 oz (175 g) melted unsalted butter
8 *amaretti* biscuits, finely crushed
extra butter for greasing
icing sugar, sifted
whipped cream for serving

For the filling
1½ oz (40 g) raisins
2 tbls brandy

3 oz (75 g) dark-brown sugar
1 tsp cinnamon
juice and grated rind of 1 lemon
5 large Cox's or Granny Smith apples
3 large cooking apples
2 oz (50 g) dry, fine breadcrumbs
2½ oz (65 g) almonds, chopped

SAME DAY AS SERVING

1. Soak raisins in brandy for at least 15 minutes.
2. Mix sugar with cinnamon and lemon rind.
3. Peel, core and thinly slice the apples. Place in a bowl and toss with the sugar mixture and half the breadcrumbs; then mix in the raisins, nuts and lemon juice.
4. Carefully unfold the filo leaves. Keep the leaves covered with a sheet of plastic. Lift off 1 sheet, place on a clean surface, brush with melted butter and sprinkle with a few tablespoons of *amaretti* crumbs. Layer with 6 more sheets of filo, brushing each with butter but only sprinkling every other layer with the crumbs. Sprinkle a few tablespoons of breadcrumbs over the last sheet and place half of the apple mixture at the bottom edge of the strip. Starting at the apple-filled edge, roll up the dough as for a Swiss roll. Place on a buttered baking tray, seam-side down, and fold ends under to seal. Brush with melted butter. Repeat to make a second strudel. Cover with cling-film so the strudels are airtight and refrigerate.

BEFORE SERVING

(APPROX. ONE AND A HALF HOURS BAKING AND RESTING TIME)

1. Preheat the oven to 190°C/375°F/Gas Mark 5.
2. Remove the cling-film and bake for about 45 minutes. Remove from the oven and sprinkle the top with sifted icing sugar. Leave for 15 minutes to 1 hour before serving. Serve with the whipped cream.

Note: Strudel can also be reheated but it is at its best warm from the oven.

APPLE CRÊPE LAYER CAKE

SERVES 8–10

Keep some crêpes handy in the freezer. They can be used in countless ways and always add a festive note. Here they are layered with apples and praline to make a wonderful dessert.

8 × 9-in (23-cm) crêpes (see
  p. 210)

For the apple mixture
3 lb (1.4 kg) Golden
  Delicious apples
juice of 1 lemon
2½ oz (60 g) sugar
1 oz (25 g) butter

For the top of the cake
1 oz (25 g) butter
2 tbls sugar

For the praline mixture
2 eggs
¼ pt (150 ml) double cream
8 oz (225 g) praline
  (see p. 231)
3 tbls Calvados

UP TO TWO DAYS IN ADVANCE

1. Make the crêpes, using two-thirds of the basic crêpe recipe. Layer with cling-film and keep refrigerated unless using the same day.
2. Whisk all the praline ingredients together. Cover and refrigerate.
3. Preheat the oven to 200°C/400°F/Gas Mark 6. Peel and core the

apples. Cut into very thin slices and toss with the lemon juice and sugar. Spread out on a large baking tray and dot with butter. Bake about 25 minutes, turning the slices occasionally, until they are tender but still retain their shape. Cool, then turn into a bowl, cover and refrigerate.

SAME DAY AS SERVING

Use a flat or shallow round baking dish from which you can serve. Grease with butter and place a crêpe, best-side up, in the centre. Spread with a layer of apple slices, then dot with several spoons of the praline. Repeat with the remaining crêpes, ending with an apple layer. Sprinkle 2 tbls of sugar over the top and dot with butter.

BEFORE SERVING
(THIRTY MINUTES BAKING TIME)

1. Preheat the oven to 190°C/375°F/Gas Mark 5.
2. Bake for 30 minutes or until the apples on top are just beginning to brown. Serve hot or warm. Can be kept warm in a cool oven for 1 hour.

APPLE-FILLED CRÊPES
WITH CALVADOS
SERVES 8

2½ lb (1.1 kg) eating apples	4 tbls orange juice
4 oz (100 g) sugar	16 crêpes (see p. 210)
5 oz (150 g) butter	extra butter for greasing
8 tbls Calvados	

UP TO TWO DAYS IN ADVANCE

1. Peel, core and thinly slice the apples. Toss with 3 oz (75 g) of sugar. Heat 3 oz (75 g) of butter in a frying-pan. Add the sugared apples and cook over low heat until the apples are tender. Raise the heat and continue to cook, stirring occasionally, until the sugar

begins to caramelize, then scrape into a bowl. Mix 2 tbls of Calvados with the orange juice and pour over the apples. Cover and refrigerate.

2. Make the crêpes. Layer with cling-film, cover and refrigerate.

SEVERAL HOURS IN ADVANCE

Lay a crêpe under-side up and spoon on some apple mixture. Roll it up and place in a well-buttered baking dish, in one layer or overlapping slightly.

BEFORE SERVING
(FIFTEEN MINUTES BAKING TIME)

1. Preheat the oven to 215°C/425°F/Gas Mark 7.
2. Melt the remaining butter and dribble over the crêpes. Sprinkle with the rest of the sugar. Bake for 15 minutes or until bubbling hot. Cover to keep warm if not serving immediately.
3. Heat the Calvados in a small saucepan. Carefully light the warmed Calvados and pour over the crêpes. Serve at once.

EASY APPLE PIE

SERVES 8–10

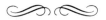

Easy because one large circle of pastry becomes both top and bottom crust. It is very good served warm with cream. It is also easy to remove the pie from the tin.

2½–3 lb (1.1–1.4 kg) Cox's or other crisp apple	grated rind and juice of 1 lemon
4 oz (100 g) sugar	8 oz (225 g) shortcrust pastry (see p. 212)
1½ tsp ground cinnamon	1 oz (25 g) butter
	cream for serving

SAME DAY AS SERVING

1. Quarter, peel and core the apples. Slice and toss with the sugar, cinnamon, lemon juice and rind.
2. Preheat the oven to 200°C/400°F/Gas Mark 6. Place a baking sheet in the centre of the oven.
3. Roll the pastry into a circle about 4 in (10 cm) larger in diameter than a 10-in (25-cm) flan tin. Place it over the tin, leaving the sides hanging over the edge. Fill with the apple slices and dot with butter. Fold the edge over the top. You should have a border of pastry with an apple centre. Bake the pie on a hot oven sheet for 45 minutes or until cooked. Cool on a rack and keep at room temperature.

BEFORE SERVING
(TEN TO FIFTEEN MINUTES REHEATING TIME)

For a warm pie reheat in a hot oven for 10–15 minutes. Serve with the cream.

CRUSTLESS TARTE TATIN

SERVES 4–6

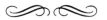

Not having a brilliant grill, I have often had to resort to caramelizing sugar in a saucepan to pour over *crème brulée*. Here is an apple dessert using the same principle from *The Gold and Fizdale Cookbook* by Arthur Gold and Robert Fizdale (Random House, 1984).

4 tbls butter
6 large tart apples, peeled,
   cored and thinly sliced
3 tbls dried currants

grated peel and juice of ½
   lemon
1 tbls brown sugar
7 oz (200 g) granulated
   sugar

UP TO THREE DAYS IN ADVANCE

1. Preheat the oven to 230°C/450°F/Gas Mark 8.
2. Butter the bottom and sides of a pie plate. Layer it with apple slices, sprinkling each layer with currants, grated lemon peel, lemon juice and brown sugar; dot with butter. Cover with foil pierced in a few places with a sharp knife. Set the pie on a baking sheet and bake for 1 hour or until the apple slices are tender. Remove the foil for the last 15 minutes. They should be moist but not sitting in liquid. If excess liquid does accumulate, remove it. Cool, then cover and refrigerate.

UP TO TWO HOURS IN ADVANCE

1. Reheat the apples in a moderate oven until just lukewarm.
2. Melt the granulated sugar in a small, heavy-bottomed saucepan with 3 fl oz (75 ml) water over medium heat. If the sugar on one side of the pan begins to turn dark before the rest, stir it. Remove from the heat as soon as the syrup has become dark amber in colour. Pour it over the apples to cover them evenly. Work as quickly as you can. Set aside in a dry atmosphere.

BEFORE SERVING

Serve on its own or with cream.

Note: If you use Bramley apples, cook them for a shorter time and watch they don't disintegrate. Other cookers, if you can find them, work better. I find it quicker to caramelize sugar without the addition of water. The sugar goes white and lumpy, but it all dissolves into an amber colour in the end.

APRICOT TART

SERVES 8

A creamy apricot tart with a hint of almonds from the *amaretti* biscuits.

6 oz (175 g) shortcrust pastry (see p. 212)	**4 oz (100 g) sugar**
1½ lb (675 kg) apricots, halved and stoned	**2 eggs**
	¼ pt (150 ml) double cream
	8 *amaretti* biscuits, crushed

──────── SAME DAY AS SERVING ────────

1. Preheat the oven to 200°C/400°F/Gas Mark 6. Place a baking sheet in the centre of the oven.
2. Roll out the pastry and line a 9-in (23-cm) flan tin. Sprinkle the biscuit crumbs on the bottom of the pastry. Place the halved apricots, cut-side up, on the crumbs in one tight layer. Sprinkle half the sugar over the fruit and bake for 15 minutes. Reduce oven temperature to 190°C/375°F/Gas Mark 5. Whisk the eggs with the remaining sugar until pale and thick. Whisk in the cream. Pour over the apricots and bake for a further 25 minutes or until custard is set and lightly coloured. Cool on a rack.

──────── BEFORE SERVING ────────
(TEN MINUTES BAKING TIME IF SERVING WARM)

Warm in a hot oven for 10 minutes if you wish to serve the pie warm. It can also be served cold.

Note: Substitute plums for the apricots and add some cinnamon for a delicious plum tart.

BLACKBERRY MOUSSE

SERVES 6

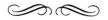

A light mousse with a delicious flavour. It can be made with fresh or frozen berries.

1½ tsp gelatine
1 lb (450 g) fresh or frozen
   blackberries
juice of 1 lemon

3–4 oz (75–100 g) caster
   sugar
¼ pt (150 ml) double cream
2 egg whites
pinch of salt

UP TO TWO DAYS IN ADVANCE
(MINIMUM EIGHT HOURS)

1. Soak the gelatine in 2 tbls of cold water.
2. Wash and pick over the blackberries. Place in a saucepan with the lemon juice, cover and simmer gently for about 8 minutes or until blackberries are soft and juicy. Rub through a sieve and return to the pan. Stir in the gelatine and dissolve over low heat – do not boil. Remove from heat, add sugar to taste and set aside until cold and beginning to thicken.
3. Whip the cream to soft peaks and fold into the purée. Whisk the egg whites with a pinch of salt and carefully fold into the mixture. Line 6 ramekins with cling-film and fill with the mousse if you wish to turn them out or fill a serving dish. Cover and refrigerate until set. Serve with additional cream if desired.

CRYSTAL CURRANTS

SERVES 6

Cold sparkling currants are a great treat – the very best way I know of enjoying them. This recipe can be made only with currants that are dry.

2 lb (900 g) fresh dry redcurrants (not frozen)	**1 lb (450 g) raspberries (optional)**
8 oz (225 g) caster sugar	*Garnish*
	currant leaves (if available)

ONE DAY IN ADVANCE
(MINIMUM EIGHT HOURS)

Carefully remove stalks from the currants, using the prongs of a fork. Keep them as dry as possible. Place in a shallow bowl and layer with the sugar. Refrigerate, uncovered, turning them carefully in the sugar one time after several hours.

BEFORE SERVING

If you are using the raspberries, arrange a pile on one side of the plate and a pile of the crystal currants. Garnish with currant leaves.

FRUIT SOUP

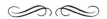

A very refreshing fruit salad to round off your meal

10 passion fruit	**2 ripe mangoes**
1 ripe pineapple	**caster sugar**
6 kiwi fruit	*Garnish*
juice of 2 oranges	**fresh small mint leaves**

SEVERAL HOURS IN ADVANCE

Cut passion fruit in half, scoop out the insides and place in a blender. Blend for about 10 seconds to detach the membranes from the black seeds. Strain through a fine sieve, rubbing as much juice through as possible. Mix with the orange juice and some caster sugar. It should be tart but sweet at the same time. Cover and refrigerate.

AS LATE AS POSSIBLE

Cut the flesh of fruits into attractive pieces. Place in a bowl and pour over the passion fruit juice. Cover and refrigerate.

To serve: Serve, if possible, in glass bowls or goblets garnished with a few small mint leaves.

GINGER PEARS

SERVES 6

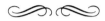

Poached pears stuffed with stem ginger are very good and very easy to make.

6 ripe but firm pears, Passacrassana or Comice	***For the poaching syrup***
½ lemon	**2 oz (50 g) sugar**
6 tbls stem ginger, cubed	**juice of 1 lemon**
2 tbls ginger syrup from the stem ginger jar	**2 cloves**
¼ pt double cream	**½ cinnamon stick**
1 tbls rum	**pear peelings**
1 tsp sugar	

ONE DAY IN ADVANCE

1. Place syrup ingredients in a saucepan with 1 pt (600 ml) of water, dissolve sugar over moderate heat and bring to the boil.
2. Peel and halve the pears. Immediately rub them with the cut lemon. Place them in the poaching syrup and simmer until just tender. Be sure the pears are covered in the syrup. Scoop out the core with a small spoon and place in a serving dish in one layer.
3. Boil the poaching syrup until reduced to ¼ pt (150 ml) and pour over the pears. Cool, cover with cling-film and refrigerate.

SEVERAL HOURS IN ADVANCE

Place some ginger and syrup in each pear. Whip the cream and add the rum and sugar. Keep refrigerated until serving.

Grilled Quinces

SERVES 6

3 quinces
3 oz (75 g) sugar
3½ fl oz (100 ml) white wine

juice of 1 lemon
¼ pt (150 ml) double cream,
 lightly whipped

UP TO ONE DAY IN ADVANCE

1. Peel, halve and core the quinces. Reserve the peelings.
2. Place the sugar, 3½ fl oz (100 ml) water, wine, peelings and lemon juice in a saucepan. Bring to the boil, add the quinces, cover and simmer until the quinces are soft. Cool in the liquid, then cover and refrigerate.

SEVERAL HOURS IN ADVANCE

1. Place the fruit in a shallow gratin dish, cut-side up. Cover with cling-film and set aside.
2. Boil the liquid until reduced to 2 fl oz (60 ml). Strain and cool, then fold into the cream.

BEFORE SERVING
(FIVE MINUTES GRILLING TIME)

Heat grill to highest heat. Pour the cream over the quinces and grill for about 5 minutes or until lightly browned.

Note: Serve with a home-made biscuit if you have the time. Other fruit can be grilled by the same method.

HAZELNUT MERINGUE CAKE WITH RASPBERRIES

SERVES 8

Perhaps this scrumptious dessert suffers from overexposure, but it is an all-time great and impossible to tire of.

5 oz (150 g) hazelnuts
4 egg whites
pinch of salt
7 oz (200 g) vanilla caster
   sugar
½ tsp vinegar

Garnish
fresh mint leaves

For the filling
½ pt (300 ml) double cream
1½ lb (750 g) raspberries

——— SEVERAL WEEKS IN ADVANCE ———

1. Preheat the oven to 180°C/350°F/Gas Mark 4. Line the bottoms of two 8-in (20-cm) sandwich tins with greased paper.
2. Spread hazelnuts on a baking sheet and bake for 8 minutes or until nuts are lightly toasted. Rub the nuts between a towel to remove the skins. Grind the nuts in a food processor, flicking the machine on and off to achieve a consistency like very coarse sand.
3. Reduce the oven temperature to 150°C/300°F/Gas Mark 2.
4. Whisk egg whites with salt until stiff. Whisk in 2 tbls of sugar, then fold in the remaining sugar, a few tablespoons at a time. Fold in the vinegar and then the nuts. Divide the mixture between the two tins and level the tops with a palette knife.
5. Bake for 1¼ hours. Cover tops if they colour too much. Leave in tins for 5 minutes before turning out on to a rack. Peel off the paper, cool, then store in an airtight container.

——— SIX HOURS IN ADVANCE ———

Leave raspberries at room temperature if frozen.

—— THREE TO FOUR HOURS IN ADVANCE ——

1. Whip the cream.

2. Spread half the cream and raspberries on one meringue. Top with the other meringue, spread cream over top and pile with raspberries. Decorate with mint leaves. Keep in the refrigerator to facilitate cutting.

Note: If you are storing meringues for any length of time, it is prudent to dry them off in a turned-off oven after baking.

LEMON DELICIOUS

SERVES 3–4

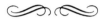

An accurate name for this pudding, which bakes into a light cake mixture on top and lemon curd below. It is at its best served warm.

2 oz (50 g) butter
4 oz (100 g) sugar
1 oz (25 g) plain flour
2 eggs, separated
grated rind and juice of 1
    lemon

½ pt (300 ml) milk
extra butter for greasing
¼ pt (150 ml) single cream
    for serving

SEVERAL HOURS IN ADVANCE

Cream the butter with the sugar. Sift over the flour and stir in. Beat in the egg yolks, lemon rind and juice. Set aside.

ONE HOUR IN ADVANCE

Beat the milk into the lemon mixture. Whisk the egg whites until stiff and fold into the batter. Pour into a 2-pt (1.1-L) greased soufflé dish.

BEFORE SERVING

(THIRTY-FIVE MINUTES BAKING TIME)

1. Preheat the oven to 180°C/350°F/Gas Mark 4.
2. Place the dish in a roasting pan. Pour enough boiling water in the pan to come about 2 in (5 cm) up the side of the dish. Bake for 35

minutes or until just set. Leave the oven door open and keep warm in the water bath. The middle of the pudding will sink but don't worry. Serve from the dish and pass the cream separately.

LIME ROULADE
WITH KIWI FRUIT

SERVES 8

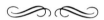

A light roulade filled with kiwi fruit and cream looks glamorous, and is also very quick and easy to make.

4 eggs	**juice of 2 limes**
5 oz (150 g) caster sugar	**pinch of salt**
3 tbls flour	**½ pt (300 ml) double cream**
grated rind of 1 lime	**10–12 kiwi fruit**

—————— UP TO ONE DAY IN ADVANCE ——————

1. Preheat the oven to 180°C/350°F/Gas Mark 4. Line a 13½ × 9½-in (33 × 24-cm) baking tin with parchment paper.
2. Separate the eggs, dropping the yolks into a large bowl and the whites into a smaller bowl, preferably copper. Add 4 oz (100 g) of caster sugar to the yolks and whisk until thick and light. Sift the flour over the mixture and fold in. Stir in the grated rind and lime juice. Whisk the egg whites with a pinch of salt until stiff, then whisk in the rest of the sugar. Fold carefully into the yolks, using a large metal spoon. Spread on to the prepared tin and bake for 15 minutes or until firm.
3. Sprinkle a sheet of greaseproof paper with caster sugar. Run a knife around the edge of the cake to loosen and turn out on to the paper. Peel off the parchment paper. Before the cake has cooled, roll it up, using the paper to help. Keep rolled in a cool place.

————— SEVERAL HOURS IN ADVANCE —————

1. Whip the cream. Peel and slice the kiwis, saving any juice and adding it to the cream.

2. Unfold the roulade, spread over the cream and sprinkle with half of the kiwi slices. Roll up the roulade and slide on to a serving platter. Surround with the other fruit slices and refrigerate.

BEFORE SERVING

Cut slices with a sharp knife heated by dipping in very hot water. You may prefer to arrange individual plates ahead of time.

Note: Other fruits such as strawberries can replace the kiwi. Edible flowers such as borage or nasturtium look great around the roulade.

MANGO MOUSSE

SERVES 6

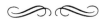

The best way to enjoy a mango is to eat it on its own and get as messy as necessary. When it is sliced for more civilized eating you lose a lot that is around the stone and under the skin. A mousse makes use of every bit of pulp and juice, and captures that special fragrance.

1 scant tbls gelatine	*Garnish*
3 ripe mangoes	***toasted slivered almonds***
juice of 1 lemon	
1–2 oz (25–50 g) caster sugar	***For the raspberry sauce***
extra lemon juice	**12 oz (350 g) raspberries**
¼ pt (150 ml) double cream	**juice of ½ lemon**
1 egg white	**icing sugar**

UP TO THREE DAY IN ADVANCE
(MINIMUM SIX HOURS)

1. Soak the gelatine in 3 tbls of cold water.
2. Peel the mangoes in a bowl to catch the juice. Cut away as much flesh as possible from the stone. Squeeze the stone to extract any extra juice. Purée the flesh in a blender or food processor and sieve if it is stringy.
3. Place the mango pulp in a saucepan with the juice of 1 lemon and

bring slowly to the boil, stirring continually. Remove from the heat.

4. Stir in the gelatine and add the sugar and extra lemon juice if needed. Set the pan over ice water until the mixture cools and begins to thicken.

5. Whisk the cream to soft peaks and fold into the purée. Whisk the egg white with a pinch of salt until stiff peaks are formed and carefully fold into the mixture. Pour into a 2-pt (1.1-L) dish. Cover and refrigerate.

SEVERAL HOURS IN ADVANCE

1. Make the raspberry sauce by sieving the raspberries and adding lemon juice and sifted icing sugar to taste.

2. Scatter some almonds over the top of the mousse and leave at room temperature. Serve with the sauce passed separately.

PASSIONATE HEARTS

SERVES 4

A heart-shaped *coeur de crème* mould has small holes in the bottom for draining. Filled with yoghurt or a light cream cheese, it is an attractive and delicious accompaniment to fresh berries or fruit sauces. The passion fruit sauce came about by some left-over sorbet.

1 egg white	**juice of ½ lemon**
8 oz (225 g) thick-set Greek yoghurt	**10 passion fruit**
caster sugar to taste	*Garnish*
3 oz (75 g) sugar	**fresh small mint leaves**

UP TO ONE DAY IN ADVANCE

1. Whisk the egg white and fold into the yoghurt. Add caster sugar to taste. Line the bottom of 4 individual heart moulds with paper towels and fill with the yoghurt mixture. Leave to drain on a plate in the refrigerator.

2. Dissolve the sugar in 3 fl oz (75 ml) of water over low heat, bring to the boil, then remove from the heat. Stir in the lemon juice.

3. Cut the passion fruit in half, scoop out the insides and place in a blender. Blend for 15 seconds to detach the membranes from the black seeds. Rub through a sieve, pressing out as much juice as possible. Mix with the sugar syrup, cover and refrigerate.

———— BEFORE SERVING ————

Turn the hearts out on to individual plates. Pour the passion fruit juice around the hearts and garnish with small mint leaves.

Note: It is not essential to drain thick-set Greek yoghurt, so this dish can be prepared, turned out of the moulds almost immediately and served.

PEACH TART
WITH ALMOND CREAM
SERVES 8–10

A lovely, rich tart for a special occasion. It is also good made with pears that have been lightly poached before being arranged in the pie.

8 oz (225 g) shortcrust pastry (see p. 212)	2 oz (50 g) caster sugar
4 tbls apricot jam	2 eggs
5 good-sized peaches	¼ pt (150 ml) double cream
4 oz (100 g) ground almonds	5 tbls Calvados or dark rum
	1 oz (25 g) toasted flaked almonds

———— UP TO ONE DAY IN ADVANCE ————

1. Preheat the oven to 215°C/425°F/Gas Mark 7. Place a baking sheet in the centre of the oven.

2. Roll out the pastry and line a 10-in (25-cm) flan tin with a removable base. Refrigerate while the oven heats. Prick the bottom

all over with a fork and line with a piece of crumbled, greaseproof paper weighted down with dried beans. Bake for 10 minutes. Lower oven to 190°C/375°F/Gas Mark 5. Remove paper with beans and bake another 8 minutes. Heat the jam and brush half over the bottom.

3. Drop the peaches, one at a time, into boiling water. Leave for 10 seconds, remove with a slotted spoon and slip off the skin. Cut in half, remove stones and cut them at a slight diagonal into thin slices. Keep the slices together and place in the pie. Flatten them out to make the spokes of a wheel. Use the last half peach, cut up, to fill the gaps.

4. Whisk together the ground almonds, sugar, eggs, cream and rum. Pour over the peaches and bake at 190°C/375°F/Gas Mark 5 for about 20 minutes or until custard is set. Glaze with the rest of the jam. Sprinkle with almonds and serve at room temperature.

Note: The pie crust can be made in advance but the filling and baking are best done on the day you plan to serve the dish.

PEAR CHARLOTTE

SERVES 8

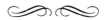

A lovely charlotte, but it needs good-flavoured juicy pears. Taste one before you make it to be sure it has good flavour.

1½ tbls gelatine	½ oz (15 g) butter
3 eggs	lemon juice
2 egg yolks	8 fl oz (250 ml) double
4 tbls *eau de vie de poire William*	cream
	2 tbls apple or orange juice
3 oz (75 g) sugar	22 sponge fingers
3 firm ripe pears, Williams or Passacrassana	raspberry sauce made from 1 lb (450 g) of raspberries (see p. 225)

UP TO THREE DAYS IN ADVANCE
(MINIMUM TWELVE HOURS)

1. Place gelatine with 3 tbls of cold water in a cup and leave for 5 minutes to sponge. Stand the cup in simmering water to dissolve gelatine.

2. Place eggs and egg yolks with 2 oz (50 g) of sugar in a bowl (preferably copper) set over a pan of very hot, but not boiling, water. Whisk with an electric beater or hand whisk until mixture is thick and light, and leaves a ribbon trail when the whisk is lifted. Take from the heat and beat in the gelatine and continue to whisk until mixture is cool.

3. Peel and core the pears. Simmer them with the butter, remaining sugar and a good squeeze of lemon juice until soft, about 5 minutes. You should have about ¾ pt (450 ml) of purée. Stir into the egg mixture. Set the bowl in ice water and stir occasionally, until the mixture starts to set. Whip the cream to soft peaks and fold into the mousse. Fold in 2–3 tbls of the *eau de vie de poire William* and more lemon juice if needed.

4. Line a 3½-pt (2-L) charlotte mould with cling-film. Mix apple or orange juice and 1 tbls of *eau de vie de poire William* in a shallow bowl. Brush the sponge fingers with the juice and line the bottom and sides of the mould. Spoon the mousse into the mould, cover with cling-film and refrigerate until well-set.

ONE HOUR IN ADVANCE

Leave at room temperature if it has set very firmly.

BEFORE SERVING

Turn the charlotte out on to a large cake plate and pour a little raspberry sauce around the edge. Serve with the rest of the sauce passed separately.

PEARS AND RASPBERRIES

A delicious combination.

**6 ripe pears such as
    Passacrassana or Comice**

**1 lb (450 g) fresh raspberries
    or frozen and thawed
juice of 1 orange**

SEVERAL HOURS IN ADVANCE

Peel and cut the pear into elegant slices. Mix with the orange juice.
Place in a bowl and seal with cling-film. Keep refrigerated.

BEFORE SERVING

Add the raspberries to the pears and serve.

RASPBERRY PEACHES

SERVES 8

**8 peaches, ripe but firm
1½ lb (675 g) raspberries,
    fresh or frozen
juice of ½ lemon
icing sugar, well sifted**

For the poaching syrup
**4 oz (100 g) sugar
1 vanilla pod
few strips of lemon peel
juice of 1 lemon**

ONE DAY IN ADVANCE

1. Place all the poaching syrup ingredients in a saucepan with 1 pt
(600 ml) water. Dissolve the sugar carefully over low heat, then
bring to the boil.
2. Drop a few peaches at a time (syrup must cover peaches) into the
simmering syrup, poach very gently for 15 minutes or until just
tender. Peel the peaches when tepid. Place in a bowl, cover and
refrigerate.

Whizz the raspberries in a blender or food processor. Rub through a sieve. Add the lemon juice and stir in just enough icing sugar to taste.

——— BEFORE SERVING ———

Place peaches on a serving dish and coat them in the sauce.

SABAYON WITH FRUIT

SERVES 4–6

This is a fabulous sauce to serve with fruit. It is so good that you can also serve it on its own, garnished, perhaps, with a few finely chopped pistachio nuts. Use this amount for 4 but increase the quantities for 6 if you are not serving any fruit.

I tsp gelatine
3 egg yolks
1½ oz (40 g) sugar
3 fl oz (90 ml) Marsala
¼ pt (150 ml) whipping
   cream

fruit such as poached pears
   or fresh peaches,
   strawberries or
   raspberries

——— UP TO ONE DAY IN ADVANCE ———

1. Place the gelatine with I tbls of cold water in a cup and leave for 5 minutes. Place the cup in a pan of simmering water and stir to dissolve gelatine.
2. Place the egg yolks, sugar and Marsala in a bowl (preferably copper) set over a pan of hot, but not boiling, water. Whisk until the mixture is thick enough to leave a ribbon trail when the whisk is lifted. Be careful not to allow the mixture to become too hot or it will curdle. Remove from the heat, whisk in the gelatine and continue to whisk until the mixture cools. The bowl can be set in cold water to speed this up. Whip the cream and fold carefully into the *sabayon*. Cover and refrigerate.

3. Poach the pears if you are using them (see p. 246).

(see p. 246)

BEFORE SERVING

Prepare the fresh fruit if you are using it. Place a small mound of *sabayon* in the centre of each plate and surround with the fruit.

Note: Sauterne or Grand Marnier are delicious substitutes for the Marsala.

SUMMER PUDDING

SERVES 8

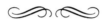

Not another recipe for summer pudding, you may well say, but try it and you will see why it is included. It is hard to imagine anything better. I freeze both raspberries and redcurrants so I can make this in the winter. My American friends won't leave until they have had a good big slice. The currants are sieved so it isn't too seedy, but the raspberries are left alone.

1 small farmhouse white loaf, 1–2 days old	**juice of ½ lemon**
1½ lb (675 g) redcurrants	**1½ lb (675 g) raspberries**
caster sugar to taste	*Garnish*
	few sprigs of redcurrant

UP TO TWO DAYS IN ADVANCE

1. Slice the bread and remove the crusts. Line a 3-pt (1.7-L) pudding basin with the slices, cutting them to fit. Reserve a few slices for the lid.
2. Save a few redcurrants for a garnish. Heat the rest gently in a saucepan, crushing a few with a fork to start the juices flowing. Cover and simmer for a few minutes until juicy. Sieve, rubbing through as much juice as possible. Add the lemon juice and sugar to taste. Keep it nice and tart.
3. Dip the slices of bread, lining the basin, in the redcurrant purée. Replace the soaked bread back in the basin. Pour in the raspberries and then add the rest of the redcurrant purée. Place a layer of bread

on top. Place a layer of cling-film loosely over the top. Find a plate that will fit in the basin and press the bread down. Place a 2-lb (900-g) weight on the plate. Refrigerate for 8 hours or up to 2 days.

BEFORE SERVING

Slip a knife around the inside edge and turn out on to a plate. Garnish with a few sprigs of redcurrant and serve.

WINTER FRUIT SALAD

SERVES 8–10

A glass bowl layered with a selection of plump dried fruit is a perfect winter pudding.

1 lb (450 g) prunes
1 lb (450 g) dried apricots,
   preferably Hunza
8 oz (225 g) figs
4 oz (100 g) raisins
4 oz (100 g) sultanas
1 stick cinnamon
6 cloves
4 blades of mace

½ pt (300 ml) dry white wine
½ pt (300 ml) double cream
½ pt (300 ml) yoghurt

Garnish
**blanched julienne of orange
   and lemon peel or toasted
   slivered almonds**

UP TO FOUR DAYS IN ADVANCE
(MINIMUM ONE DAY)

Soak all the dried fruit individually in enough water to cover overnight.

UP TO THREE DAYS IN ADVANCE

1. Using a small saucepan, simmer the prunes with their soaking water, cinnamon, cloves, mace and wine for 15 minutes or until tender. Remove the prunes with a slotted spoon and place in a serving bowl.
2. Add the apricots to the saucepan and simmer for about 5 minutes

or until soft. Remove to the bowl and repeat with the figs, raisins and sultanas. Strain over the liquid, having first reduced it if there is too much.

SEVERAL HOURS IN ADVANCE

Whip the cream to soft peaks, then fold into the yoghurt. Keep refrigerated until you are ready to serve.

BEFORE SERVING

Garnish with the orange and lemon peel, or almonds, and serve.

BANANA ICE-CREAM

SERVES 10–12

More a sorbet than an ice-cream, with a wonderfully light consistency and an excellent flavour.

1 pt (600 ml) milk	**5 oz (150 g) sugar**
1 vanilla pod, split	**5 ripe bananas**
lengthwise	**¼ pt (150 ml) double cream,**
5 egg yolks	**lightly whipped**

UP TO ONE WEEK IN ADVANCE
(MINIMUM EIGHT HOURS)

1. Bring milk with the vanilla pod to just below the boiling point. Take off the heat, cover and leave to infuse for 10 minutes.
2. Meanwhile, whisk the yolks with the sugar until thick and light. Whisk in the hot milk, then return to the pan. Stir continuously, using a wooden spoon, over very gentle heat until the custard thickens enough to coat the spoon. Remove from heat and cool.
3. Process or mash the bananas with a fork to make a purée. Do not blend.
4. Fold the bananas into the custard, then fold in the cream.
5. Freeze according to your ice-cream maker's instructions; or freeze to a slush, whisk and continue to freeze until set.

ONE TO TWO HOURS IN ADVANCE

Place ice-cream in refrigerator to soften slightly.

CHOCOLATE PRALINE
ICE-CREAM

SERVES 8

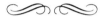

If you haven't time to make your own chocolate ice-cream, you can transform a good variety by adding home-made praline.

¾ pt (450 ml) milk
4 egg yolks
3 oz (75 g) sugar
5 oz (150 g) plain
 eating-chocolate,
 chopped

4 oz (100 g) praline (see
 p. 231)
½ pt (300 ml) double
 cream

UP TO THREE WEEKS IN ADVANCE
(MINIMUM EIGHT HOURS)

1. Bring the milk to just below the boiling point.
2. Meanwhile, whisk the egg yolks and sugar together. Whisk in the hot milk and return to the pan. Stir continuously, using a wooden spoon, over very gentle heat until the mixture thickens enough to coat the spoon. Remove from the heat and stir in the chocolate until dissolved. Leave to cool.
3. Lightly whip the cream and fold into the chocolate mixture. Fold in the praline. Freeze according to your ice-cream maker's instructions; or freeze to a slush, whisk and continue to freeze until set.

ONE HOUR IN ADVANCE

Remove ice-cream from freezer before serving.

Note: Plunge a scoop in hot water and shake dry before using. Keep reheating after every few scoops.

COFFEE GRANITA

SERVES 8

2 pts (1.2 L) strong freshly brewed espresso coffee	**½ pt (300 ml) whipping cream**
3 oz (75 g) sugar	**1 oz (25 g) caster sugar**

——— UP TO ONE WEEK IN ADVANCE ———
(MINIMUM TWELVE HOURS)

1. Make the coffee and add about 3 oz (75 g) of sugar – just enough to sweeten slightly.
2. When the coffee has cooled, place in a tin and freeze until solid.
3. Plunge the bottom of the frozen coffee container into very hot water for a few seconds, turn the coffee out, cut into chunks and process until it forms small crystals. Return to the tin, cover and keep frozen until served.

——— BEFORE SERVING ———

1. Chill wine glasses in which to serve the granita.
2. Lightly whip the cream and add the caster sugar.
To serve: Serve in the chilled glasses with the cream poured over the top.

Note: Any water ice that has gone too solid or has crystallized can be softened and made smoother by processing just before serving.

COFFEE RUM ICE-CREAM

SERVES 10–12

2 tbls instant coffee	**2 pt (1.2 L) vanilla**
2 tbls dark brown sugar	**ice-cream (see p. 268)**
3 fl oz (75 ml) dark rum	

(MINIMUM ONE DAY)

Dissolve coffee and sugar in 1 tbls of boiling water; stir in the rum. Soften ice-cream in a blender or food processor, add rum mixture and mix just long enough to blend. Freeze overnight.

ONE HOUR IN ADVANCE

Place in refrigerator before serving.

HALVA ICE-CREAM
SERVES 6–8

Jane Grigson's recipe and always a hit. Buy halva cut from a long block rather than the small packets. Delicatessens and health food stores usually stock it.

3 large eggs	4 oz (100 g) halva (any
2 oz (50 g) caster sugar	flavour), crumbled into
½ pt (300 ml) whipping	small pieces
cream	

UP TO THREE WEEKS IN ADVANCE
(MINIMUM EIGHT HOURS)

1. Whisk the eggs and sugar with an electric beater until the mixture is light and thick enough to leave a ribbon trail.
2. In another bowl whip the cream to soft peaks and mix in the halva. Fold this into the egg mixture.
3. Pour into a 2–2½-pt (1.1–1.4-L) capacity container. Cover and freeze.

FIFTEEN MINUTES IN ADVANCE

Leave ice-cream at room temperature to soften.

Note: Chopped sesame crunch is a good topping. Simply heat 4 oz (100 g) each of sugar and sesame seeds with 2 oz (50 g) of butter. Stir continuously until the mixture turns a good caramel colour. Pour on to an oiled marble surface or into an oiled tin and chop when cold. Store in an airtight container.

ICE-CREAM SUNDAE

SERVES 6

This was the most popular ice-cream dish at Schrafft's in New York City when I was a teenager. It is due for a revival.

2 oz (50 g) almonds
1 tbls oil
½ tsp salt

½ pt (300 ml) hot-fudge
sauce (see p. 226)
1½ pts (900 ml) vanilla
ice-cream (see p. 268)

———— UP TO SIX DAYS IN ADVANCE ————

1. Drop the almonds into boiling water. Boil for 1 minute. Drain and slip off the skins. Preheat the oven to 180°C/350°F/Gas Mark 4. Spread the nuts in a tin and bake for 5 minutes. Add the oil and shake the pan to coat the nuts. Sprinkle over the salt and bake for another 5 minutes. Keep an eye on them and take them out when they are lightly toasted. Drain on paper towels. Store in a container when cold.
2. Make the sauce and store in the refrigerator.

———— BEFORE SERVING ————
(FIVE MINUTES REHEATING TIME)

1. Reheat the sauce in a *bain-marie*.
2. Serve a scoop of vanilla ice-cream with some sauce poured over the top and a few almonds scattered over.

Note: Remember to take the ice-cream out of the freezer about 1 hour before serving; or place in the refrigerator for about 1½–2 hours before serving.

MANGO SORBET

SERVES 8–10

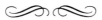

A tin of mango pulp, available in Indian shops, makes very good sorbet. It is less expensive than using fresh mangoes, and is very quick and easy to use.

3 oz (75 g) sugar
1 pt (600 ml) tinned or fresh
   mango pulp

juice of 2 lemons
icing sugar, sieved

——— ONE WEEK IN ADVANCE ———
(MINIMUM EIGHT HOURS)

1. Dissolve the sugar in 6 fl oz (175 ml) of water over low heat, bring to the boil. Boil for a few minutes, then cool.
2. If using fresh mangoes, purée the flesh in a blender or food processor. Mix pulp with lemon juice and cooled syrup. Taste for flavour – you are after a sharp, yet sweet, taste. Add more lemon juice or sieved icing sugar as necessary.
3. Turn into a container and freeze. When half frozen, whisk until smooth, return to freezer and leave until set. Alternatively, allow it to set and whizz it in a food processor just before serving.

PASSION FRUIT SORBET

SERVES 6–8

This is the best sorbet I have ever tasted or made. Don't wince at the number of passion fruit – the result is very special.

12 oz (350 g) sugar
24 passion fruit

juice of 1 lemon

1. Dissolve the sugar carefully in 12 fl oz (400 ml) of water over low heat. Bring to the boil and boil hard for a few minutes to slightly reduce the syrup.
2. Cut each passion fruit in half and scoop out the insides. Place in a blender and blend at low speed for 30 seconds to detach the membranes from the seeds. Strain through a sieve, pressing out as much juice as possible. Add the lemon juice and the cooled syrup. The mixture should taste sharp but sweet at the same time. Adjust if necessary by adding more lemon juice or sugar.
3. Freeze in an ice-cream maker or whisk the sorbet in a blender or food processor when half frozen and return to the freezer until set.

Note: If fresh-fruit sorbets are frozen quickly (20 minutes in the I C T C Gelato Chef) and eaten soon after, the flavour is at its most intense. They lose flavour with time, so try and make them as close to the time you intend to serve as possible.

PEAR SORBET

SERVES 6

A refreshing and beautifully flavoured sorbet. It looks very splendid served in a *tuile* cup.

juice of 2 small lemons	**icing sugar, sifted**
6–7 large ripe pears,	***eau de vie de poire***
Williams, Comice or	***William***
Passacrassana	

— UP TO TWO TO THREE DAYS IN ADVANCE —
(MINIMUM TWELVE HOURS)

1. Place the lemon juice in a heavy-bottomed saucepan.
2. Quarter, peel and core the pears, then cut into chunks and toss with the lemon juice. Poach gently in the lemon juice until soft, then cool.

3. Process or crush the cooled pears to a purée. Whisk in a few spoons of icing sugar and taste. Aim for a sharp, yet sweet, taste. Freeze in an ice-cream maker or in a freezer, whisking when half frozen in the usual way.

THIRTY MINUTES IN ADVANCE

Leave in the refrigerator to soften.
To serve: Serve in scoops with 1–2 tbls of *eau de vie* sprinkled over the top.

PEPPERMINT ICE-CREAM

SERVES 8–10

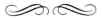

Ice-cream made with an Italian meringue works well in the freezer. It doesn't crystallize and has a light, mousse-like texture.

2 egg whites	**1–2 drops green food**
pinch of salt	**colouring**
5 oz (150 g) sugar	**½ pt (300 ml) double cream**
juice of ½ lemon	*Garnish*
3–4 drops oil of peppermint	**fresh mint leaves**

UP TO SEVEN DAYS IN ADVANCE
(MINIMUM SIX HOURS)

1. Whisk the egg whites with a pinch of salt with an electric beater until stiff.
2. Dissolve the sugar in the lemon juice and 3 fl oz (75 ml) of water. Bring to the boil and boil hard for 3 minutes. Pour over the whites in a steady stream while beating at top speed. Continue to whisk

until the mixture is thick and meringue-like. Add the peppermint oil and the colour.

3. Lightly whip the cream to soft peaks and fold into the meringue. Place in a container and freeze.

ONE HOUR IN ADVANCE

Remove from freezer and place in refrigerator.
To serve: Serve in scoops garnished with the mint leaves.

VANILLA ICE-CREAM

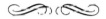

A good home-made vanilla ice-cream is delicious just served on its own, but it also can be the basis for a variety of excellent desserts. Some suggestions are on pp. 262 and 264.

1 pt (600 ml) milk	4 oz (100 g) sugar (vanilla
1 vanilla pod, split	sugar if possible)
lengthwise	½ pt (300 ml) double cream
5 egg yolks	1 tsp vanilla essence (not
	flavouring)

UP TO THREE WEEKS IN ADVANCE
(MINIMUM ONE TO TWO HOURS IF USING
AN ICE-CREAM MACHINE)

1. Bring the milk and vanilla pod to just below the boil. Take off the heat, cover and leave to infuse for 15 minutes. Scrape some of the black seeds from the pod into the milk.
2. Whisk the egg yolks and sugar together until thick and pale. Whisk in the milk, then return the mixture to the saucepan. Place over very low heat, stirring constantly with a wooden spoon, until the custard thickens slightly. Your finger should leave a clear trail when drawn across the back of the spoon. Do not allow the custard to come near the boil. Strain into a bowl. Whisk occasionally as it cools.
3. Whip the cream to the soft peak stage and fold into the cool custard. Taste and add the vanilla essence if needed.

4. Follow your ice-cream maker's instructions for freezing.

Note: If you don't have an ice-cream maker, use the recipe for Halva ice-cream (see p. 263) and omit the halva. Use 4 oz (100 g) vanilla sugar and 1 tsp of vanilla essence.

CHOCOLATE CAKE
WITH KUMQUATS

SERVES 8–10

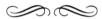

This is really more of a cooked mousse with a chocolate glaze top. It should be served in thin wedges with some kumquats and syrup – a delectable treat.

For the cake
scant 2 oz (50 g) cake flour
5 oz (150 g) caster sugar
3 large eggs
3 oz (75 g) plain chocolate
1 oz (25 g) cocoa powder
4 oz (100 g) unsalted
  butter

For the glaze
4 oz (100 g) plain chocolate
1 oz (25 g) unsalted butter
2 tbls milk

For the kumquats
1 lb (450 g) kumquats or
  tiny clementines
5 oz (150 g) sugar

———— UP TO TWO DAYS IN ADVANCE ————

1. Preheat the oven to 150°C/300°F/Gas Mark 2.
2. Grease an 8-in (20-cm) shallow, round cake tin and line with parchment paper. With an electric whisk, beat the flour, sugar and eggs for about 10 minutes or until the mixture is very thick and leaves a ribbon trail when the whisk is lifted. Melt the chocolate, cocoa and butter in a double saucepan over boiling water, add to the egg mixture and whisk for another 6 minutes. Pour into the tin and bake for 25 minutes. Remove from the oven and leave in the tin for 10 minutes before turning out on to a cake rack.
3. Melt the glaze ingredients together and pour over the cake while it is still warm. Cover and refrigerate when completely cold.

4. Wash the kumquats and halve lengthwise. If you are using clementines, cut each fruit into 8 segments. Place in a pan with the sugar and ½ pt (300 ml) of water. Bring to the boil and cook very slowly for 30 minutes. Set aside.

BEFORE SERVING
(FIVE MINUTES REHEATING TIME)

Reheat the kumquats and serve warm with slices of the cold cake.

Note: The cake is delicious served warm from the oven. Hard to do for dinner parties but worth trying if the rest of the menu allows. It is also very good without the kumquats but served with a pistachio sauce.

CHOCOLATE CHESTNUT MOUSSE CAKE

SERVES 10

4 oz (100 g) plain chocolate
4 eggs, separated
7 oz (200 g) sugar
8 oz (225 g) tinned
   unsweetened chestnut
   purée
1 tsp vanilla essence

pinch of salt
½ pt (300 ml) double cream
4 tbls cocoa powder
3 tbls strong coffee
2 tbls caster sugar
Garnish
cocoa powder

UP TO ONE DAY IN ADVANCE

1. Preheat oven to 180°C/350°F/Gas Mark 4. Line a 13½ × 9½-in (33 × 24-cm) Swiss roll or biscuit tin with baking parchment.
2. Melt the chocolate in the top of a double saucepan over hot, but not boiling, water. Beat the egg yolks with three-quarters of the sugar, then beat in the chestnut purée, vanilla and the melted chocolate. Sieve the mixture into a clean bowl.
3. Whisk the egg whites with the salt until stiff, add the remaining sugar and whisk until glossy. Using a metal spoon, fold a quarter of

the egg whites into the chestnut mixture. Carefully fold in the rest of the whites and spread over the prepared tin. Bake for 15–20 minutes. Leave in the tin to cool, then cover in cling-film and leave in a cool place.

SEVERAL HOURS IN ADVANCE

1. Whip the cream. Dissolve the cocoa in the coffee and add to the cream with the caster sugar.
2. Cut the cake into three equal strips and sandwich with the cream. Sieve a layer of cocoa over the top and serve in thin slices.

Note: A good variation is to fill the cake with whipped cream to which you have added several chopped *marrons glacé*.

CHOCOLATE MARQUISE

SERVES 10

A marquise is the king of chocolate puddings and usually contains over a pound of butter and nearly a dozen eggs. Here is my less rich version – still incredibly luscious and chocolaty.

6 oz (175 g) plain chocolate, cut into pieces	3 oz (75 g) caster sugar
5 oz (150 g) butter, cut into small pieces	2 tbls white rum
1½ oz (40 g) cocoa powder	½ pt (300 ml) double cream
2 eggs	22 sponge fingers
	small cup of strong black coffee, unsweetened

UP TO FOUR DAYS IN ADVANCE

1. Line a charlotte mould 6½ in (16 cm) in diameter with cling-film, leaving an overlap around the top edge to ease turning out. Melt the chocolate in the top of a double saucepan over hot, but not boiling, water. Whisk in the butter and then the cocoa, and remove from the heat. Whisk the eggs and caster sugar over a bowl of hot water until the mixture is very thick and leaves a ribbon trail when the whisk is lifted. Using a metal spoon, carefully fold in the

chocolate mixture and rum. Whip the cream to the soft peak stage and fold into the chocolate. Brush the sponge fingers with the cold coffee and line the bottom and sides of the mould, cutting them to shape where necessary. Spoon in the chocolate mixture, cover with cling-film and refrigerate.

ONE HOUR IN ADVANCE

One hour before serving turn the marquise out and leave at room temperature.

EASY CHOCOLATE PUDDING
SERVES 4–6

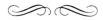

A no-time-to-cook pudding.

6 oz (175 g) soft white breadcrumbs
2 tbls powdered instant coffee
4 oz (100 g) dark brown sugar

2 tbls cocoa powder
¾ pt (450 g) whipping cream
6 tbls rum or brandy

UP TO TWO DAYS IN ADVANCE
(MINIMUM ONE DAY)

1. Mix the dry ingredients together and set aside for a few hours.
2. Whip the cream lightly. Layer a dish with half of the crumb mixture. Sprinkle over half the rum and cover with half the cream. Repeat these layers, cover the dish with cling-film and refrigerate overnight or up to 2 days. Serve very cold.

Mocha Roulade with Praline Cream

SERVES 8

Roulades have a lot going for them. They are quick to make and very light to eat. And the spiral slices have a professional look.

4 eggs, separated
6 oz (175 g) caster sugar
1 oz (25 g) cocoa powder
4 tbls very strong coffee or
   1½ tsp instant coffee,
   dissolved in 3 tbls water
pinch of salt

icing sugar for dusting
½ pt (300 ml) double or
   whipping cream
2 oz (50 g) praline (see p. 231)
Garnish
praline

UP TO ONE DAY IN ADVANCE
(MINIMUM THREE HOURS)

1. Preheat the oven to 180°C/350°F/Gas Mark 4. Line a 13½ × 9½-in (33 × 24-cm) Swiss roll tin with baking parchment.
2. Whisk the yolks with the sugar until pale, then whisk in the cocoa and coffee.
3. Whisk the egg whites with a pinch of salt until stiff. Fold a few tablespoons of the whites into the chocolate mixture to lighten, then pour the chocolate mixture on to the whites and fold in carefully. Pour into the prepared tin and spread level with a palette knife.
4. Bake for 15 minutes or until just set.
5. Sprinkle a sheet of greaseproof paper with icing sugar. Run a knife around the edge of the cake to loosen and turn out on to the paper. Peel off the parchment. Before the cake has cooled roll it up, using the paper to help. Keep rolled in a cool place.

SEVERAL HOURS IN ADVANCE

1. Whip the cream and fold in the praline.
2. Unfold the roulade, spread with the cream and reroll, sliding it on to a serving platter. Refrigerate and just before serving sprinkle the top with icing sugar and praline.

THREE CHOCOLATE TERRINE

SERVES 8–10

The only way to describe this is as a chocolate spectacular. Three different chocolate textures, colours and tastes are layered together and create a chocoholic's dream. It isn't difficult to make and can be done days in advance or even frozen.

For the cake layer
2 oz (50 g) butter
¾ oz (20 g) cocoa
1 egg
4 oz (100 g) caster sugar
1 tsp vanilla essence
1 oz (25 g) flour

For the chocolate-cream layer
6 oz (175 g) plain chocolate, broken into small pieces
½ pt (300 ml) double cream

For the white-chocolate mousse layer
1 tsp gelatine
1 oz (25 g) liquid glucose
8 oz (225 g) white chocolate, broken into small pieces
2 egg yolks
pinch of salt
½ pt (300 ml) double cream

—— UP TO THREE DAYS IN ADVANCE ——
(MINIMUM ONE DAY)

1. *For the cake layer:* Preheat the oven to 180°C/350°F/Gas Mark 4. Line the bottom of an 8-in (20-cm) square tin with parchment paper. Melt the butter over low heat, then stir in the cocoa and remove from the heat. Whisk the egg with the caster sugar, then add the cocoa mixture and vanilla essence. Sift the flour over the top and fold in. Turn into the tin and bake for 20 minutes. Leave in the tin for 5 minutes, then slide a knife around the edge and turn out on to a rack. Line a 2-lb (900-g) loaf tin with cling-film, leaving an overlap at the top to help unmould later. Cut a piece of cake to fit the bottom of the loaf tin and place in the tin.

2. *For the chocolate-cream layer:* Melt the plain chocolate in a double saucepan set over hot, but not boiling, water. Bring half the cream to the boil in a small saucepan, remove from the heat and beat in the chocolate gradually. Place in the refrigerator to cool. Whip the remaining cream. Whip the cold chocolate cream until it lightens in

colour and increases in volume, then fold in the plain whipped cream. Turn in to the tin and spread level. Keep refrigerated.

3. *For the white-chocolate layer*: Soak the gelatine in 2 tbls of water. Bring 2 fl oz (60 ml) of water with the glucose to the boil. Remove from the heat, cool for 1 minute, then stir in the gelatine until dissolved. Stir the white chocolate into the liquid. When the mixture is blood temperature, stir in the egg yolks and salt. Whip the cream and fold into the chocolate mixture. Pour into the tin, cover with cling-film and refrigerate for at least 24 hours.

BEFORE SERVING

Unmould 1–2 hours before serving, the later the better. Lift the terrine out of the tin by the cling-film. Cut into very thin slices, using a sharp knife heated in very hot water and dried before slicing. Place a slice in the centre of each dessert plate.

WHITE CHOCOLATE TERRINE

SERVES 10

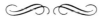

A fashionable dessert that looks particularly stunning surrounded with chocolate sauce. It has a wonderful creamy texture and taste.

1 tsp gelatine	pinch of salt
12 fl oz (350 ml) double cream	1 thin Genoise sponge, to cover top
2 tbls liquid glucose	
10 oz (275 g) white chocolate, chopped	*For the chocolate sauce*
	4 oz (100 g) caster sugar
3 egg yolks	2 oz (50 g) cocoa powder

UP TO THREE DAYS IN ADVANCE
(MINIMUM ONE DAY)

1. Soak the gelatine in 3 tbls of cold water. Whip the cream to soft peak stage. Bring 2 fl oz (60 ml) of water and the glucose to the boil, remove from the heat and add the gelatine. Stir until completely dissolved, then stir in the white chocolate until smooth. Add the

egg yolks while the mixture is warm, then add a pinch of salt and fold in the cream. Place the mixture in a 2-lb (900-g) loaf tin and cover with a layer of the sponge, cut to fit. Cover the tin and refrigerate for at least 24 hours.

2. *For the sauce*: Simply dissolve the sugar in ¼ pt (150 ml) of water, bring to the boil and stir in the cocoa. Set aside until needed.

BEFORE SERVING

Turn out 1–2 hours before serving, the later the better. Place the tin in very hot water for a few seconds and then turn out. Slice with a sharp knife heated in very hot water and dried before slicing. Place a slice on each plate and surround with some chocolate sauce; or present the terrine and slice at the table.

Note: Chocolate-dipped leaves on the white chocolate are an attractive way of decorating the white mousse.

CARAMEL MOUSSE

SERVES 6–8

A gorgeous caramel-flavoured mousse.

1½ tsp gelatine	2 tbls caster sugar
4½ oz (135 g) sugar	½ pt (300 ml) double cream
5 eggs, separated	pinch of salt

UP TO TWO DAYS IN ADVANCE

1. Soak the gelatine in 3 tbls of cold water.
2. Using a small, heavy-bottomed saucepan, dissolve the 4½ oz (135 g) of sugar over low heat with 2 tbls of water. Bring to the boil and cook until syrup turns a rich brown caramel. Swirl the pan from time to time to help the sugar caramelize evenly. Remove from the heat and gradually add 4 tbls of water, stirring to dilute the caramel. Be careful, as caramel may spit. Wait about 5 minutes, then stir the gelatine into the hot caramel. Whisk the egg yolks with the caster sugar until light and thick, add the caramel and continue to whisk

until mixture is fluffy. Whip the cream and fold into the mixture, then whisk the egg whites with a pinch of salt until stiff but not dry and gently fold into the caramel. Spoon into a serving dish or individual dishes, cover and refrigerate until serving.

Note: It is tricky to get the caramel just right. If it is too pale when removed from the heat, the flavour will not be strong enough. If it burns it will be bitter. Wait until it turns a rich brown caramel colour remembering that it will continue to darken a bit after it is removed from the heat.

CHESS PIE

SERVES 6–8

A lovely pecan and walnut pie from America.

6 oz (175 g) shortcrust pastry (see p. 212)	3 oz (75 g) walnuts
4 oz (100 g) butter	3 oz (75 g) pecans
6 oz (175 g) soft light-brown sugar	1 large cooking apple, grated
1 egg	cream or ice-cream for serving
¼ pt (150 ml) double cream	

—— UP TO ONE DAY IN ADVANCE ——

1. Preheat the oven to 190°C/375°F/Gas Mark 5. Place a baking sheet in the centre of the oven.
2. Roll out the pastry and line a 9-in (23-cm) flan tin.
3. Cream the butter with the sugar, add the egg gradually, then stir in the cream, nuts and grated apple. Pour into the tin.
4. Bake on the hot baking sheet for 30 minutes. Turn off the oven and leave the pie for another 15 minutes. Cool on a rack.

—— BEFORE SERVING ——
(FIFTEEN MINUTES REHEATING TIME)

1. Preheat the oven to 190°C/375°F/Gas Mark 5.

2. Bake the pie on a hot baking sheet for about 15 minutes to warm. Serve warm with cream or ice-cream.

Note: Flavour ½ pt (300 ml) of whipped cream with 1 tbls of caster sugar, 2 tbls of rum and 1 tbls of mixed ground nutmeg, cinnamon and ginger. Serve with the pie.

COCONUT CRÈME BRULÉE
SERVES 8

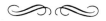

2 pts (1.1 L) double cream
6 oz (175 g) desiccated
  coconut
1 vanilla pod, split
  lengthways

2 eggs
2 egg yolks
caster sugar

UP TO THREE DAYS IN ADVANCE
(MINIMUM EIGHT HOURS)

1. Bring the cream, coconut and vanilla pod slowly to the boil. Remove from the heat, cover and leave to infuse for 10 minutes.
2. Remove vanilla pod, rinse, dry and save for another use. Whizz cream and coconut in a blender or food processor. Sieve back into the rinsed pan, rubbing through as much coconut cream as possible.
3. Beat eggs and yolks together in a large pudding basin. Reheat the cream to just under the boiling point. Pour on to the eggs, while whisking, until blended. Place basin over a pan of barely simmering water and stir until cream is very thick. It will continue to thicken as it cools. Pour into custard ramekins, cool, then cover and refrigerate.

SEVERAL HOURS IN ADVANCE

1. Heat grill to highest setting.
2. Sprinkle custards with a thin, even layer of sugar. Place about 3 in (8 cm) below heat source and grill for 5 minutes or until sugar has caramelized. Watch carefully and move them around so they caramelize as evenly as possible. Leave in a dry place.

Note: You can place the custards in the freezer for about an hour before caramelizing. This can prevent the custard cooking under the grill.

GINGER CREAM

SERVES 4

A light mousse-like cream well-flavoured with stem ginger and rum.

1½ tsp gelatine
2 tbls ginger syrup from
    stem ginger
2 eggs, separated
2 tbls caster sugar

¼ pt (150 ml) milk
3 tbls rum
2 oz (50 g) stem ginger,
    chopped

——— UP TO THREE DAYS IN ADVANCE ———

1. Soak the gelatine in the ginger syrup.
2. Whisk the egg yolks with the caster sugar in a bowl. Heat the milk in a heavy-bottomed saucepan to just below a simmer. Whisk into the egg yolks in a steady stream, pour back into the pan and stir over very low heat until thickened. Do not allow it to come near a simmer. Remove from the heat and stir in the gelatine. Place over ice and stir until it begins to set. Stir in the rum and chopped ginger. Whisk the egg whites until stiff and carefully fold into the custard. Line 4 ramekins with cling-film. Don't worry about the creases. Pour in the custard, cover and refrigerate.

——— BEFORE SERVING ———

Turn out and serve.

RICOTTA AMARETTI TART

SERVES 8

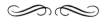

You can find *amaretti* in supermarkets now. These small Italian macaroons have an intense flavour and make delicious pie crust.

5 digestive biscuits	**1 egg**
16 amaretti	**4 oz (100 g) sugar**
3 oz (75 g) butter	**2 oz (50 g) ground almonds**
1 lb (450 g) ricotta cheese	*Garnish*
3 egg yolks	**a few crushed amaretti**

—————— UP TO TWO DAYS IN ADVANCE ——————

1. Preheat the oven to 190°C/375°F/Gas Mark 5. Place a baking sheet in the centre of the oven.
2. Crush the digestive biscuits and the *amaretti* in a food processor or with a rolling pin. Melt the butter and mix with the crumbs. Press into the bottom of a 10-in (25-cm) flan tin with a removable base. Bake on the sheet for 10 minutes or until lightly browned. Cool on a rack and lower oven to 180°C/350°F/Gas Mark 4.
3. Mix the ricotta with the egg yolks, whole egg, sugar and ground almonds. Turn into the tin and bake on the sheet for 1 hour or until top is golden. Cool on a rack, then remove from tin. Don't worry if the cake sinks a bit. Refrigerate if not eating the same day. Cover first with foil or cling-film.

—————— BEFORE SERVING ——————

Garnish the top with a sprinkling of *amaretti* crumbs.

Note: Ricotta is very perishable. It should have a light crumbly texture and a mild flavour. When you find a shop that stocks it, check on the delivery day and buy it then. Although you can make this tart in advance, it is at its best when prepared on the day of serving.

Saffron Yoghurt Hearts

SERVES 8

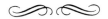

Greek yoghurt with its wonderful thick consistency can be used in place of cream in many desserts. This is a favourite of mine. A heart-shaped *coeur de crème* mould has small holes in the bottom for draining. You can get away with only buying one small mould if you drain your cream first in a muslin-lined sieve. The single mould can then be filled and turned out in succession.

big pinch of saffron threads	**2 × 8-oz (225-g) carton of**
2 tbls rose water	**thick-set Greek yoghurt**
4 green cardamom pods	**3 oz (75 g) caster sugar**
2 oz (50 g) shelled pistachio	**2 egg whites**
nuts	

—————— UP TO ONE DAY IN ADVANCE ——————

1. Soak the saffron in the rose water for 30 minutes.
2. Remove the black seeds from the cardamom pods and grind using a pestle and mortar.
3. Heat nuts in a moderate oven for about 8 minutes. Rub off the dry skin and chop them very finely. Set aside.
4. Line the bottom of 8 *coeur de crème* moulds with paper towels. Cut out 8 bases even if you are using one mould.
5. Mix the yoghurt with the saffron, its soaking liquid, the cardamom and half the sugar.
6. Whisk egg whites until stiff, then whisk in the remaining sugar. Fold into the yoghurt. Taste and add more sugar if you think it needs it. Spoon into the moulds (or into a muslin-lined sieve if you have only one mould; leave on a dish to drain). Keep in the refrigerator or a cool larder.

—————— THIRTY MINUTES IN ADVANCE ——————

Turn hearts out on to individual plates and garnish with the chopped nuts. If you have used one mould reline with a fresh paper base after each turning out.

Note: Saffron loses flavour with time, so try and make the hearts the same day as serving.

INDEX

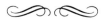